INTERNATIONAL AND HISTORICAL ROOTS OF AMERICAN HIGHER EDUCATION

REFERENCE BOOKS IN
INTERNATIONAL EDUCATION
(VOL. 18)

GARLAND REFERENCE LIBRARY
OF SOCIAL SCIENCE
(VOL. 633)

Reference Books in
International Education

Edward R. Beauchamp
General Editor

INTERNATIONAL AND HISTORICAL ROOTS OF AMERICAN HIGHER EDUCATION

W.H. Cowley
Don Williams

GARLAND PUBLISHING, INC. • NEW YORK & LONDON
1991

Library of Congress Cataloging-in-Publication Data

Cowley, W.H. (William Harold), 1899–
    International and historical roots of American higher education /
W.H. Cowley, Don Williams.
        p.   cm. — (Reference books in international education ; vol.
18) (Garland reference library of social science ; vol. 633)
    Includes bibliographic references (p.   ) and index.
    ISBN 0–8240–4697–8 (alk. paper)
    1. Education, Higher—United States—History. 2. Education,
Higher—History. 3. Universities and colleges—United States—
History. I. Williams, Don, 1928–   . II. Title. III. Series.
IV. Series: Garland reference library of social science ; v. 633.
LA226.C8   1991
378.73—dc20   91–15161
                                                                   CIP

Printed on acid-free, 250-year-life paper
Manufactured in the United States of America

To our wives
Jean and Kathleen

SERIES EDITOR'S FOREWORD

This series of reference works and monographs in education in selected nations and regions is designed to provide a resource to scholars, students, and a variety of other professionals who need to understand the place of education in a particular society or region. While the format of the volumes is often similar, the authors have had the flexibility to adjust the common outline to reflect the uniqueness of their particular nation or region.

Contributors to this series are scholars who have devoted their professional lives to studying the nation or region about which they write. Without exception they have not only studied the educational system in question, but they have lived and travelled widely in the society in which it is embedded. In short, they are exceptionally knowledgeable about their subject.

In our increasingly interdependent world, it is now widely understood that it is a matter of survival that we understand better what makes other societies tick. As the late George Z.F. Bereday wrote: "First, education is a mirror held against the face of a people. Nations may put on blustering shows of strength to conceal public weakness, erect grand façades to conceal shabby backyards, and profess peace while secretly arming for conquest, but how they take care of their children tells unerringly who they are" (*Comparative Method in Education*, New York: Holt, Rinehart & Winston, 1964, page 5).

Perhaps equally important, however, is the valuable perspective that studying another education system provides us in understanding our own. To step outside of our commonly held assumptions about schools and learning, however briefly, and to look back at our system in contrast to another, places it in a very different light. To learn, for example, how the Soviet Union handles the education of a multilingual society; how the French provide for the funding of public education; or how the Japanese control admissions into their universities enables us to understand that there are alternatives to our familiar way of doing things. Not that we can often "borrow" from other societies; indeed, educational arrangements are inevitably a reflection of deeply rooted political, economic, and cultural factors that are unique to a society. But a conscious recognition that there are other ways of doing things can serve to open our minds and provoke our imaginations in ways that can result in new approaches that we would not have otherwise considered.

Since this series is designed to be a useful research tool, the editors and contributors welcome suggestions for future volumes as well as ways in which this series can be improved.

Edward R. Beauchamp
University of Hawaii

CONTENTS

ix

Contents

PREFACE

The writing of this book began over forty years ago. W.H. Cowley had left the presidency of Hamilton College, accepted a faculty position at Stanford, and now could devote his full scholarly efforts to a better understanding of the operations of colleges and universities. Over the next several decades Cowley committed his considerable energy to studying the history of American higher education. A good portion of that history derives from foreign models, so in the process he became an authority on the international roots of the American system.

By the time I came to Stanford in the mid-1950s, Cowley had adopted the practice of inviting his students to review his manuscript. He hadn't finished it, he explained, but in the meantime he hoped that we might point out the strengths and weaknesses in the present draft. He actually built his weekly seminars around these criticisms, which proved an excellent pedagogical device.

A decade later I returned to Stanford in a post-doctoral capacity to help Cowley with his manuscripts. He was still refining his history and had, in fact, turned his attention to completely rewriting the opening chapter on Greek higher education. The ultimate perfectionist, he still wanted to make more improvements. As time passed, however, and more and more people asked, "When will Cowley finish his book?," the necessity for its meeting an ever-higher standard grew.

When Cowley died in 1978, he still had not finished the task. I continued to use the manuscript in my courses, however, constantly editing it to accommodate changes suggested by scholars in the field. Were he alive today, Cowley would most definitely want to make further refinements in the manuscript. He would not even recognize some chapters in the present draft, because they are now almost totally my own work.

I have aimed the book in its present form at two groups: those who teach courses on the historical or international roots of American higher education and those who, for other reasons, take an interest in colleges and universities. Persons in both groups may conclude upon finishing the book that taken by itself it does not suffice. I agree. Cowley once called it "A Short History of American Higher Education," and that it is. When I teach using this text I treat it as a starting point, supplementing it with other readings specific to the period. For instance, Goodchild and Wechsler, working under the auspices of the Association for the Study of Higher Education, have produced *The ASHE Reader on the History of Higher Education*. Used in conjunction with Cowley-Williams, the ASHE reader should provide good coverage of the subject.

The bibliographic essays at the close of each chapter identify recent references I have found most useful. Because I am not aware of a great deal of recent writing on the Greek, Roman, Byzantine, or Islamic periods, I have included sources written in earlier decades, but for periods that follow I have limited my sources to those appearing in 1970 or after. In the case of the twentieth century I limited myself to sources written after 1979.

I genuinely hope my readers will let me know their impressions of this book. In this way I can continue learning more about a subject that has so intrigued me during the more than three decades that I have dealt with it. Meanwhile, Mr. Cowley, wherever he is, can go about the next revision—on which I am quite certain he is still working.

Don Williams
Seattle
March 1991

International and
Historical Roots of
American Higher Education

CHAPTER ONE

Origins of Higher Education in the Western World: Sixth Century B.C.–133 B.C.

> Greece was the mother of Europe, and it is to Greece that we must look in order to find the origin of our modern ideas.
>
> (Whitehead, 1928, p. 8)

A comprehensive survey of the continuum of higher education would begin with the apprenticeship of religious, medical, legal, and governmental leaders in nonliterate societies. It would then trace the rise of educational institutions following the invention of writing in the ancient civilizations of Asia and North Africa. Then it would scan the early seats of learning in Egypt, Persia, Babylonia, India, and China. In particular it would sketch the operations of such Asian centers as the Buddhist city of Nalanda where, in the century prior to Plato's opening of his Academy, there arose an institution which during its heyday housed "ten thousand students, one hundred lecture rooms, great libraries, and six immense blocks of dormitories four stories high" (Durant, 1935, p. 559).

Such a thorough-going review would show how these early fountainheads of knowledge and wisdom influenced Greece, the pivotal source of Western civilization, but nothing so ambitious will be attempted here. Instead, since "Greece was the mother of Europe" and hence the grandmother of Europe's transoceanic offspring, the origins of American colleges and universities will be traced no farther than Grecian educational institutions.

The Rise and Fall of Athens

Early in the fifth century B.C. Athens and Sparta joined forces to repel the invading Persians in the series of victories that began with Marathon. In pride and self-confidence Athens, which had borne the brunt of the war, envisioned itself at the head of a great Hellenic empire so powerful that the Persian menace would be forever curbed. Seeking to make this dream a reality, it organized the Delian League into which it drew over 350 cities. This imperialistic development raised the ire of Corinth, Sparta, and their allies, which, after the Persian threat waned, organized to check the tormenting growth of Athenian supremacy. At the end of the resulting Peloponnesian War in 404 B.C., its enemies all but destroyed Athens. It made, however, a spectacular—yet short-lived—recovery that terminated in the even-worse disaster of 338 when Philip of Macedon overran the Greek city-states and eviscerated "the glory that was Greece."

Over a period of about two hundred years that glory had been woven by the work of a procession of wondrous men in the arts, philosophy, political thought, and embryonic natural science that always will be honored. An abbreviated list includes Aeschylus, Anaxagoras, Aristotle, Democritus, Euripides, Heroditus, Isocrates, Pericles, Phidias, Plato, Protagoras, Pythagoras, Socrates, Sophocles, and Thucydides. Several of these people engaged in Hellenic higher education, and to their efforts the next few pages are devoted.

The Hellenic Higher Education

The Pythagorean Museum: During the sixth century Pythagoras cultivated studies of mathematics, music, acoustics, and geometry. Both a mystic and a polymath, Pythagoras established in southern Italy a well-housed *museum* (home of the muses) with an advanced *encyclios paideia* (circle of studies). Its male and female members not only investigated mathematical and related problems but also followed a strict discipline of purity, silence, self-examination, and dietary taboos. The group flourished for about a century, until its enemies suppressed it and dispersed its adherents. Some of them, however, carried forward the study of mathematics and powerfully affected the thinking of Plato and the programs of the Academy as well as those of later higher schools.

Thus did mathematics become the fundamental subject that it has been ever since.

The Sophists: Athenians, in contrast to the laconic Spartans, were congenital talkers who discussed everything under heaven and in the heavens themselves. The most curious of them began about the eighth century to meditate about the rotation of the planets, and, perhaps building on the knowledge of the Egyptians and Persians, Thales is reputed to have predicted the eclipse of the sun on May 28, 585. Others struggled with the perennial problem of the ultimate stuff of the universe, an enterprise that, after long controversies, developed into skepticism about man's ability to unlock the mysteries of nature. This, in time, produced the Sophists whose outlook Protagoras, one of the greatest of them and a friend of Pericles, phrased in the famous epigram: "Man is the measure of all things."

Differing from both the poets and the scientific theorists, the Sophists were teachers of worldly wisdom who appeared upon the scene in the more advanced Hellenic cities. Many of them traveled about Greece, with Athens becoming the Palladium of their circuits; and some of them who did not originate in Athens made it their home. There the most popular became extremely wealthy, charging the equivalent of $5000.00 for a three- to four-year course of training, a huge sum since skilled craftsmen earned about twenty-five cents a day (Marrou, 1956, p. 80).

Both the hereditary aristocracy and the nouveau riche plutocrats sent their sons to the Sophists, the former to prepare them for political leadership, the latter to give them the polish and skills of gentlemen. Probably many of them promoted high political and personal morals, but succeeding ages know them only from the writings of their fourth-century enemies. Isocrates and Plato, in particular, castigated them for their success-at-all-costs formulas, Plato adding the accusation that they not only neglected but also derided spiritual concerns and commitments. Whatever the truth, undoubtedly the mercenary Sophists whose teaching applauded opportunism and cunning helped set the stage for the debacle that followed the devastations of the Great Plague and the victories of the Spartans in the Peloponnesian War.

The Sophists travelled from city to city. Marrou has succinctly summarized their methods:

To make himself known, to demonstrate the excellence of his
teaching and to give a sample of his skill, [the Sophist] would
give a sample lecture either in a town through which he happened
to be passing or in some panhellenic sanctuary like Olympus,
where he could take advantage of the international assembly that
gathered there for the games. The lectures might be either a
carefully thought-out discourse or a brilliant improvisation on
some theme or other, a free debate on any subject chosen by his
audience. . . . In his efforts to impress his audience, the (S)ophist
was not afraid to claim omniscience and infallibility—adopting a
magisterial tone, a grave or an inspired manner, and pronouncing
his decisions from a throne high up in the air; and sometimes, it
seems, even donning the triumphal costume of the rhapsodist with
his great purple robe (Marrou, 1956, pp. 80–81).

The Sophists did not develop higher educational structures even
though they performed a higher educational function. Such structures
did develop during the Hellenic period, however, and four are mentioned
here. Two of the four—the Pythagorean Museum and the school of
Isocrates—did not survive into the Hellenistic Period, but the other
two—Plato's Academy and Aristotle's Lyceum—continued for centuries
and hence must be more fully described. I shall start, however, with
Plato's teacher, Socrates.

Socrates: Neglecting his family and his trade of stone-cutting,
Socrates spent his time discussing ethical and religious problems
wherever he could find an audience—in the salons of the wealthy, in the
market place, and in the outdoor gymnasia. He declared that he knew no
answers to the complex questions he raised, but his method of
dialectical probing (obstetrics, he called it) led others to find their own
answers. Since he lived twenty-four centuries before the publish-or-
perish syndrome came into vogue, he left no writings, and so
succeeding generations have known him through the caricatures of his
contemporary, Aristophanes, the *Memorabilia* of Xenophon, and,
especially, the dialogues and epistles of Plato.

The Rhetorical School of Isocrates: His estates destroyed by the
Peloponnesian War, the wealthy Isocrates became a teacher of rhetoric
and oratory on the Aegean island of Chios. Returning to Athens, he
established about 392 a top-flight school that left its stamp on all
subsequent education. Neither a mystic nor an abstract philosopher,

Isocrates propounded practical wisdom and trained his students for politics. In Athens this primarily meant teaching them to think clearly, to deal with commonsense problems, and to speak and write persuasively.

In his celebrated inaugural address, "On the Sophists," with which he opened his Athenian school Isocrates inveighed against those teachers who betrayed their high calling by coaching their students in verbal trickery and by inculcating low morals in general. He also paid his critical respects to the dialectical method the followers of Socrates employed and that Plato would emphasize in his soon-to-be-founded Academy. He called it "empty chatter, mere hair splitting" (Jaeger, 1944, Vol. 3, p. 59).

The educational ideas Isocrates propagated projected the rhetorical studies into permanent preeminence. He described his educational philosophy as follows:

> This is my definition of the educated man. First he is capable of dealing with the ordinary events of life, by possessing a happy sense of fitness and a faculty of usually hitting upon the right course of action. Secondly, his behavior in any society is always correct and proper. If he is thrown with offensive or disagreeable company, he can meet it with easy good-temper; and he treats every one with the utmost fairness and gentleness. Thirdly, he always has the mastery over his pleasures, and does not give way unduly under misfortune and pain, but behaves in such cases with manliness and worthily of the nature which has been given to us. Fourthly (the most important point) he is not spoiled or puffed up nor is his head turned by success, but he continues throughout to behave like a wise man, taking less pleasure in the good things which chance has given him at birth than in the products of his own talents and intelligence. Those whose soul is well tuned to play its part in all these ways, those I call wise and perfect men, and declare to possess all the virtues; those I regard as truly educated (Norlin, 1929, Vol. 2, p. 391).

About a decade before his death at the age of ninety-eight, Isocrates closed his school. Its short duration of four decades helps explain why many educational historians have paid so much less attention to it and to Isocrates than to Plato and his long-lived Academy.

The Academy: Plato left Athens after the restoration of the Athenian Republic in 403 and travelled about the Mediterranean, possibly visiting Egypt. On one of his tours he studied with the Pythagorean scholars Archytas and Timaeus, who made him a devotee of mathematics. From them and from other Pythagoreans he probably also absorbed the non-Socratic other-worldliness that permeated his teaching.

Perhaps stimulated by what he learned of the earlier Pythagorean museum, Plato about 387 bought land in a walled park sacred to the memory of the hero Academos on the outskirts of Athens and founded the Academy. Honoring the Muses as did the Pythagorean school, it had at least one well-furnished building over whose portal appeared the inscription *Medeis ageometretos eisisto*—"Let no one enter here without geometry." His students typically came from wealthy families, their elegant dress (caps, cloaks, and canes) calling forth barbs from the comic poets of the time. Standard studies included the Pythagorean theory of numbers, advanced geometry, and speculations about science. Chiefly, however, Plato and his disciples explored social issues— education, jurisprudence, politics, sex—in lectures and informal seminars, an organized curriculum apparently never taking form during Plato's time.

In and through the Academy Plato essayed to educate Athenians and Greeks from other states for public service. There he also wrote his famous dialogues and epistles to diffuse his teaching among educated Greeks. There he laid the foundation of analytical philosophy. There his successors continued to teach until the Emperor Justinian closed the institution nine centuries later in deference to the imperial "university" in Constantinople.

The Lyceum: About twenty years after Plato opened the Academy a seventeen-year-old Macedonian, son of the physician of Philip Second's father, became one of Plato's students and assistants and continued as such until Plato's death two decades later. Apparently disappointed that Plato in his will named his nephew to succeed him as head of the Academy and, in any case, disagreeing with Plato's excessive conceptualism, Aristotle and some other members of the Academy staff departed for Mysia across the Aegean where they organized their own small study group under the patronage of its ruler, Hermias, whose adopted daughter Aristotle married. Later he undertook biological investigations in various cities and then accepted the invitation of Philip, who had recently become the Macedonian ruler, to tutor the young Alexander the Great. Then at the age of forty-nine, three years after the battle of Chaeronia (338), he returned to Athens and organized the Lyceum, so named because of its location in a grove sacred to Apollo Lyceius and the Muses.

The Lyceum closely resembled the Academy in its physical arrangements, but it had a much wider intellectual scope. Aristotle and his associates were interested in everything, including subjects ignored by Plato. The work in the physics of music by his student and colleague, Aristoxenus, for example, remained authoritative until the Renaissance, and the botanical classification of Theophrastus, his successor as head (scholarch) of the Lyceum, continued to be the standard until Linnaeus published his taxonomies in the late eighteenth century. Aristotle himself pioneered the study of biology and, indeed, of most other basic disciplines. His books in a number of them—anthropology, ethics, law, logic, metaphysics, physics, politics, psychology, poetry, rhetoric—remained for centuries mandatory reading for all who went beyond elementary study.

Aristotle influenced higher education primarily and potently in two ways: his Lyceum vastly extended the scope of subjects taught and investigated, the sciences prominently included, and in its instruction and research, it emphasized the principle that generalizations must be derived from the careful observation and classification of facts rather than, as Plato held, from speculation and logic. As will be seen in the next section the museums of the Hellenistic period honored both concepts, but thereafter they went into eclipse and would not come out into the open again until the Renaissance.

The Lyceum never fully recovered from the circumstances that forced Aristotle to flee Athens upon Alexander's death in 323. Nationalistic Athenians had long believed him to be an agent of the expanding Macedonian empire, and when Alexander died, their pent-up hatred impelled Aristotle to leave for one of the Aegean Islands where the next year, aged sixty-two, he died. Theophrastus succeeded him as scholarch, after his death in 287, the Lyceum gradually descended into desuetude.

The Hellenic Educational Legacy: The Academy and the Lyceum survived in one form or another throughout the Hellenistic centuries and beyond, but though the intellectual center of gravity moved to Alexandria and other museums, Athens lived on as the philosophical capital of antiquity and as the "mother of arts and eloquence" (Milton, 1671, Vol. IV, p. 240). All efforts to reconstruct its earlier greatness failed, but students came from near and far to study with its teachers, especially those associated with the Academy. Cicero studied there under Plato's successors just before the beginning of the Christian era; Longinus, the most learned man of the third century, A.D. taught in Athens for thirty years; and during the following century, the Academy concurrently enrolled such personages as the Emperor Julian and two of the four fathers of the Greek Orthodox Church—Basil and Gregory of Nazianus.

The Hellenic educational legacy has nourished every succeeding age, and like all the progeny of European institutions of higher education, American colleges and universities embody ideas and practices that originated in the four schools described in this chapter— the subjects taught, the fundamental methods used in teaching them, the debates about values and purposes, the conflicting concepts concerning the nature and techniques of research. In brief, "the glory that was Greece" reverberates on every college campus and will so long as civilization endures.

Interculturation—the Hellenistic Period

Titles given to historic eras seldom adequately illuminate them. Such names typically obscure some of their most vital characteristics and hence obstruct efforts to see them "steadily and whole." Consider, for example, "the Hellenistic Age." Historians have used the title qualmlessly, but critics point out that the name connotes to the general reader that the culturation process moved in one direction only, that is, from Greece to less civilized peoples. These critics recall that highly advanced civilizations had flourished in Asia Minor and Egypt several thousand years before Greece began to emerge from barbarism, that these early societies had been the primary agents in stimulating Hellenistic creativity, and that Alexander the Great must be regarded as a spectacular accelerator of the *inter*culturation that from time immemorial had been in process throughout the areas surrounding the eastern Mediterranean.

The conviction also grows that the term has served to conceal if not to flout the Asian (Near Eastern) and Egyptian components of the rapidly evolving culture of the period after Alexander's death, and, most important of all, that it reflects the arrogant provincialism of the Western world so odious to present-day Asian and African nations.

Herein, "Hellenistic" will refer to a fusion of Greek and Eastern cultures. The era began with Alexander's invasion of Asia Minor in 334 B.C. and continued until Egypt became a Roman province three hundred years later. The "Roman centuries," which overlapped the latter part of the Hellenistic period, which, in turn, overlapped the Byzantine, will be discussed in the next chapter.

The Ephebia: At some unknown date after the Peloponnesian War Athens, emulating Sparta, established a third educational level below the museums for youths aged eighteen to twenty, the ephebic level. Later other cities followed suit. Civil governments financed and directed these schools, called *ephebia*, primarily as instruments in the early years of military preparation and experience. During these military years Athens, like Sparta, made attendance compulsory, but in later years the emphasis turned to the development of body and mind, attendance became voluntary and enrollments low. The importance of the ephebias in the Roman period, when they became more similar to modern liberal arts colleges and catered to the sons of the wealthy, has been confirmed by historians (see, for example, Marrou, 1956, pp. 256–60), but they had minimal bearing upon the higher educational structures now to be considered.

Alexandria: Alexander has been credited by tradition with founding seventy cities, but, whatever the number, Alexandria at the western end of the Nile Delta towered above all the others in the Hellenistic world. Alexander himself marked it out after conquering Egypt in 331–30. He or one of his remarkable staff discerned that how an engineering tour de force (joining the large offshore island of Pharos and a small fishing village on the mainland by means of a 300-yard causeway) would make it the best harbor and naval base in the Mediterranean. The Ptolemies completed building the city after the first head of that dynasty had entombed its founder's mummified body in a flamboyant museum in the royal section of the city.

In the partitioning of territory after Alexander's death, Egypt and Libya fell to the lot of Ptolemy Soter (Preserver). He acquired the latter name because of his protection of Rhodian independence during twenty years of warfare among Alexander's generals and their progeny for control of his empire. When the Battle of Ipsus in 301 confirmed Ptolemy's hold on Egypt, he established the Ptolemaic dynasty and "engaged no more in war with any of the rival kings" (Bevan, 1919, p. 36).

Soon thereafter Ptolemy founded the Alexandrian museum-library, his greatest achievement (Parsons, 1952). Almost certainly the inspiration for it came from Demetrius Phaleron, a student at the Lyceum of Theophrastus and, possibly, of Aristotle. Demetrius Phaleron had been governor of Athens for a decade ending in 307 and took refuge in Alexandria when the Wars of the Successors forced him to flee for his life. Demetrius envisioned Alexandria as a second and greater Athens, and what Soter accomplished toward the conversion of the vision into reality, his son and successor Ptolemy II (Philadelphus) carried forward with so much enthusiasm that some historians have called him the founder. Because of the several fires that destroyed Alexandria's early records, no one knows how the credit for conceiving the enterprise(s) should be allocated, the opening date(s), and much else including the relationship of the museum and library.

Getting the institution(s) underway required recruiting the requisite learned men by providing them with materials for their studies and arranging for their physical well-being. In all of these enterprises Demetrius played a key, and probably the leading, role. As a disciple of Aristotle, he plotted out a program consonant with the scope of the Lyceum and its encyclopedic master. This meant finding and enticing to the conspicuously rich Alexandria gifted people in all intellectual fields—not only several varieties of scientists, mathematicians, and astronomers but also philologists, philosophers, and poets. The number decided upon appears to have been one hundred who, except for projects undertaken at the request of the king, would be free to pursue their own interests and to teach or not in accord with their own desires.

In the ancient world the tools of learning consisted almost entirely of papyrus scrolls. Sizeable libraries of these had been accumulated by Egyptian and Asian rulers, and Alexander's generosity had enabled Aristotle to acquire many of them as well as scrolls from Western sources. Ptolemy commissioned Demetrius to purchase all available scrolls and thus to build up a great scholarly library for the use of his assembled savants and literati. A French investigator, believing that the museum preceded the library, has summarized the results:

> It (the library) had still to be organized; no one was better fitted for that difficult task than Demetrius. On his recommendation Ptolemy bought, among other works, everything that had been written on the art of government. . . . If we can trust various ancient statements, it harboured no less than 200,000 volumes at the end of Ptolemy Soter's reign, and Demetrius, whom the king questioned on this subject, flattered himself with the hope of having 500,000 in his charge (Couat, 1931, pp. 136–37).

The Alexandrian museum and library, probably housed together and administratively coordinated, have frequently been referred to as a university. Over time the teaching function expanded, so the name applies despite the fact that "university" did not become a current term until the Middle Ages. At the outset the institution seems to have been rather like the School of Advanced Studies near Princeton University or perhaps in part like the Center for the Advanced Study of the Behavioral Sciences adjacent to Stanford. Early in its history, however, it made a transition comparable to that of Rockefeller Institute for Medical Research, which after almost a half century as a research organization, added the teaching function of a few advanced students and in 1965 changed its name to Rockefeller University.

Another important fact about the University of Alexandria or, as some writers have called it, the University of Egypt was that the Ptolemies built and financed it, its scholars (to be referred to from this point as professors) receiving salaries from the state treasury. It had the distinction, therefore, of being one of the first state-supported universities of the Western world. A president (*epistates*) headed the administrative staff which, considering the intricate bureaucracy that enmeshed the Ptolemaic government, may have been formidable. Among other things the administrators looked out for the physical comfort of the professors, operating a dining hall or halls, for example, and possibly arranging for or even supplying residences. They also protected the professorial prerogatives of exemption from taxation, military service, and the like.

Athens: Alexandria cannot be credited with all these advances. During the Hellenistic era, for instance, the Academy in Athens underwent as many as five restructurings. The first or Old Academy stayed faithful to Plato's philosophical doctrines and to his strong interest in mathematics and astronomy. The second and third (sometimes called the Middle Academy) switched to the skeptical point of view first propounded by Pyrrho the century after Plato's death. The fourth swerved toward Stoicism (which will be discussed later). The fifth, generally called the New Academy, flourished during the last pre-Christian century and sought to reconcile Stoicism not only with Platonism but also with the teachings of Aristotle.

As described above, Aristotle's Lyceum declined in importance in the decades following his death. Probably many factors contributed to its decline, but two seem especially significant: the establishment of the Alexandrian Museum-Library and the bequeathal by Theophrastus, Aristotle's successor, of his own and Aristotle's library to a nephew named Neleus. The first of these considerations seems so self-evident as not to require elaboration beyond pointing to the great resources of Ptolemy Soter and the fact that scholars have ever been alert to the relationship of higher budgets and higher learning. Neleus, although a student at the Lyceum, lacked scholarly interests, and the collection fell into several different hands following his death. The largest portion remained in a cave for nearly two hundred years, more or less disintegrating. Later acquired by an Athenian collector-scholar, it was claimed by Sulla as Roman booty when he subdued Athens. Soon thereafter Andronicus of Rhodes, the eleventh *scholarch* of the Lyceum, took on the task (presumably under commission from Sulla) to prepare and publish the writings of both Aristotle and Theophrastus. His work has been one of the primary sources of all later editions in all languages and also of some basic terms of Aristotle, but its publication caused hardly a ripple in the intellectual world of the last Hellenistic century. The scope of philosophy had been narrowed by the dominant Stoics to ethics with the result that few Athenians understood Aristotle. Nor did the scientifically oriented Alexandrians pay much attention to Aristotle's writings. There as elsewhere interest in such matters had drastically diminished. Fortunately a set of the complete writings of Aristotle found its way to Persia, where it was translated into Arabic. From these translations by Muslim scholars, Europeans began in the twelfth and thirteenth centuries to become acquainted with the encyclopedic Aristotle.

Epicurus: In 307 Demetrius Phaleron, educated in the Lyceum and for a decade the ruler of Athens, fled to Alexandria because of a new and potent twist in Macedonian politics. That year or the next a young philosopher named Epicurus, scion of a noble Athenian family which had moved to the island of Samos, transferred his activities from the Aegean to Melita, a suburb of Athens. There he purchased a house and spacious garden, established a school known as The Garden, and began teaching what came to be called the Epicurean philosophy. When he died thirty-seven years later he willed the property to his follower, Hermarchus, the first of a succession of scholarchs who would govern the school during its approximately six hundred years of life.

Most Greeks considered the city-state to be the foundation of Hellenic culture, and its collapse, followed by more than a quarter of a century of chaotic warfare among Alexander's generals and their families, made for abounding pessimism. This feeling, in turn, pulled in the boundaries of philosophy that Plato and Aristotle had so spectacularly extended, ethics and moral education becoming the all-absorbing topic of the new-type philosophers, including Epicurus. The nature of man, not of the physical world, engrossed his thoughts. He resurrected the all-but-forgotten atomic theory of Leucippus and Democritus, but he had no scientific curiosity per se. His Roman follower Lucretius (96?–55 B.C.) immortalized this rudimentary Greek atomic theory in his great work, *De Rerum Natura*, but its known characteristics largely explain why the name Epicureanism soon came to denote the exact opposite of its creator's point of view.

Apparently no one thought ill of Plato or of the Academy because it admitted women, but Epicurus's anti-clericalism and his staunch refusal to condone the fast-spreading superstitions from Asia Minor so nettled his enemies that they erroneously associated the coeducation of The Garden with his basic ethical concept, namely, that pleasure is the ultimate good. By this he meant the subjective or spiritual pleasure that follows from self-control, moderation, and prudence, but his opponents maintained that he applauded sensualism. They might better have pointed to two real counts against the program of The Garden: first, its neglect of scientific investigation; second, its strong tendency to encourage students to seek the ultimate pleasure of imperturbability (*ataraxia*) by substituting contemplation for action. This latter count against Epicureanism probably explains why so few of the world's eminent doers have been its adherents.

Zeno: Zeno, a contemporary of Epicurus, projected the opposing philosophy of Stoicism, so named because Zeno and his successors taught in one of the several *stoa* (buildings with colonnades or cloisters) in the center of Athens. A native of Cypress and a Phoenician, Zeno had been a merchant, an accident converting him into a philosopher. Diogenes Laertius told the story:

> He was shipwrecked on a voyage from Phoenicia to Piraeus with a cargo of purple. He went up into Athens and sat down in a bookseller's shop [where he picked up Xenophon's *Memorabilia of Socrates*]. He was so pleased that he inquired where men like Socrates were to be found. Crates passed by in the nick of time, so the bookseller pointed to him and said, "Follow yonder man." From that day he became Crates's pupil, showing in other respects a strong bent for philosophy, though with too much native modesty to assimilate Cynic shamelessness (Vol. 1, p. 113).

Shamelessness constituted one of the central doctrines of the Cynics, the beatniks of the Hellenistic world. Complete individualists, they declared the purpose of life to be the pursuit of happiness through virtue and that virtue could be attained only by self-sufficiency and hence by sneering at social conventions. Unable to swallow the Cynic panacea, Zeno spent the next twenty years sampling the thinking of the variegated scholars and pundits of Athens and of other cities. Then about the year 300 he launched his own career as a moral philosopher in the Stoa Poikile, so named because Polygnotus, the foremost painter of the Periclean Age, had decorated its cloister. There Zeno continued to teach for more than three decades, and there, or nearby, students congregated to study with his intellectual heirs until the middle of the third Christian century. Stoic centers also took form in other Hellenistic cities; and, well before Rome became an empire, the eclectic philosophy of Stoicism had achieved primacy.

Some of the scholarchs of the Academy and of the Lyceum, for example, became proponents of Stoicism, and most leading Romans adopted its tenets. Further, the Stoic outlook influenced Christianity directly through St. Paul who grew up in Tarsus, a major Stoic stronghold, and indirectly through later Christian theologians. Like the Epicureans whom they deplored, the Stoics accented ethics to the disastrous neglect of many of the broader interests (scientific in particular) sponsored during their halcyon days by the Academy, the Lyceum, and the Alexandrian Museum-Library.

The Stoics did not, however, entirely neglect higher learning. They gave significant attention to the study of language, some of their work in grammar and literary criticism surpassing that of the

Alexandrians. In the course of time this interest veered some Stoics toward the educational views of Isocrates, a shift that, merging with the attention given rhetoric by the Peripatetics of the Lyceum, established the subject as the paramount study of Roman education.

Zeno and Epicurus established their schools in Athens because for over a century it had been the heartland of philosophy and education. Their schools' durability together with that of the Academy and Lyceum assured the City's intellectual eminence and attracted many private teachers, especially of non-scientific subjects. The more successful of these became residents who taught in their homes or in one or another of the stoas, but some continued in the itinerant tradition of the earlier Sophists. Meanwhile the city's fame in drama, poetry, and the fine arts lived on unimpaired by the monumental scientific reputation of Alexandria. The largess of the descendants of Alexander's successors and other benefactors illustrates the resulting emotional appeal of Athens for Greeks and later for Romans. Ptolemy II in 250 B.C. erected a large gymnasium for it close to the *Agora* (marketplace); one of the kings of Pergamum adorned the Acropolis with bronze statues; two others of that house built stoas, that of Attalus II being famous for centuries; and a Syrian king whose ancestor had been one of Alexander's generals initiated work on the colossal temple of Olympian Zeus that would be carried forward by Augustus and completed more than two and a half centuries later by Hadrian. During his reign (117–38 A.D.) Hadrian, whose mother had become an Epicurean, considerably increased the size of the city by extending its wall, built temples for the worship of Hera and Zeus Panhellenius, and erected a huge library (the Hadrian Stoa) some of whose columns still stand. Later during the same century the wealthy scholar-politician Herodes Atticus built the city a stadium with a seating capacity of 44,000 and a theater (the famous Odeum) accommodating 5,000.

Other Hellenistic Seats of Learning

The glow which emanated from the mingling during the Hellenistic centuries of Hellenic and Asiatic cultures illuminated in some degree every city of the period. At least a half score of them established higher schools such as those of Athens and Alexandria, those of Pergamum and Rhodes sparkling so brightly that at least one of them—Pergamum—must be commented on briefly.

A series of betrayals converted the fortress city of Pergamum into the capital of an extensive kingdom that became wealthy enough to rival—and in the fine arts, at least, to equal—Alexandria and Athens. The half-Greek eunuch, Philataerus, governor of the city during the War of the Successors, began the double-dealing by selling out to the Seleucids to whose lot had fallen the Alexandrian satrapy of Syria. In this fashion Pergamum became a semi-independent principality. Upon his death Philataerus bequeathed it, considerably enlarged, to a nephew whose successor, Attalus I, defeated the invading Gauls about 230 B.C., broke away from Syria, and expanded the kingdom further. The fourth member of the Attalid dynasty (Attalus was the name of three of the six rulers of Pergamum) conspired during his reign (197–160 B.C.) with the rising Roman power to weaken the Seleucid dynasty further. With Roman help he controlled the entire coast of the Aegean as well as territories deep in its hinterland.

Like many other celebrated families founded and augmented by famous malefactors, the Attalids became devoted sponsors of learning and culture. They not only gave of their wealth to adorn Athens, for a period they also subsidized the Academy. Chiefly, however, they coveted eminence for their capital city. Several of the distinguished scholars they invited to head the Pergamene Library declined, but during the first half of the second pre-Christian century the Stoic rhetorician, Crates, accepted. He and his successors, well supplied with Attalid gold, made their collection of about 200,000 scrolls almost as famous as that of Alexandria (Antony gave it to Cleopatra and thus to Alexandria.).

The scholars associated with the Library did work in grammar, rhetoric, and literary criticism comparable to that of Alexandria and Athens, but the accomplishments of the associated Museum have not excited historians of science. The famous younger contemporary of Archimedes, the mathematician Apollonius, had been born in Pergamum and had perhaps even been financed by Attalus I, but he found Alexandria more congenial. Several centuries later Galen, a native Pergamene, also departed for Alexandria although he received his first training degree in the medical school that, even before the Attalids, had been established in the outskirts of the city. Meanwhile Attalus III, who brought the dynasty to an end by bequeathing the kingdom to Rome in 133 B.C., did botanical research but his research was practical, not scholarly. The fame of Pergamum rests not on its science or on its literary achievements but primarily on its memorable works of art, on the invention of parchment, and on the educational activities of its professors.

The defeat of the Gauls during the 230s accentuated the ambition of the Attalids to make Pergamum a beautiful city. To commemorate the victory, Attalus I brought to Pergamum the best architects and sculptors of the period and commissioned them to build an altar to Zeus. The frieze of the resulting edifice, seven and a half feet high and extending 350 feet around the sides of the mammoth altar, depicts the battles of the gods (the Pergamanians) against the giants (the worsted Galatians). One of the most famous as well as most beautiful of ancient works of art, the frieze has been in the possession of the Berlin Museum for the past century. Roman museums preserve two other famous survivals of the golden age of Pergamene art—the statues of the "Dying Gaul" and the "Wounded Gaul."

The Perpetuation of Greek Ideas in Later Centuries

Pergamum, Rhodes, Athens, Alexandria, and other Hellenic centers of higher education perpetuated and expanded upon the beginnings made earlier by Pythagorus, Isocrates, Plato, Aristotle, and others during the Hellenic era. In so doing they ensured a continuation of Greek higher educational ideas long after the Greek nation itself had been absorbed into other empires. In the chapter which follows it becomes readily apparent that the Romans, Byzantines, and Moslems, while occasionally contributing new areas of knowledge, housed such activities in structures basically Hellenic or Hellenistic. Not until universities began to appear in western Europe during the Middle Ages did a new kind of higher educational structure appear. From the medieval and Reformation universities grew today's American colleges and universities.

Bibliographic Notes

Among the few recent publications dealing with Hellenic or Hellenistic higher education is Bruce Kimball's *Orators and Philosophers* (1986). Kimball provides historic insight into the content and meaning of the "liberal education." He builds his thesis around the opposing approaches Isocrates and Plato took to the higher learning, Isocrates focusing on the education of the orator and Plato on the philosopher. Kimball continues his analysis through most of the periods covered in this book.

Dewald's chapter in Grant and Kitzinger (1988) focuses on the teaching of rhetoric and oratory in Greece starting with Homeric times and extending into the Roman period. She provides an excellent contemporary overview of the period, covering in good detail much of the material in Chapter One of this book. Lloyd's chapter in this same publication deals more with Greek philosophy but in the process provides further information about the schools wherein these philosophers taught and the major topics studied. Lentz (1989) compares Plato, the Sophists, Isocrates, Aristotle, and others especially in terms of the oral tradition that influenced life in Hellenic times.

Beyond these more recent sources the most helpful materials come from earlier authors. Smith (1955) covers a broad range of cultural and educational history, focusing on seven early civilizations: Mesopotamia, Egypt, India, China, Greece, Rome, and the Jews. Clarke (1971) writes in some detail about the teaching of grammar, rhetoric, mathematics, and music in ancient Greece and Rome. Lynch (1972) devotes his book to Aristotle's Lyceum: the site, the education possessed by his students when they arrived at his door, other institutions of those times, the functioning of his school at its height, and its eventual destruction at the hands of Sulla in 86 B.C.

Important among even earlier texts are Marrou (1956), Jaeger (1944), and Sarton (1952 and 1959).

CHAPTER TWO

Higher Education During the Roman, Byzantine, and Islamic Civilizations: 800 B.C.–1600 A.D.

> The historical importance of Roman education is not to be found in any slight variations or additions it may have made to classical education of the Hellenistic type, but in the way it managed to spread this education through time and space.
>
> (Marrou, 1956, p. 391)

> Surprising as it may seem, there is to begin with a whole area where, strictly speaking, the old classical school never came to an end—in the Greek East; for Byzantine education was a direct continuation of classical education.
>
> (Marrou, 1956, p. 452)

> It is hard for us, pigeonholed in Christendom, to realize that from the eighth to the thirteenth century Islam was culturally, politically, and militarily superior to Europe.
>
> (Durant, 1957, p. 695)

In the same year that Philip II of Macedonia completed his subjugation of Athens and her sister Greek city-states, another people in a series of local battles succeeded in gaining dominance over their neighbors in the Latin League of central Italy. Some 63 years later in 275 B.C. these people further extended their boundaries and gained control over all of the Italian peninsula, including the Greek colonies in southern Italy.

Worrying constantly over the intentions of their neighbors, the Romans sought by any means at their disposal to neutralize the threats as they perceived them. Thus they continually extended their boundaries until they reached to the north into the British Isles, to the south along the Mediterranean coastline of Africa, to the west to the Atlantic and to the east far into Persia. Some centuries later the neighbors did indeed become a decided threat; and, aided by deterioration in the fabric of Roman society itself, the barbaric peoples of the north overthrew the Roman government.

Further to the east, however, new civilizations arose. Byzantium, in the fourth and fifth centuries avowedly Roman and in later centuries increasingly Hellenistic in orientation, preserved and extended the Greco-Roman heritage. To the south the Islamic civilization during the seventh century began spreading its influence into Persia and along the southern shores of the Mediterranean all the way into Spain. Even more than Byzantium, Islam during the centuries that followed further extended the boundaries of human knowledge as well as helped to preserve the literature and knowledge of classical times.

The Hellenistic Flavor of Roman Higher Education

Roman history divides into at least three periods: the monarchy, which ended in 509 B.C., the Republic, which ended in 27 B.C., and the Empire, which ended in 476 A.D. The peak centuries—the first century B.C. plus the first two centuries A.D.—mark the period of greatest higher educational activity, but first some of the accomplishments of the earlier years require attention.

Higher Education During the Period of the Republic: Roman education until approximately 240 B.C. remained almost solely the concern of the family, especially of the male head of the family, the paterfamilias. Higher education at this time consisted of a father's taking his son with him to the seats of government where the son could observe the goings-on. Sometimes apprenticed to a friend of the father—perhaps someone "noted for his gifts in the conduct of public affairs or in law or as a speaker" (Moore, 1936, p. 213)—the son would increasingly enter into public affairs until he was judged competent to assume an adult role there.

This pattern changed because of the growing influence of the Greeks during the last two centuries of the Republic. Increasingly the Romans brought Greeks, either as slaves or as freedmen, into their homes and communities, in most instances to school their children but in some cases also to provide an intellectual atmosphere in which to entertain their guests. Among the latter instances is the so-called Scipionic Circle, which centered about the Greek historian and scholar, Polybius, who became in the second century B.C. the protege of Scipio Africanus the Younger. Scipio's friendship with Polybius and with the Latin writers Terence and Laelius gave him a lasting reputation as a patron of the arts. Polybius wrote of him, and so did Cicero in *De Republica* and *De Amicitia*.

Roman higher education, much as with the Greeks, concentrated largely on rhetoric. As such it followed closely in the tradition of the Sophists and of Isocrates. Having completed their secondary schooling under the *grammatici* and in many cases having then donned the *toga virilis*—symbol of their manhood—these were "young men preparing for public life and destined to speak before the senate, the law courts, and the people gathered before the Rostra" (Moore, 1936, pp. 213–14).

Although Cicero and Quintilian would have emphasized and even exceeded the more humanistic bent of Isocrates, the great bulk of rhetores remained narrowly utilitarian in their approach. "The *rhetor Latinus*," wrote Marrou,

> . . . aimed at teaching his pupil how to master the art of oratory as handed down traditionally in the complex system of rules, methods and customs that had gradually been perfected in Greek schools from the time of the Sophists. It was all laid down in advance: one learned the rules, and then practised how to use them (1956, p. 382).

Student exercises took two forms: the *suasio*, a political speech drawing upon historical examples, and the *controversia*, in which the person pleaded for or against some established legal issue.

Although they enjoyed a status and income higher than the grammatici, the *rhetores* held a low station in life until well into the period of the Empire, at which time certain of them received special dispensations from the Emperor. In the meantime they would have to suffer the usual problems of attracting students and obtaining their tuition once having attracted them.

Upon completing their studies with the rhetor, certain young Romans would travel abroad, where they put the finishing touches on their education. Sometimes this further study consisted simply of more rhetoric, but it might also include philosophy. Centers for this activity were Alexandria, Smyrna, Antioch, Rhodes, and—above all—Athens. Cicero, for example, studied at the Academy in Athens and at the Museum in Rhodes, and Julius Caesar studied at Rhodes.

During the period of the Empire which followed, the work of the rhetors and the great Hellenistic higher educational centers continued. Increasingly higher education became the concern of the Roman state. While this increased concern brought wealth and status to the "professors" of that day, it also put limits on their work.

Higher Education During the Period of the Empire: Rhetorical training continued as the major form of higher education in the Empire. Add to it the schooling in law, the increasing government involvement in higher education, and the growth of Hellenistic higher educational structures in parts of western Europe not reached in earlier centuries by the Greeks, and one has a grasp of the major features of the later Roman higher education.

The rhetor in Empire times, especially during the first and second centuries A.D., came increasingly to receive government support. Part of the time this support came from emperors and other officials in the form of private philanthropy, but many communities during this period also provided funds to support a rhetor. They also built structures wherein the rhetors might teach. Here appeared:

> . . . rooms like exedras, arranged like little theatres and opening out on to the forum porticos at the far end: such are schola in Trajan's forum, the exedra in Augustus' forum in Rome, and the exedras by the north portico of the capitol in Constantinople (Marrou, 1956, p. 382).

With this support, however, came government controls, those officials in most cases deciding who should occupy the chair in question. Competition for the chairs increased in ferocity as the rewards to the incumbents rose.

Athens during the reign of the Flavians experienced a rebirth of the glory it had known three and four centuries earlier. Even under Nero, an unregenerate Greekophile, the sister city of Corinth enjoyed special favors, but under Vespasian, Trajan, Hadrian, Antoninus Pius, and Marcus Aurelius Athens itself flourished. Several of these men had studied under Greek tutors as youths, and they carried within them a lifelong reverence for Greece and its culture.

Vespasian began the practice by endowing at Rome chairs of Latin and Greek rhetoric and supporting them with annual salaries. He further relieved all grammarians, rhetors, physicians, and philosophers from certain public duties. Trajan extended these special privileges, and under Hadrian the support reached new levels. This emperor sought to reunite the Greek nation, with Athens as its capital, and he beautified the city with many new buildings, a number of which served educational purposes. Greek studies had special favor with Hadrian and with his successor, Antoninus Pius, who extended salaries and special privileges to men of learning throughout the Empire and who established a publicly supported chair of rhetoric in Athens. Marcus Aurelius in turn established a second chair in rhetoric and endowed chairs in each of the four schools of philosophy, showing his intention of making Athens once more a great center of learning.

Meanwhile, Rome itself during Hadrian's reign built a center of learning and named it the Athenaeum in honor of the Greek city. Here Greek and Roman teachers and writers displayed their talents, and hundreds of students flocked to the city. Their number grew so great, in fact, that it became necessary to decree the length of time they could stay and to establish the age at which they must leave and return to their home communities.

Throughout the Empire these schools flourished. Hellenistic in their emphasis and supported by the communities wherein they were located, schools such as the one in Tarsus had a reputation equal to that of Athens, although in the case of Tarsus they catered primarily to local students. Centers appeared in Smyrna, Berytus, Antioch, and Ephesus, while Alexandria regained the glory it had known under the Ptolemies. In Gaul, for instance, Treves, Autun, Toulouse, Lyon, Reims, and several other cities supported higher education, their fortunes waxing and waning according to their capacity to attract scholars. Spain, Germany, and North Africa (Carthage) in like manner had their centers.

In practically all of these instances, however, the spectre of government interference—which had overshadowed state-supported higher education since the early days of Alexandria—hung over the scholars of the Roman empire. Hadrian's mother, Plotina, for instance, meddled in the affairs of the Epicurean school in Athens, and usually the emperors retained the right to select the occupants of the learned chairs that they endowed. As beneficiaries of the state the scholars, much as with the Alexandrian scholars before them, knew better than to delve critically into political matters. The government dominance reduced the brilliance of the schools of the later Roman period, and at least one writer has attributed the eventual decline of Roman higher education to increasing governmental control (Cramer, 1939).

But Rome itself had gone into decline, and after the death of Marcus Aurelius few emperors showed any serious appreciation for literature or for learning. The Severi gave some support, and Constantine restored some of the salaries and privileges of the professors, but for the most part Roman higher education never again achieved the level it had known earlier.

Before leaving this section, the Roman system of legal education deserves attention. Marrou has commented:

> The one really great original feature of Latin education was in fact the opportunity it provided of a legal career. On this point alone does the perfect parallel between Greek and Latin schools break down. Having left philosophy and—for a long time at least—medicine to the Greeks, the Romans created their own original type of higher education with the law schools (1956, p. 387).

Within Roman society persons who knew law, could interpret it, and apply it at the appropriate moment enjoyed a high status. Government depended upon such people, and their training became increasingly vital. Before Cicero's time this schooling proceeded on an apprenticeship basis, but largely because of Cicero's influence, schools began to appear which offered more than simply practical experience. Large legal consulting organizations, for instance, began offering courses, and teachers of law taught an established body of materials over a set period of four or five years. In addition legal scholars began putting the elements of Roman law in order, the accomplishments of Gaius, Ulpianus, Papianus, and Paulus deserving special mention.

Later in the sixth century under the Byzantine Emperor Justinian this kind of activity would reach its peak.

The New Empire in the East—Byzantium

While the Roman civilization after the sixth century declined in importance, another entered the scene that both preserved important elements of the Greek and Roman cultures and added important elements both to the general history of the world and to the more specific history of higher education.

The capital city of the Byzantine empire was Constantinople. Built by the first Christian Roman emperor, Constantine the Great, on the site of the ancient city of Byzantium, Constantinople opened with flamboyant ceremonies in 330 A.D. Called New Rome by the Emperor, the city by the Bosporus gave the Latins a strong base from which to pursue their dealings with the troublesome Persians to the east. It also provided a site closer to the origins of the Christian faith from which Constantine could undertake his new religious alliance.

In the centuries that followed the Empire knew several periods of special prosperity, periods when power over the Mediterranean and many of the lands surrounding it rested in the Emperor's hands. Certainly in its beginning under Constantine the capital city had its first sense of the prosperity that was to come, and the Empire grew in wealth during the next two centuries, especially under Theodosius II in the fifth century and even more so under Justinian in the sixth. The Empire declined after Justinian's reign, the period between 610 and 717 (during which the Islamic civilization began its rise to prominence) marking one of its darkest moments, but it recovered under the Isaurian dynasty (717–867), Leo III, Constantine V, and Theophilus leading the way. By this time the Byzantine empire had gained an identity of its own, truly Eastern, more Greek than Roman. The Isaurian emperors contributed mightily to this new identity, and during the so-called Macedonian dynasty that followed (867–1081), Byzantium reached the height of its glory. Its realm by this time extended from the Danube to Syria in the east and to southern Italy in the west.

With the death, however, of Basil II in 1025 the Empire descended into new darkness, reversed itself momentarily under the Commeni, but then early in the thirteenth century faced a new threat.

"Friends" from the west, Crusaders bent on regaining control over the Holy Lands, and Italian merchants seeking new sources of wealth cast covetous eyes on the eastern Empire. In 1204 Constantinople fell to the Crusaders, who then controlled it for half a century. Exploited by westerners, racked with class strife from within, no longer possessed of a strong national identity or pride, the Byzantines found themselves in serious trouble. Finally, only the capital city itself remained; and, although the schools still operated (actively supported, in fact by the Paleologi, the emperors of this period), Byzantine art once again flourished, and the city remained under Christian control for another century, the end was in sight. It came on May 29, 1453, at the hands of Mohammed II and his Turkish army.

Byzantine Higher Education: As one might expect, the status of higher education in the Byzantine empire grew and diminished largely according to the fortunes of the Empire and to the proclivities of the men or women who reigned at its head. Some emperors (Leo III, for example, destroyed schools whose teaching conflicted with his iconoclasm) worked to the detriment of higher education. Others, however—notably Constantine I, Theodosius II, Justinian, Theophilus, many of the Macedonian and Commenian rulers, and the Paleologi— gave it abundant support. Theodosius II, for instance, founded in 425 what later historians have called "the state university of Constantinople," which continued—except for occasional periods of inactivity—for ten centuries, until the very end of the Empire in 1453.

This institution quickly overshadowed Athens in importance. When in 529 Justinian, by forbidding the teaching of philosophy and law in the Greek city, put an end to any significant higher education there, the die was cast. Justinian sought by this action to concentrate the intellectual resources of the Empire in Constantinople, although he did permit the continuation of the law school in Berytus.

Controlled at the beginning by Theodosius and the Constantinople city council, this institution housed 31 teachers and their classrooms in one building. Subjects taught ranged from grammar, letters, medicine, and law to philosophy—only theology, by Imperial edict, remaining outside the curriculum. Scholars, in the tradition of Alexandria, had access to great libraries, where the treasured literature of classical times, especially that of the Greeks, was kept. Professors received a state salary, and, if they lived in a praiseworthy manner and taught with distinction for twenty consecutive years, they could expect to retire with the title of Count of the First Order.

The "university" at Constantinople served mainly to prepare civil servants for the government, which required great numbers of them. The demand for government workers thus ensured the well-being of higher education, but so did the continuing reverence of the Byzantine people for classical culture.

As perpetuators of the Western tradition, the scholars at Constantinople and Berytus produced their most singular contributions in the teaching and further codification of Roman law. Justinian, whose closing of the Athenian schools produced such a negative effect in that city, nevertheless had much to do with the advancement of legal scholarship in Byzantium. In an effort, for example, to set high standards in legal education he closed the many low-quality institutions in the Empire and left only two law schools open, those in Berytus and Constantinople. Here he supervised the development of new strong programs. Professors from these cities participated in the codification efforts, Theophilus from Constantinople assisting with the *Code*, a colleague from Constantinople and two from Berytus writing the *Institutes*. These materials, plus the constitutions (the *Novels*, for which the Emperor also obtained professorial help), made up the *Corpus Juris Civilia*, which constituted the curriculum of the law school during Justinian's time. Students completed the *Institutes* and began the *Digest* during the first year, heard lectures on the Digest for another two years, spent a fourth year studying the remainder of the *Corpus* individually, and in the fifth year concentrated on the private study of the *Code*.

After Justinian's death higher education in the Byzantine empire underwent a series of fluctuations. Peak periods came when later emperors sought to renew the stature of legal studies as Justinian had done or to restore the literary or scientific studies of the earlier Hellenistic civilization. The Emperor Theophilus (829–842), for example, gave Leo the Mathematician a public lectureship during his reign, and Basil I and Leo VI later in the same century initiated some of the most important post-Justinian legal scholarship of Byzantine times. Indeed higher education in Constantinople during the ninth century reign of Caesar Bardas regained many of the characteristics given it originally by Theodosius II, the faculty consisting, for instance, of laymen who taught philosophy, geometry, astronomy, rhetoric, but no theology (Mango, 1965, p. 114). Emperor Constantine VII "The Purpleborn," (912–959) went so far as to provide subsidies for literary education, and the teachers he supported taught geometry, philosophy, rhetoric, astronomy, grammar, arithmetic, music, law, and medicine. Not only did this Constantine provide professorships, he also set aside a splendid income for the maintenance of students. The eleventh century also saw a flurry of activity, Constantine XI funding schools of law and letters and supporting professorships in both.

When in the thirteenth century Constantinople fell to the French armies of the Fourth Crusade, its scholars scattered in several directions. Some of them fled east to Nicaea and came into close contact with the Persian culture. Others moved west, taking with them their knowledge of classical culture, much of which the Europeans had long since forgotten. Those who fled to Nicaea returned to Constantinople when their hosts retook the city. They restored their schools, only to be driven out again once and for all in the successful Turkish invasion of Constantinople concluded in 1453. By this time a number of Byzantine scholars had begun teaching in western Europe, one of the first of these having been a Greek, Manuel Chrysoloras, who attracted great attention in Florence, Pavia, Milan, Venice, and (possibly) Rome. Treasured in western Europe were the legal documents and the classical literature which these Byzantine scholars had preserved, and it is to them that present-day scholarship owes a debt.

The Byzantines contributed little *new* knowledge. Theirs was more a holding action, but in this they served later societies well. Living in the shadow of the Hellenistic culture, they absorbed some of its spirit, and, although they added little to literature, they never forgot their debt to their Hellenic and Hellenistic predecessors and hence preserved their works. From Byzantine libraries western Europe eventually obtained many of the versions of the writings of the Greeks, and because of the work of Byzantine scholars the Roman law was preserved and strengthened. Rivalling these contributions, however, and in some ways surpassing the Byzantine civilization in the richness of its contribution to the higher learning, was that of Islam.

The Flowering of the Islamic Civilization

During its seven centuries of florescence the Islamic culture made a lasting impact on the lands it conquered and upon its neighbors. For example, the Abbasid Caliphate, while it presided over the disintegration of the massive empire it had inherited from its Umayyad predecessors, achieved amazing progress in scholarship, literature, science, and a host of other fields, not to mention trade and industry. This progress began in the area of Baghdad in the eighth century and developed in later centuries in Persia, Egypt, and Spain. In the latter regions the now independent dynasties developed cultural centers that soon rivaled Baghdad, and in the process the Arab culture gave way to the interculturating influences of the people the Arabs had conquered—notably the Spaniards, Persians, Jews, Greeks, Syrians, and Egyptians. Holding all these people together culturally, if not politically, was the Arabic language, rich in vocabulary and well suited to tying together the range of peoples embraced by the Islamic faith. This language served well, too, the Islamic higher education from which the Western world gained much during the tenth to thirteenth centuries. To trace this legacy, one begins with the Nestorian Christians, who arrived in Persia in the fifth century.

Islamic Higher Education: When the Byzantine Emperor Zeno in 439 forced a group of Nestorian Christians to leave their schools in Edessa, they found a ready haven awaiting them in Nisibis in Persia. Here the monarch Piruz allowed the Nestorians religious and intellectual freedom, and here they assumed increasing responsibilities—translating the classics into Arabic, teaching, writing, and heading the Persian hospitals. To be sure, their effort (like that of medieval scholars in Europe centuries later) went largely into reconciling the writings of Aristotle to Christian dogma, but they nevertheless played a role in bringing further classical learning to what was to become the Islamic world.

Persians of this period depended largely upon the Nestorian Christians for their contact with classical culture, but they did not limit themselves to drawing upon the Greco-Roman civilization. Well prior to the advent of Islam, they had begun operating a number of centers for higher learning—in Nisibis, Harran, Ctesiphon, Nishapur, and Jundi-Shapur—and here the classical philosophy and science of Greeks,

Romans, Syrians, Jews, and Hindus merged. Scholars translated documents from these varying cultures into a common language and amplified the knowledge gained thereby into new discoveries and theories.

Jundi-Shapur, the best known of these cities at the time, epitomized the blending of cultures. Its academy dates from mid-third century to as late as 1340, and during those years scholars studied subjects ranging from medicine, Hindu literature, astronomy, and mathematics to philosophy. The academy reached its zenith in the sixth century, when it became a sanctuary for intellectuals from many parts of the world. To Jundi-Shapur, for example, came Damascius, the last head of Plato's Academy, and eight of his colleagues following Justinian's closing of the Athenian schools of philosophy. Damascius and the others taught in the academy, then moved on to Alexandria.

The seventh century marks the rise of Islam and the subsequent Arabic subjugation of Persia and much of the southern Byzantine empire. "The ink of the learned is as precious as the blood of the martyrs," declared Mohammed, and centers such as Jundi-Shapur continued to flourish despite the political and religious changes occurring around them. The center for scientific studies, for instance, remained at Jundi-Shapur even after the Arabian conquest.

In the Islamic era, especially under the Abbasid dynasty, Baghdad developed as a particularly exciting center for the higher learning. Beginning in the eighth century chiefly as a research and translation center, Baghdad's Bail-al-Hikmah (House of Wisdom) in later centuries came to share the reputation of Cordova in Spain as the outstanding center of higher education to develop in the Islamic world.

During the eighth century the Islamic quest for new knowledge accelerated, Jabir ibn Haiyyan (a contemporary of Charlemagne) undertaking new studies both in the sciences and in philosophy. During this century paper replaced parchment in Baghdad, and by 900 the city housed one hundred book vendors with libraries and private collections, some of the latter so large as to require several hundred camels to transport them.

The tenth and eleventh centuries, with the establishing of the Fatimid's new capital city of Cairo, saw also the founding of two great higher educational structures, one of which still operates today. In 972, only four years after establishment of the city, the Fatimids built a mosque, al-Azhar, the "Fair One." Sixteen years later it became a school, was closed under Saladin, but later became the symbol of traditional Islam. The only one of the great Islamic "universities" remaining, it has long been a major seat of learning for Islam. The Dar al-'Ilm or Dar al-Hikmah rose in Cairo in 1005 for the teaching and propagation of the liberal Shi'ite doctrine of that time. Like the Bail al-Hikmah, Dar al-'Ilm had a scientific curriculum as well as the usual other Islamic research pursuits: Greek philosophy, mathematics, medicine, and the major work in theology.

Totah found reference in the literature to 238 higher educational structures, "though that may not be more than one-tenth of the true number" (1926, p. 23). Except for Spain—where mosques performed the educational function—institutions called *madaris* spread throughout the Empire. Here higher education flourished, and the numbers of such institutions grew. In Damascus alone were 74 madaris, in Cairo 74, in Jerusalem 41, Aleppo 14, Tripoli 13, and Mosul nine (Totah, 1926, p. 23). The larger of these schools had principals who appointed professors who in turn were subject to the patron's (sultan of the community or caliph—or their aides) approval. Professors had assistants who repeated the lectures after class to the students who hadn't been able to copy them completely. The teachers themselves, not the institutions, gave diplomas to those who had studied with them. Consequently, "students did not seek institutions but sought eminent scholars, prized their inspiration, and prided themselves on obtaining certificates from them" (p. 53). Except for his submission to institutional authority regarding his orthodoxy, "the professor was, practically, all in all. He was the textbook and the curriculum" (p. 98). It was common for serious students to learn everything a teacher could offer, receive his certificate, and go on to others. Thus Abu al-Wazim Sulaiman—during thirty-three years—studied under a thousand professors from Mesopotamia to Egypt, and Tax al-Islam abu Said studied under 400.

This keen interest in learning led, by the ninth and tenth centuries, to the translation into Arabic of eight of Plato's books, nineteen of Aristotle's, ten of Hippocrates's, and twenty-six of Galen's plus others by Euclid, Archimedes, and Ptolemy. By the eleventh century the Islamic interest in scholarly pursuits had reached full flower, both in the eastern sector dominated by Baghdad and the western sector dominated by Cordova. Higher education had come to Spain in the tenth century, and centers developed not only in Cordova but also in Seville, Toledo (the major center for translation in western Europe), Granada,

Marcia, Almeria, Valencia, and Cadiz. Such centers usually developed around great libraries (Cordova's contained 600,000 volumes by the late tenth century).

The eleventh century, the "golden era of Islamic culture," spawned numerous important men of learning. They include the fabled Omar Khayyam, mathematician-astronomer and poet—the greatest scientist of his time; the philosophers al-Farabi and al-Masudi ("the Pliny of Islam"); the mathematicians Ibrahim ibn Sinan and al Khwariznu (who gave the term "algebra" to the West); the historian Abu al-Hasan Ali al Masudi ("one of the earliest Muslims to suggest the concept of the evolution of life from the physical inanimate plane upward to the plant, animal, and human planes" [Nakosteen, 1964, p. 155]); Avicenna, whose *Canon of Medicine* fixed the classification of sciences used in medical schools of Europe from 1000 to 1300; and the encyclopaedist Abu Rayhan al-Biruni, who wrote on subjects ranging from geography, mathematics, astronomy, physics, poetry, and philosophy to medicine. Persian literature also reached its heights during this period in the person of Firdawsi, whose epic 60,000-verse *Shah Namah* ("Book of Kings") served as the inspiration for generations of poets.

The curricula in Islamic centers covered a broad range. They included mathematics (algebra, geometry, and trigonometry), science (chemistry, physics, and astronomy), medicine (anatomy, surgery, pharmacy, and specialized medicine), philosophy (logic, ethics, and metaphysics), literature (philology, grammar, poetry, and prosody), social sciences, history, geography, politics, law, sociology, psychology, jurisprudence, and theology (comparative religions, history of religions, study of the Koran, religious traditions, and other religious subjects) (Nakosteen, 1964, p. 62). New centers of learning arose, two in Baghdad—Nizamiyyans and the Mustansiriyyah—especially flourishing as one sought to outdo the other. LeStrange has written concerning the Mustansiriyyah:

> We are told that in outward appearance, in stateliness of ornament and sumptuousness of furniture, in spaciousness and in the wealth of its pious foundations, the Mustansiriyyah surpassed everything that had previously been seen in Islam. It contained four separate law schools, one for each of the orthodox sects of the Sunnis, with a professor at the head of each, who had seventy-five students . . . in his charge, to whom he gave instruction gratis. The four

professors each received a monthly salary, and to each of the three hundred students one gold dinar a month was assigned. The great kitchen of the college further provided daily rations of bread and meat to all the inmates. According to Ibn al-Furat there was a library in the Mustansiriyyah with rare books treating of the various sciences, so arranged that the students could easily consult them, and those who wished could copy these manuscripts, pens and paper being supplied by the establishment. Lamps for the students and a due provision of olive oil for lighting up the college are also mentioned, likewise, storage places for cooling the drinking water; and in the great entrance gate . . . stood a clock . . ., announcing the appointed times of prayer, and marking the lapse of the hours by day and by night. Inside the college a bath house . . . was erected for the special use of the students, and a hospital . . ., to which a physician was appointed whose duty it was to visit the place every morning, prescribing for those who were sick; and there were great store-chambers in the Madrasah provided with all requisites of food, drink, and medicine (LeStrange, 1900, pp. 267–68).

The Mustansiriyyah, founded in 1234, was contemporary with the European universities of Salerno, Bologna, Paris, and Oxford.

Descriptions such as this document the very real, but rarely reported, contributions of the medieval Moslem civilization. From Islam, moreover, came efforts at measuring the size of the earth, the idea of teaching the roundness of the earth by use of a globe, the practice of dissection in anatomy, the use of anesthetics in surgery, and the manufacture of potash, alcohol, nitrate of silver, nitric acid, sulphuric acid, and corrosive sublimate (Nakosteen, 1964, p. 53). Much of what European professors talked about and wrote about in the eleventh to thirteenth centuries was either Greek or Islamic. Roger Bacon, for example, lectured on Moslem science. Not until the mid-sixteenth century advent of Copernicus in astronomy, Paracelsus in medicine, and Vesalius in anatomy did Moslem-Hellenistic science give way to the "new concepts of man and his world" (Nakosteen, 1964, p. 194).

By this time, too, the Islamic civilization had succumbed—to the Mongols in the east and to the Christians in the west—and the responsibility for carrying further the work of Islamic scholars fell to those who taught and studied in the newly established universities of western Europe. Before moving to these institutions, however, it is necessary to mention two peoples—the Jews and the Africans south of the Sahara—who came into contact with Islamic higher education and made their own contributions to it.

The Jews had operated schools long before the rise of Islam; in fact, there appeared in Jerusalem in the second or first century B.C.

> . . . a sort of university or academy—an institution composed of the scribes (sages and teachers), whose pupils having outgrown the schools, gathered around them for further instruction and were called, therefore, *talmide hakamin* (disciples of the wise) (Singer, 1906, Vol. 2, p. 147).

Instruction in the Jewish institutions centered about the study of Jewish law from the Torah, and this concern continued dominant in the later Islamic period. Despite their destruction of the Temple in Jerusalem in 70 A.D. the Romans did not crush the Jewish culture. With the general easing of restrictions against Christians in the centuries that followed, the Jews also enjoyed a tolerance that permitted their schools to grow. Christian disfavor worked against the Jews, but they welcomed the much greater tolerance given them by the followers of Mohammed in later centuries. Gradually, as the Islamic empire spread along the shores of the Mediterranean to Spain and east into Babylonia, the Jews moved with it; and in most large Islamic cities appeared a Jewish quarter. Here arose schools, the more advanced of these similar to the earlier "university" in Jerusalem, where the major concern was, as before, with Jewish religious law. In addition to this concern, however (and at times as a complement to their religious studies), the Jews explored other fields—notably astronomy, medicine, and translation. In these areas the Jews excelled, and for their accomplishments they require mention in the present chapter.

Motivated by the intricacies of the Hebrew lunar calendar, the Jews became intimately familiar with the heavens. This familiarity stood them in good stead in the related area of navigation, and the maps they drew and the instruments they perfected contributed singularly to the age of exploration that opened near the close of the Islamic period.

Medical schooling, it appears, may have served as a part of the "liberal education" given the Jews in their higher schools (Neuman, 1942, Vol. 2, p. 108). Jewish physicians attended the ruling families of Europe and the Islamic world, and their research contributed mightily to the store of medical knowledge passed on to the European universities by the Arabs in the eleventh through the thirteenth centuries.

Jewish work in translation, finally, goes back at least to the early days of Jundi-Shapur and seems to suggest a traditional Jewish role as a translator. Again this work aided them primarily in their religious studies; but such studies, which required a knowledge of Greek, Latin, Arabic, and other tongues, made them the logical translators of the early European medieval period. Perhaps the best known of the Jewish translation centers appeared in Toledo in Spain in the twelfth century.

Much as the Islamic culture countenanced and actually drew strength from the Jews in its midst, so did it encourage the spread of higher learning to new areas. One such instance of this phenomenon appeared during the fourteenth to the sixteenth centuries south of the Sahara in the city of Timbuktu. Sometimes called the "seaport of the Sahara," Timbuktu served as a rich center for trade between peoples of the desert and those who lived along the Niger River and its tributaries westward to the Atlantic. Inevitably the Islamic faith reached Timbuktu, and with it came respect for the higher learning. Because of its size and wealth Timbuktu, as with other large Islamic cities, attracted numerous scholars, whose fame spread throughout much of the continent and made Timbuktu one of the greatest sub-Saharan university centers of its time. Thus it remained until invaded by the Moroccans at the close of the sixteenth century.

By this time higher education had taken a new form on the continent of Europe, and to this new institution the next chapter turns. The original higher educational institutions of the western world, commencing with Pythagorus's Museum and including Plato's Academy, the Hellenistic museums, the Byzantine "state universities," and the Islamic madari, established the intellectual basis of Western thought and much of the curricular content of the western education that followed.

Bibliographic Notes

Recent publications on the Roman period include Kimball (1986), which continues the history of the liberal arts into Roman times, showing how Cicero and Quintilian, much in the tradition of

Isocrates, sought to bridge the gap articulated by Socrates and Plato between oratory and knowledge. Kimball also describes the emergence of the so-called seven liberal arts during Roman times and shows their influence during the centuries that followed.

Wooten's chapter in Grant and Kitzinger (1988) shows the strong influence of the Greeks on Roman education but also reveals how the more practical-minded Romans put less effort into philosophy and more into rhetorical studies. Wooten provides good details as to the character of these rhetorical studies.

Clarke (1971) discusses the teaching of the liberal arts and philosophy during Roman times and included a chapter on the impact of Christianity on the curriculum and teaching in higher education. He also provides a chapter on the role of the Byzantine empire in maintaining the Greek-Roman tradition. Papalas (1981) describes education in the time of Herodes Atticus, a Greek millionaire living during the revival of intellectual life in Athens in the second century A.D.

Turning to less-recent sources on the Roman period, few accounts are more complete than that of Marrou (1956), who shows the strong influence of the Greeks during this period but also gives the Romans full credit for the quality of the legal education that they developed. Other earlier sources include Smith (1955), Sarton (1954), Cramer (1939), and Moore (1926).

Geanakoplos (1984) has provided glimpses of Byzantine education in the form of commentaries on and translations of primary documents from this period. Included are Theodosius's "Regulations for Professors," an account of the reestablishment of the higher school in Constantinople during the time of Constantine IX, Constantine's "Rule of Law," Michael Psellus's comments on rhetoric and philosophy as taught in the eleventh century, an account by Anna Comnena of transgressions on academic freedom during the twelfth century, and a description of the revival of the higher schools in Constantinople by Michael VIII in the thirteenth century.

Rice (1967) reviews the influence of ancient Greece on the Byzantine culture and the role the Byzantines played in turn in transmitting the ancient culture to western Europe during the Middle Ages. Material appears here on the Patriarchal School, a religious institution separate from the so-called "state university of Constantinople, as well as on a third "university" established in 1045 in Constantinople for the training of civil servants. Earlier sources on the Byzantine period include Marrou (1956), Butler (1948), Hussey (1937), and Bury (1912).

Readers should watch for a new book by Stanton on Islamic higher education. In the meantime they will want to read Chaudhri (1982), who has chapters on the important role of the higher education teacher in Islamic society, the people who assisted him in his work, the setting where his students lived, the equipment available to him, the use he made of textbooks, his approach to examinations (including the use of riddles), the degrees and diplomas awarded by his institution, and his approach to classroom management. Clarke (1971) has included a short section on the role of the Arabs in adjusting ancient learning to their own literature and culture. Daniel (1975) and Watts (1972) provide chapters dealing with much the same subject. Makdisi (1981) writes in good detail about the Muslim colleges of law, with special attention to Baghdad in the eleventh century.

A most helpful earlier source is Nakosteen (1964). He provides rich detail on the scholarly contributions of the Persian precursors to the Islamic civilization, then proceeds to show the valuable role that Islam itself played, not only in preserving the classical literature of ancient times but also in adding to it in many fields. Tritton (1957) describes in detail the thinking and the way of life of the Muslim scholar. Tritton includes chapters on the Muslim institutions of higher education and the conditions under which they operated, the curriculum, and the books that were studied. Other useful earlier sources on Islamic higher education include Totah (1926) and LeStrange (1900).

CHAPTER THREE

The Growth of Universities in Europe: 742–1662

> There is a cropping time in the generations of men, as in
> the fruits of the field, and sometimes, if the stock be
> good, there springs up for a time a succession of splendid
> men.
>
> (Aristotle, *Rhetoric*, Book Two, Chapter 15)

Historians style the eleventh through the fourteen centuries as Europe's
rebirth or Renaissance, but the great European power saltation that
spawned it had several earlier phases beginning with the reign of
Charlemagne in the ninth century. In two steps this chapter traces the
rise of universities during this period: first, their medieval origins in the
twelfth and thirteenth centuries, and second, their transformation during
the "revival of learning" in the fourteenth and fifteenth centuries.

The Rebirth of European Universities

Although intellectual stirrings had somewhat aroused Europe
during the reign of Charlemagne, not until the year 1000 passed did the
Western world break out of the cocoon of the Dark Ages into a period
of sustained growth. Hastings Rashdall, the English authority on
medieval universities, has written, for example, that "the beginning of
the eleventh century represents, as nearly as it is possible to fix it, the
turning-point in the intellectual history of Europe" (1936, Vol. 1, p.
33). With the passing of the first Christian millennium a new
anthropocentric spirit surged through Europe, and in every avenue of

41

human activity conspicuous developments followed one another in rapid succession. The chief elements of this growth included the following:

- Urban centers began to grow in wealth and power, and the Italian city-states, Venice in particular, became vigorous trading centers with Byzantium, the Islamic world, and Asia. In addition, the Crusades brought Europeans into touch with Islam and also more effectively with Byzantium. Through these leavenings Europeans learned that other peoples surpassed them intellectually and socially, and gradually they began to modify their semi-barbaric ways.

- Far-reaching inventions began to transform technology. For example, in the tenth century three relating to the use of the power of horses came into use: the horse collar, the horseshoe, and the tandem harness. They strikingly improved agricultural production, altered both military methods and the institution of chivalry, and precipitated significant shifts in community and rural life.

- Roman law revived. It had never been entirely superseded in the cities and towns of Italy or in the territories that the Romans had conquered; but it had lain fallow until the appearance of Irnerius (1050–1130) and other legal scholars, whose lectures led to the organization of the University of Bologna.

- In medicine the writings of Hippocrates and Galen had reigned supreme throughout the Dark Ages, but Arabian and Jewish physicians, striking out in new directions, began to influence European medical concepts and practices. The University of Salerno appears to have come into existence in the eleventh century largely because of Arabian medical infiltration.

- More of Aristotle's writings became available. Europe during the Dark Ages had known only his work on logic, *The Analytics*. Through translations from Islamic Spain and importation from Byzantium, during the twelfth and thirteenth centuries, Europe learned of Aristotle's other encyclopedic writing. The papacy originally banned but eventually approved them, and shortly Aristotle's influence surpassed Plato's and also Saint Augustine's, which had long dominated Christian thought.

• Developing the idea of the corporation, Europeans began to organize new groups such as trade guilds, political units in towns and provinces, and artisan guilds. All were "universities"—that is, corporations. Guilds of scholars and guilds of students also sprang up—the *universitas magistorum* and the *universitas scholarium.*

• Religious orders began to multiply and to radiate throughout Europe. In the sixth century Benedict had established one of the first European monasteries at Monte Cassino; in 910 an offshoot at Cluny had been founded; and from it in 1098 a group of monks departed to organize the Cistercian order. Monasteries in the British Isles and elsewhere maintained classical manuscripts, which became useful to the universities after they were established. The monastic conception, however, had already begun to lose both its vigor and its popularity, whereupon the mendicant orders incubated, among them the Carmelites (White Friars) and the Franciscans (Gray Friars) in 1210, the Dominicans (Black Friars) in 1215, and the Augustinians about 1250. Some of their units established elementary and secondary schools, and the more important of them, particularly in France and England, organized colleges and universities associated with the monasteries.

• Secondary education quickened. During the Dark Ages a few choir, cathedral, and collegiate schools had been instituted, but, like Alcuin's school at the palace of Charlemagne, they served only small numbers of students. The Benedictine monasteries also conducted schools, but the big developments in secondary education came after the millennial year. Here Gerbert, who had studied in an Islamic Madrasah (the singular of *madrasi*) in Spain and who became Pope Sylvester II (999–1003), had a wide influence. He introduced into the Cathedral School at Reims the higher studies of which he had learned from the

Moslems, and from there they spread to other cathedral schools and to a lesser extent to the monastery schools. These mutations helped prepare the way for the universities of northern Europe, the University of Paris developing from the cathedral school of Notre Dame and the monastery school of St. Genevieve.

The universities of Paris and Bologna burst into life during the twelfth and thirteenth centuries as did a number of other universities, including Oxford. Their vitality made it clear that an irresistible trend had begun, and soon kings, rulers of smaller states, and the town councils of the free cities of Italy founded comparable institutions under a variety of names. The designation *studium generale* soon became standard. Not until the fifteenth century did *universitas* replace it.

Bologna and Paris set patterns for two quite different kinds of *studia* and instead of considering medieval universities in general, one must deal with the Italian—or what might better be called the southern type—and Parisian or northern type. At first they had little in common, but in later centuries they slowly coalesced.

Consider first the southern variety of medieval university. What eventually came to be called the University of Bologna took form gradually as the result of conflicts that broke out among four groups of people: first, the private teachers of law who had been offering instruction in Bologna for centuries to anyone who would pay their fees, second, the students from all corners of the continent who in the eleventh century began to flock there in large numbers because of the reputation of Irnerius and of other compelling teachers, third, the merchants who—like their successors in academic communities everywhere ever since—made teachers and students pay through the nose for the wherewithal of life, and fourth, the city officials who with the revival of Roman law during this period grew increasingly strong and active. Bologna had few religious roots. It began as a law school and only later developed faculties of medicine, theology, and philosophy.

Although the faculty members of Bologna organized guilds, they operated for some time as private entrepreneurs. Each professor charged students what he thought the traffic would bear and collected his fees personally or through an assistant who also served as a recruiter of new students. Hence at Bologna and the other *studia* which followed its leadership, the student guild immediately got the upper hand, and, indeed for several centuries effectively controlled the university. The students and not the professors, therefore, elected from among their number the rectors or chief administrators, and students held the other administrative posts.

During the fourteenth century, however, some of the professors joined forces with the city government against the students, the common enemy of both. Following a neglected precedent of various cities during the Hellenistic and Roman eras, they got the town to appoint them public professors. As such, they received salaries from the public purse. This action led to the founding of lay boards of control to supervise their salary payments, and from this source American higher education eventually derived its system of external control.

The University of Paris and its northern progeny had a quite different origin from that of Bologna and the southern universities modelled after it. Bologna germinated primarily because extraordinary teachers of civil law attracted hordes of students, but Paris budded as a cathedral school and bloomed as the supreme center for the study of dialectics and of theology because of the masterful teaching there of such men as William of Champeaux and his student and rival, Peter Abelard. Significantly, the Prince of the Scholastics, Thomas Aquinas, an Italian, spent sixteen years of his relatively short life at the University of Paris and at other northern centers of learning rather than in Italian universities.

In contrast to their counterparts in Bologna, Parisian professors were all clerics attached to churches or monasteries or otherwise under ecclesiastical discipline. They could not, therefore, function in the same self-contained manner as the teachers of Bologna. As individuals they did, however, have the traditional right to place their stamp of approval upon their students, a right which led to the supremacy at Paris of the teaching guilds over the student guilds or "nations." Parisian students planned to become teachers themselves, but they could not find positions without the endorsement of their masters.

Perhaps the greatest misconception held of medieval universities is the belief that they chiefly promoted non-utilitarian, "liberal" education. Nothing is less true: above all they were occupationally oriented. *The universities of Europe from the beginning gave their chief attention not to general or "liberal" education but to specialized professional education.* Salerno arose as a medical school, Bologna as a law school, and Paris as a training ground for theologians and scholars.

As Rashdall wrote in his authoritative work on the medieval institutions:

> The rapid multiplication of universities during the fourteenth and fifteenth centuries was largely due to a direct demand for highly educated lawyers and administrators. In a sense the academic discipline of the Middle Ages was too practical. . . . [M]ost of what we understand by "culture," much of what Aristotle understood by "noble use of leisure," was unappreciated by the medieval intellect (1936, Vol. 3, p. 456).

In short, European universities began as, and except for Oxford and Cambridge, have remained, primarily professional schools. Their faculties or divisions of medicine, law, and theology trained doctors, lawyers, and theologians, and their "superior faculty of the arts," or philosophy gave professional instruction in Aristotle's moral, mental, and natural philosophies to students seeking advanced degrees and academic careers. Although some higher faculties required the bachelor's degree granted by the "inferior faculty of the arts," the so-called seven liberal arts (grammar, rhetoric, logic, arithmetic, geometry, astronomy, and music) which they purveyed were merely preliminary. They did not interfere with the controlling occupational point of view of the universities, and eventually European educators pushed them down into secondary education.

A second serious misconception of medieval higher education regards the universities as autonomous "republics of scholars," operating without external controls. The universities achieved some degree of autonomy by playing church authorities off against civil rulers, but they could not avoid regulation. Authoritative historians of the University of Paris, for example, leave no doubt that the Bishop of Paris and the Chancellor of the Cathedral Church of Notre Dame controlled the University during its early period and that the papacy later kept it and other universities under continuous although usually magnanimous surveillance.

By the fifteenth century, moreover, civil governments both in France and England grew strong enough to supersede the church in the affairs of the universities. In 1573, for example, the Parliament of Paris declared the University of Paris to be a secular rather than an ecclesiastical institution, and in his statues of 1600 Henry IV assumed full responsibility for the University. Civil government in Italy assumed control of universities even earlier. As mentioned above, lay boards of academic control appeared in Italy primarily because professors by becoming salaried public teachers sought to free themselves from the despotic domination of the student guilds. Paying the professors required that the treasury allocate funds for the purpose, and this led to the appointment of groups of officials and citizens to administer the grants and later also to supervise their recipients. The Council of Florence established the first such board in 1348, but the majority of them got underway during the following century. They went by various names, two of which, slightly modified in translation, continue in use today in the United States: "boards of curators" and "boards of governors." Rashdall described their appearance and activities as follows:

> In the course of the fourteenth and fifteenth centuries such a body . . . was established by the city government or prince in all Italian universities, and the real control of the university more and more passed to this body of external governors, which by the sixteenth or seventeenth century succeeded in destroying the student autonomy or reducing it to a shadow (1936, Vol. 1, p. 212).

Thus some two hundred years before the founding of the first American college and at least half a century before Columbus set sail to discover the Americas, the primary progenitors of American boards of trustees had begun to take command of Italian higher education.

A third misconception of medieval higher education affirms that, because the students of the northern institutions took holy orders, the universities were quiet retreats for serious study and pious contemplation. The Middle Ages may perhaps rightly be called "the age of faith," but student life abounded in quite worldly interests and activities. Witness the early ballads of the wandering *Goliardi*, the fact that the only duty of the High Steward of Cambridge even today is "to attend to the hanging of any undergraduate," and the revealing, although admittedly extreme events that began on St. Scholastica's Day, 1355, at Oxford. On that holy day a group of students—all tonsured to betoken their ecclesiastical status—imbibed too much alcohol in an Oxford tavern and in a dispute with the landlord cut open his head with a jug. His friends came to his rescue and among other things rang the bell of the townsmen's church to summon other friends. They came in such formidable numbers that some of the students rang the much bigger bell of the University church to call students from the colleges and monks from the monasteries to join the fray. The riot subsided that night but continued the next day. An Oxford historian has dramatically reported what happened then:

> Next morning . . . the townsmen were already collecting their forces and calling in allies from the country-side. They were determined not to miss so good an opportunity of settling accounts with the spoilt children of the Church. . . . Again the bells clanged and the armies mustered, and a fierce and much more dangerous fight ensued. The scholars tried to shut the gates, but the country-men poured through them—two thousand strong, it was said, with a black flag at their head. The clerks were overpowered and took refuge in their Halls and Inns. But the Halls and Inns were fired and pillaged. Cries of "Slay, Slay, Havoc," resounded through the night.

The battle continued into a third day, and

> . . . again the mob broke into the Halls. Scholars were beaten, wounded, killed. . . . Some were . . . carried off and tortured, their tonsured crowns flayed "in scorn of the clergy" (Lyte, 1886, pp. 162–68).

The toll of the combat among the townsmen seems not to be recorded, although one estimate puts the total killed on both sides at fifty. The University reported six dead, twenty-one dangerously wounded and a large number missing; and because of the battle, the City of Oxford annually paid fines and obeisance to the University of Oxford for the next 470 years.

Still another fallacy about the original universities needs correction: the belief that they understood what we today call "research." The research techniques for discovering empirical facts have a much more recent origin than the universities, which until the nineteenth century emphasized the techniques of dialectic.

During the Middle Ages Christianity continued to fear and fight "pagan learning," but following the tenth century it sloughed off some of its religious fundamentalism and accepted that part of the Hellenic heritage immediately at hand, namely Aristotle's logic. Thus appeared the dialecticians whose debates exemplified the intellectual life of the high Middle Ages and culminated in the brilliant writings of Thomas

Aquinas in the thirteenth century. Aquinas stands aloft as one of the most phenomenal logicians of history, but his works include no new objective facts and do not stress those then known. He synthesized Christian doctrine with Aristotelian philosophy, but his age believed available knowledge to be complete and hence in need only of interpretation, not expansion.

Like Aquinas, the teachers in all four faculties of the medieval universities devoted their energies to theorizing and limited their investigations to logic and often to splitting hairs. Students, too, found their chief intellectual activity through disputation—not, however, on the question, as frequently alleged, of the number of angels that could stand on the head of a pin, but on such freighted problems as whether Adam and Eve had navels.

A major limitation on such questions, it must be remembered, consisted in the necessity of disputants to conceptualize within the framework of Christian dogma. They questioned accepted dogma at their peril, and even Aquinas barely escaped excommunication. The concept of academic freedom would not take form until the seventeenth century, when the Italian philosopher, Campanella (1568–1639), introduced the slogan, *Libertas philosophandi*—"freedom to philosophize." Until then dialectical discussions amounted to little more than what theologians have come to call apologetics.

Throughout the Middle Ages and, indeed, well into the nineteenth century the dialectical method ruled supreme in the universities and still flourishes in most theological thinking. Never, however, has it encouraged experimental research. Dialecticians need only "propositions" and strive only for "logical consistency," regardless of the factual significance or veracity of the proposition under debate. Experimental research obviously could not move ahead until the dethronement of the dialectical method. Galileo and Francis Bacon opened the campaign against it in the seventeenth century, but until the nineteenth century experimental research would not seriously affect most universities.

To recapitulate, despite their limitations, "the universities and the immediate products of their activity may be said to constitute the greatest achievement of the Middle Ages in the intellectual sphere," as Rashdall noted (1936, Volume 1, p. 3). Primarily concerned with training the limited kinds and numbers of professional men needed, they also provided the chief intellectual arena of the period. As the

Renaissance gained momentum, however, the saltation that had created them swept on, and other institutions wrested their intellectual leadership from them. Not until the nineteenth century would they recapture it.

The Universities and the Revival of Learning

During the fourteenth century, when the universities of western Europe had become great institutions of professional learning, the wealthy Italian city-states fostered a vigorous cultural movement in painting, sculpture, architecture, and literature. Dominated by a succession of extraordinarily creative men—including Petrarch, Boccaccio, Leonardo da Vinci, and Michelangelo—this artistic explosion resulted largely from the vast admiration of Renaissance patricians for "the glory that was Greece and the grandeur that was Rome." This admiration also nourished anthropocentrism; that is, interest in human life as opposed to the other-worldly orientation of the medieval world.

The revival of humane learning and the re-evaluation of pagan antiquity that accompanied this mighty cultural saltation spread three mighty rivers of thought and action throughout Europe—the literary, the aesthetic, and the scientific. Of these three, however, the universities dismissed aesthetics, almost completely rejected science, and slowly accepted literature. The Herculean changes occurring in Renaissance society, however, slowly pushed them into modernity.

As indicated above, the medieval universities served essentially as professional schools. To educate the nobility and gentry, a separate educational system flourished during medieval times: the feudal system of schooling centered in palaces, castles, and manor houses. It trained the knights, courtiers, and gentlemen and ladies of the landed aristocracy. As feudalism declined, this educational pattern languished and eventually vanished. Then with the rise of wealth of the new commercial entrepreneurs the universities took over the task of civilizing their sons. In this way the universities during the Renaissance and the Reformation—and especially those of England and France—added to their purpose of professional training that of inculcating what went by the name of "polite learning." They shifted, in other words, from purely occupational education to cultural education, a return, be it noted, to the *raison d'etre* of the Hellenic institutions of two thousand years earlier.

Samuel Eliot Morison, Harvard's tercentennial historian, has described the situation as it developed in England's two universities during the sixteenth and seventeenth centuries when the gentry all but evicted the tonsured students of the medieval era:

A new upper class was arising. Enriched by the woolens trade and overseas commerce, glutted by the spoils of the abbeys, families like the Cecils, Russells, Greshams, and Winthrops wished to educate their sons as gentlemen, and prepare them for active life. Oxford and Cambridge colleges were appropriate dwellings for such youth. They offered an opportunity, in luxurious surroundings and congenial company, to read the polite literature which Erasmus told them was necessary for a gentlemen's education. It is true that the University did not admit the logic of the situation—Englishmen seldom do. All college students were supposed to be clerics, and behave as such. There was no objection to their smoking or drinking in moderation; but they were forbidden to dress as men of rank, or to indulge in field sports such as hawking, hunting and coursing with greyhounds, to keep dogs in college, bear arms, carouse in taverns, view bull-and-bear baitings, or visit "bawdy Barnwell and Sturbridge Fair." Of course all these forbidden things were done.

One can hardly exaggerate the importance of this intrusion of "young gentlemen" into the English universities, for there they remained. . . . Owing to the fact that England simultaneously received the reformation, the renaissance, and this notion of a gentleman's education, there was brought about an unwilling compromise between gentility and learning, a rubbing of shoulders between the poor scholar and the squire's son, that has made the English and American college what it is today: the despair of educational reformers and logical pedagogues, the astonishment of Continental scholars, a place which is neither a house of learning nor a house of play, but a little of both; and withal a microcosm of the world in which we live (1935, pp. 54, 56).

The change in clientele that Morison described revolutionized Oxford and Cambridge life, determined the scope of American college life, and in large measure accounts for the intermingling of learning and living, of work and of play, that makes Anglo-American higher education so different from that in most of the rest of the world. With this change in clientele and its resulting shift in university purposes, the fifteenth and sixteenth centuries also witnessed a significant transition in university curriculums. Oxford and Cambridge, for example, like Paris from which they sprang, had begun with the four faculties of law, medicine, theology, and philosophy typically found in medieval universities. Their law and medical faculties, however, soon disappeared: the Inns of Court took over instruction in secular law; and the hospital schools of London and other cities largely expropriated the teaching of medicine. This left Oxford and Cambridge with theology and philosophy, no longer organized in separate faculties. Continuing with the theological preoccupations of the earlier period, they also began to give attention to classical literature.

Even here, however, as throughout Europe, the introduction of the New Learning of the classical period and the learned tongues of Hebrew, Arabic, and Syriac raised furious controversies that abraded the universities for the next two centuries. Oxford, as Morison showed, passed through "a period of violent opposition to the new learning" (1935, p. 52). Similarly, when Erasmus took up residence at the University of Louvain in 1521, he found the Dominicans and Franciscans united in opposition to the new learning.

Even in Italy literary study made slow progress. There, wrote Rashdall, universities were "above all things places of professional study, and their professors were long the enemies of humanism" (1936, Vol. 2, p. 251). Not until the Reformation, in fact, would literary humanism triumph over the scholasticism of the Church and the professional orientation of the universities.

The greatest victory of the New Learning came in the fourth decade of the sixteenth century. Stimulated by Erasmus, Francis the First in 1530 established chairs in the ancient languages at the College of France. Five years later Henry the Eighth of England followed his example at Oxford and Cambridge by creating the five Regius professorships which have continued ever since—one each in Divinity, Hebrew, Greek, Physic, and Civil Law.

Science, on the other hand, did not fare so well: another three centuries passed before it achieved status. Maintaining their medieval indifference to "scientific research," the universities continued along the time-honored road of dialectic. The rest of the world's interest in argumentation began to wane during the revival of classical learning, however, and the pioneering scientific work of Copernicus depressed it even further.

A few universities during the sixteenth century did, however, sponsor research. At Padua—which had become the world's greatest medical center and at which Copernicus studied—Vesalius, Fallopio, and Fabricius revolutionized anatomy by reintroducing the dissection of the human body; and at Leyden soon after its founding in 1575, Joseph Scalinger, Grotius, and Armenius pioneered in social, literary, and theological research. The Dutch universities at Leyden, Utrecht, and Groningen equipped themselves in the seventeenth century with scientific laboratories, and at Leyden the professors gave their major attention to the discovery and development of new knowledge. Modern science and *pari passu* the modern world got their greatest stimulus, however, from the seventeenth century work of Francis Bacon and Galileo.

In 1605 appeared Bacon's *The Advancement of Learning*, fifteen years later his more widely known work, the *Novum Organon*—the "New Tool"; that is, the tool of experimental science as opposed to Aristotle's *Organon* or tool of logic. Two quotations from these books forcibly illustrate the new scientific point of view:

> Men commonly take a view of nature as from a remote eminence, and are too much amused with generalities; whereas, if they would descend, and approach nearer to particulars, and more exactly and considerately examine into things themselves, they might make more solid and useful discoveries (1605, Book Four, Chapter Three).

> Man . . . understands as much as his observations . . . permit him and neither knows or is capable of more (1620, opening epigram).

Bacon died in 1626, but his writings did not begin to have a wide influence until after the Puritans became a power in English life shortly thereafter. Among their reforms the Puritans attempted to remold the two English universities along Baconian lines by making scientific research dominant. For various reasons they failed, and their defeat meant that Oxford and Cambridge would all but reject the experimental sciences until late in the nineteenth century.

In Italy Galileo's efforts succeeded little better. Everyone knows of Galileo's troubles with Cardinal Bellarmine and his religious associates, but his difficulties with his own academic colleagues better illuminate the crisis within the universities that the new breed of scientists caused. A professor of mathematics first at Padua and later at Florence, Galileo in 1583 formulated the principle of the pendulum and in 1589 the law of falling bodies. Then on the night of January 7, 1610, he discovered the satellites of Jupiter. After further observations through his self-manufactured telescope, he concluded that he had made a discovery of the first importance. He published his findings and sent reprints, together with a hundred or more new telescopes which he had made, to the princes and the learned men of Europe. Thereupon fury broke loose. The princes and some of the scholars acclaimed him, but as one of his biographers expressed it, "the Aristotelians were furious" (Fahie, 1903, p. 101). Typical of them was Galileo's celebrated colleague at Padua, Jules Libri, who refused to look through Galileo's telescope. Aristotle had made no mention of such absurdities as Jupiter's satellites, and ipso facto it had none. Professor Libri could not bring himself to break away from the authority of antiquity, nor could Professor Francesso Sizzi of Florence who the year after Galileo's discovery wrote:

> There are seven windows given to animals in the domicile of the head, through which the air is admitted to the tabernacle of the body, to enlighten, to warm and to nourish it. What are these parts of the microcosmos? Two nostrils, two eyes, two ears, and a mouth. So in the heavens, as in a macrocosmos, there are two favorable stars, two unpropitious, two luminaries, and Mercury undecided and indifferent. From this and many other similarities in nature, such as the seven metals, etc., which it were too tedious to enumerate, we gather that the number of planets is necessarily seven. Moreover, these satellites of Jupiter are invisible to the naked eye, and therefore can exercise no influence on earth, and therefore would be useless, and therefore do not exist (quoted in Fahie, 1903, p. 103).

Galileo's astronomical investigations represented the new emphasis upon scientific observation, but they brought him into conflict not only with the dialecticalism of the learned world but also with the reigning geocentrism of the Church. His subsequent harassment together with the suppression of such other scientists as the Dominican monk Giordano Bruno led to the almost complete interdict of experimental science in the universities of Italy and hence, since Italian thought stood foremost in Europe, throughout European countries in general.

The scientists' failure in all but rare instances to bring the new sciences into the universities led to the birth of a new type of institution to perform the research which the universities disdained: the academy or scientific society. In Naples in 1560 appeared the first of these societies, the *Accademia Secretorium Naturae* but because its members met secretly, the Neapolitans judged them to be in league with the devil, and the Pope forced them to disband. Others, however, grew up elsewhere in Italy, among them the Roman *Accademia di Lincie* (Society of Linxes), organized in 1603 with Galileo as one of its early members, and the Florentine *Accademie del Cimento* (Academy of Experiment) that commenced in 1657 but disintegrated ten years later when its patron, Leopold Medici, became a cardinal. In today's terminology these were largely underground organizations, and, although they disbanded, three later scientific societies in England, France, and Germany grew conspicuously and incalculably influenced the development of scientific research.

In England in 1662 Charles the Second chartered the Royal Society, which took as its motto *Nullius in Verba* ("Nothing by means of words") to declare its commitment to the experimentation for which Oxford and Cambridge had scant sympathy. In France Louis XIV established the Academie des Sciences in 1666. The French Revolution closed it, but it reopened under Napoleon to follow a history comparable to that of its British counterpart. In Germany in 1700 Frederick of Brandenburg through the initiative of Leibnitz chartered the Berlin Academy as the *Societas Regi Scientiarum*, and in 1812 it combined with the University of Berlin to form the first of the great modern research universities.

Some scientific work, of course, did manage to get done within the universities: that already mentioned, for example, in anatomy at Padua, in classical philology at Leyden, and in medicine at Edinburgh. Moreover, the Universities of Halle and Gottingen immediately admitted the natural sciences upon their founding in 1694 and 1737. On the whole, however, the universities of the Renaissance and Reformation deserved the rebuke which John Stuart Mill hurled at them:

> . . . universities and academical institutions, which had once taught all that was then known, but, having ever since indulged their ease by remaining stationary, found it for their interest that knowledge should do so too—institutions for education, which kept a century behind the community they affected to educate, who, when Descartes appeared, publicly censured him for differing from Aristotle, and, when Newton appeared, anathematized him for differing from Descartes (1882, Vol. 1, p. 53).

Descartes, it should be noted, never held a professorship in any university, and although Newton served as the Lucasian professor of mathematics at Cambridge for twenty-odd years, he left Cambridge to devote the last thirty years of his life to directing the Royal Mint and the last twenty-four to the presidency of the Royal Society. Few of Europe's foremost philosophers and scientists from the seventeenth century to the middle of the nineteenth century, moreover, had university berths, although some held professorial titles in the institutes of their day. Consider the physical scientists Boyle, Cavendish, Davy, Faraday, Herschel, Laplace, Lavoisier, Leibnitz, Lyell, Priestley, and Tyndal; the biological scientists Buffon, Cuvier, Darwin, Galton, Harvey, Hunter, Huxley, Jenner, and Wallace; or the social scientists and philosophers Bacon, Bentham, Berkeley, Condillac, Diderot, Gibbon, Hobbes, Locke, the two Mills, Montesquieu, Quesnay, Ricardo, Rousseau, Spencer, Turgot, and Voltaire. These thinkers were more often members of scientific societies or men of affairs, rarely university professors.

In short, by and large the universities throughout the Renaissance and Reformation looked more to the past than to the future. They followed their own interest in "intellectual" problems and in the spirit of Plato disdained the Herculean scientific, artistic, technological, commercial, and political developments so luxuriantly blooming beyond their walls. After much opposition they admitted the study of classical Greek and Hebrew, but they held tightly to subjects that could be handled by dialectics and pushed aside the experimental and observational sciences. The modern university would not appear, therefore, until in the nineteenth century those responsible for higher education accommodated themselves to the new world which had grown up around them.

Bibliographic Notes

Nineteenth century scholars gave particular attention to the medieval universities, but contemporary writers have not entirely ignored the subject. Cobban (1975) provides, for example, a book-length treatment of the medieval university, useful in that it reflects scholarship undertaken since Rashdall's monumental effort, thus adding and correcting in light of subsequent scholarship. Rudy (1984) supplies a general history of universities in Europe that opens with a chapter on the Middle Ages and follows with a chapter on the Renaissance.

In his third chapter Kimball (1986) turns to the role of the liberal arts during the Middle Ages and shows how these subjects took a more philosophical turn during this period. Gilbert pays special attention to the so-called "seven liberal arts," both as to their origins and their impact on the medieval university. Wagner (1983) also focuses on the liberal arts, his book containing chapters on each of the seven liberal arts as well as providing insight into the role these subjects and others played in the medieval curriculum. Piltz (1981) provides a well-written review of learning in northern Europe during the Middle Ages, including the origin and spread of the "seven liberal arts," the thinking of Aristotle and his impact on the universities, the curriculum and the modes of teaching it, and the role of scholasticism in these institutions.

Ferruolo (1988) uses the medieval university, especially Paris, as his setting within which to explore the value of a liberal education. Given the greater opportunity for lucrative employment for the graduates of the law and medicine faculties of the medieval university, he asks, what attracted students to the arts and theology faculties and what careers did they assume following graduation? In a similar vein Bullough (1970) uses medical education in the medieval university as an example of the role institutions play in determining which occupations achieve the status of professions.

Hyde has a chapter in Baldwin and Goldthwaite (1972) describing the early distribution of influence within the university at Bologna. This same publication also contains a chapter by Berger covering some of the same issues in the context of the University of Paris during 1418–1450.

Some of the most active publishing today on the history of higher education deals with Oxbridge. Leader (1988) writes, for instance, the first of what eventually will become a four-volume series on the history of Cambridge. In this volume, which concludes with the year 1546, Leader covers the beginnings of the University, the settings within which scholars studied, the curriculum, the approaches to teaching, and some of the changes that occurred during the fourteenth through the sixteenth centuries.

Catto (1984) provides probably the richest source of information on Oxford, starting with the twelfth and extending through the sixteenth century. Also important as a source on the history of Oxbridge is Cobban (1988). Note particularly Cobban's opening chapter on the place of the medieval university in the history of higher education. There follow extended chapters dealing with Oxbridge in every detail, including the colleges and halls, governance, town-gown relations, student life, teaching and the curriculum, and relations with the Church.

Green's shorter history of Oxford (1974) will serve those seeking less detail and a broader time range (to 1973). Rowse's (1975) history of Oxford begins with the origins of the town itself and continues with the rise of the university and its colleges. Rowse also includes material on the conflict between humanism and dogma during the Renaissance. Lytle (1974) describes the relationships that existed between the scholars at Oxford and their patrons. By "patrons" Lytle means the people of wealth and power who in one sense made it possible for the scholars to continue their work but in another sense held authority over them.

Turning to later periods, Kittelson and Transue (1984) have edited a series of essays which, in addition to Bologna and Paris, includes material on universities that emerged in Germany and Poland during the fourteenth and later centuries. Gabriel (1977) edited the proceedings of a conference in San Francisco on the economic history of universities. Included is a paper by Verger on the cost of degrees and examinations in universities of southern Europe, a paper by De Ridder-Symoens on the financial and organizational structure of the University at Orleans, and Gieysztor's analysis of funding provided the University of Cracow in Poland. Pegues also provides an essay in the Gabriel publication on philanthropy in the universities of the thirteenth to the fifteenth centuries.

Swanson (1979) writes about the pivotal roles universities and people within them played during the period of the Avignon papacy. Ijsewijn and Paquet (1978) edit some thirty papers on the late Middle Ages. Included are papers in English by Van Eijl on the founding of the University of Paris, by Gabriel on "Intellectual Relations between the University of Louvain and the University of Paris in the Fifteenth Century," by Kibre on "Arts and Medicine in the Universities of the Late Middle Ages," by Ker on "Oxford Libraries before 1500," and by Bullough on "Achievement, Professionalization and the University."

All "roads" to the history of the medieval universities lead back to Rashdall (1895). For an immensely readable (but totally undocumented) summary of this history, see Schachner (1938).

CHAPTER FOUR

Reformation Influences: 1519–1584

Reform is always the creation of new usages.
(Ortega y Gasset, 1944, p. 46)

While scientific research was indeed slow to develop in the universities of the Renaissance and the Reformation, it did appear in a few Reformation universities. This period is also important for the structural patterns which developed for administering universities and colleges, patterns which colonial Americans followed when they started founding their colleges in the seventeenth century.

Of all the names associated with the Reformation—from John Wycliff to John Huss to Martin Luther—that of John Calvin emerges as most important to the story here unfolding. A book that strives, in other words, to describe the history of American higher education must give primary attention during the Reformation to the Geneva theocrat whose ideas on the church, state, and education so clearly influenced the early founders of American colleges. Beginning with Calvin's Academy in Geneva, there followed institutions in the Netherlands, Scotland, Ireland, and England that reflected his ideas and that guided American colonists when they became concerned with higher education.

The Lutheran influence, on the other hand, is not so direct. Distrustful of the close ties of most medieval universities to Rome, Luther and his educational advisor, Philip Melanchthon, attacked the universities most severely, calling them hellish temples of Moloch and synagogues of corruption that turned students into pagans. Under such attacks the universities in the regions influenced by Luther faded badly. In Heidelberg in 1525, for example, the University enrolled fewer students than it had faculty, and at Basel a year later the university there had but five students. Luther and Melanchthon sought through their attacks on universities to break their ties with Roman Catholicism; they did not seek to destroy higher education *per se*. In subsequent years Protestant institutions in such cities as Wittenberg, Marburg, Tubingen, Leipzig, Konigsberg, and Jena thrived. Few if any of the founders of American colonial colleges came, however, from these institutions. Lutherans did populate parts of the middle colonies; Luther's books and those of his followers found their place on the shelves of many a colonial library, and Melanchthon's theories on primary and secondary education have had a lasting influence on Western civilization. The fact remains, however, that the colonial colleges drew their models not from Luther's middle Europe but instead from Swiss, Dutch, Scottish, Irish, and English institutions that had come under the influence of John Calvin.

The chapter begins with Calvin's Academy in Geneva, then moves to Leyden in the Netherlands, to the Scottish universities, to Trinity College in Dublin, and finally to Emmanuel College at Cambridge. From Emmanuel came many of the early settlers of the Massachusetts Bay colony, including John Harvard.

The Academy at Geneva

A product of two of the universities Luther and Melanchthon so severely attacked, John Calvin brought to Geneva in 1541 the theological and literary education of Paris and the legal education of Orleans. Already banished from Paris for his Protestant leanings and later removed from Geneva for his overly zealous efforts to reduce sin in that city, Calvin returned to Geneva in 1541 at the bidding of the town fathers, there to combine his legal and theological education in developing the theocratic state that characterizes that part of the Reformation associated with his name.

Drawing upon the prodigious *Institutes of the Christian Religion*, which he had completed five years earlier, Calvin interlinked the existing civil government of Geneva with the church governing body, the Venerable Company of Pastors. The Venerable Company, in consort with a civil group known as the Small Council, controlled the day-to-day operations of government and the day-to-day lives of the people of Geneva. These two groups, one ministerial and the other lay, coordinated their efforts through an agency called the Consistory, with lay members from the Small Council holding the majority of memberships. This practice of separating civil and ecclesiastical authority but also of bringing the two groups together in a coordinating body dominated in number by lay members characterized the government of most regions that came under Calvin's influence. It would also help to shape the government of Harvard and William and Mary, the first American colonial colleges to be established.

Also characteristic of Calvin's influence was the genuine concern for a learned clergy and a lettered people. Thus Calvin in Geneva set about early to establish a secondary school. He also commenced from his early days in Geneva a series of lectures on theology. By 1559 these activities had matured sufficiently to open the Academie de Geneve, which, while it gave no degrees, soon achieved high status in Europe for the quality of its instruction in the arts, theology, and law. This eminence, combined with the role Geneva played at this time as a haven for Protestant leaders, made the city and its academy focal points in the development of the Reformation, especially in the Netherlands and Scotland. John Knox, for example, who found refuge in Geneva and came strongly under its influence, and Andrew Melville, who studied at the Academy and brought Calvin's educational practices back to Scotland, reflected the impact of the Swiss city on the Scots of that time.

In keeping with his approach to the governance of the people of Geneva, Calvin put the governance of the Academy under two groups, one lay, the other consisting of seven professors at the Academy, who managed internal affairs. The lay members came from the aforementioned Small Council of the City of Geneva. At the head of the Academy, overseeing the Council and faculty groups, sat the chief officer of the city, and under him operated the chief academic officer, who had the title of Rector.

The Geneva Academy during Calvin's day and for some years thereafter had a good reputation and attracted Protestant scholars from throughout non-Lutheran Europe (Lutherans could have no association with the Calvinists). Its faculty remained strong even after the Academy itself had fallen on difficult times, and Thomas Jefferson in casting about some two and a half centuries later for faculty for his university in Virginia seriously considered inviting the entire Geneva faculty to join him in the United States.

The University of Leyden

In the meantime, however, other institutions in the mold of the Geneva Academy appeared. The first of these was Leyden, born in the aftermath of the Netherland's successful rebellion against the Holy Roman Empire. Opened on February 5, 1575, the University by the turn of the sixteenth century "attracted the most distinguished group of scholars in northern Europe" (Morison, 1935, p. 141).

Leyden's governance showed Geneva's influence in that it again gave a dominant voice to non-academics. It differed somewhat from Geneva, however, in that these non-academics, rather than serving dual roles in city and academic government, had no role in city government. Leyden's first board of curators consisted of Ian Van der Does, Gerard Van Hoogeveen, and Cornelius de Coning. Van der Does, a former soldier, statesman, and "governor" of the city of Leyden, headed this board for a period of thirty years and receives much of the credit for the University's quick rise to eminence. His success reminds one of the Gilmans, Harpers, Washingtons, and Whites of nineteenth-century America; in fact, former Harvard President James Bryant Conant early in his term discovered Van der Does and made the following observation:

> I had always imagined that Gilman at Johns Hopkins, or Stanley Hall at Worcester, or Harper almost single-handedly building the University of Chicago, were prodigies who could arise only in this new land of enterprise. I had supposed that never before had one man had the power to build a faculty *de novo*. The account of the founding of the University of Leyden in 1575, however, proves that Gilman had a predecessor. . . . Ian Van der Does (1938, p. 317).

Van der Does concentrated his efforts on bringing to Leyden the finest scholars available. Sir William Hamilton, writing in the nineteenth century, described how Van der Does enlisted the aid of city officials, the States of Holland, and even the King of France in luring Joseph Scaliger, leading scholar of his time in Latin literature, to Leyden. Such efforts led Sir William to comment, "It is mainly to John Van der Does that the school of Leyden owes its existence" (Quoted by Conant, 1938, p. 318).

Sir William's comments caught the eye of University of Michigan President Henry P. Tappan, who quoted freely from them in his statement on the idea of a true university, delivered before the Christian Library Association in June of 1858.

These comments of Tappan, Hamilton, and Conant portray Leyden as an early precursor of the eighteenth- and nineteenth- century German universities, which, in turn, so powerfully influenced Americans in their development of the modern research university. The status accorded a meritorious faculty, the commitment of that faculty to the advancement of learning, the existence of botanical gardens and other facilities for scholarly pursuits—these and other characteristics of the university at Leyden at the start of the seventeenth century all attest to the visionary efforts of Van der Does and his colleagues.

The colonial American college was no research university by any stretch of the imagination. Such developments would have to await more than two centuries of slow, sometimes painful growth. But the seventeenth century Dutch did nevertheless have their impact on the American colonies, largely because of their willingness to harbor the Puritans and other Englishmen whose religious views did not have the support of the British government. Two prominent members of Harvard's first Board of Overseers, Hugh Peter and John Davenport, had preached to English congregations in exile in the Low Countries, and Harvard's first head, Nathaniel Eaton, had graduated from Leyden's sister institution in Franeker. Eaton, according to Morison (1935, p. 143), was probably a second choice, his Franeker mentor, William Ames, having first preference. Ames, however, died in 1633 and the offer eventually went to Eaton. These ties with the Dutch continued after the founding of Harvard, the sons of several prominent colonial clergymen undertaking their studies at Leyden, two members of the first Harvard graduating class proceeding to Leyden for their medical education, and the first Harvard man to take a Ph.D., Jeremiah Dummer, obtaining it from another of Leyden's sister institutions, Utrecht.

The Scottish Universities

In Scotland the city fathers, in keeping with the practice in Geneva, doubled their roles in both city and university affairs. Their numbers, unfortunately, did not include people of the caliber of Van der

Does, and, in the eyes of their critics, they brought more harm than good to their institutions. Scotland did, however, produce some of the early leaders of colonial American colleges.

The leader of the Scottish Reformation, John Knox, first met Calvin in 1554. Calvin's conviction that he knew the only "right" way appealed to Knox's own religious needs, and, when the Scottish people appealed to Knox in 1558 to lead them in their revolt against the Catholic Queen Mary of Lorraine, he did indeed return, lead a successful revolution, and establish a Calvinist theocracy in the northern lands.

Scotland in 1560 possessed three institutions of higher education: St. Andrews, Glasgow, and the Kings College of Aberdeen. All were little more than arts colleges, not unlike the colonial American colleges, consisting of a small body of students, a principal, four regent masters, and, at times, a professor of divinity, usually the pastor from some local church. Each regent master assumed in his turn a responsibility for the first-year students and continued with them as their sole mentor through four years of study.

In the early years of the Scottish Reformation Aberdeen added Marischall College, and the University of Edinburgh opened. These two institutions—plus the older ones after a few years of reluctant transition—assumed patterns of governance similar to Geneva and Leyden. In Edinburgh, for example, the Town Council assigned a committee of its members responsibility for the University, a committee not unlike others given responsibility for the city's water, streets, and other services. The actions of this committee came under considerable criticism from academics in later centuries, and in 1858— due at least in part to the criticisms of Sir William Hamilton—the pattern of governance was changed to one more resembling that of the present day English red brick and American state universities.

Chief architect of the curriculum of Reformation institutions in Scotland was Andrew Melville. Arriving in Geneva five years after Calvin's death, Melville found the Academy at its peak, and his teachers provided him with the models whom he emulated upon his return to Scotland in 1574. Teaching first as the principal regent at Glasgow and later as the Principal at St. Mary's College at St. Andrews, Melville instructed in a range of subjects reaching from Greek grammar, rhetoric, classic literature, mathematics, moral philosophy, and Aramaic to Syriac. His teaching and curricular concerns, especially as they related to the classical and Biblical languages, profoundly influenced several generations of students and later teachers.

In *The Founding of Harvard College* Morison refused to give Scotland much credit for patterns in the Massachusetts institution in the seventeenth century. The similarities he did identify—between Harvard's early curriculum and that of Aberdeen and Edinburgh, between the printing format of Harvard's commencement theses and that of Edinburgh, and between the practice at Harvard and in Scotland of having one instructor work with all new students of a given year through four years of college—left him largely unconvinced, mainly because he found little evidence of communication between the people of Scotland and Massachusetts. Matters did change, however, in later years, the first head of William and Mary College—James Blair—having come from Edinburgh and Benjamin Franklin's choice for the first head of what eventually became the University of Pennsylvania—William Smith—having studied in Aberdeen. Sloan (1971) has also shown the Scottish influence on eighteenth-century American higher education, especially at Princeton.

Trinity College, Dublin

Trinity College in Dublin also followed the Calvinist pattern. Its founders had visions of Trinity serving as the first of a cluster of colleges that in their combination would constitute a great university structure in the image of Oxford and Cambridge. Not unlike the situation in Massachusetts, the preponderance of its founders had attended Cambridge. The founders did not succeed, however, in duplicating Oxbridge in Ireland.

Trinity remains important, nevertheless, to the story here unfolding, mainly because under its Puritan founders it continued the patterns of the Calvinist Reformation. At Trinity, as in Geneva and Aberdeen and later at Harvard and William and Mary, one finds two governing bodies responsible for the institution. One, the Board of Visitors, consisted of lay members; the other, the Board of Fellows, consisted of the "head" and members of the faculty of the College. Harvard to this day has retained this bicameral board arrangement (although the faculty has long since lost its membership on either board to lay members), and William and Mary continued such an arrangement until the first decade of this century. One other of the colonial institutions, Brown University, has retained the bicameral arrangement, although its two boards apparently conduct much of their business in the same room with each other.

Trinity also has importance, finally, to the colonial American colleges in that certain of the colonial leaders had some exposure to the Dublin institution. This includes Thomas Parker, pastor at Newbury in Massachusetts, and and a member of the prominent Winthrop family, John, Jr., who later became Governor of Connecticut.

Emmanuel College, Cambridge

The ties between higher education in the New World and the Old, admittedly tenuous at times, become decidedly stronger when one studies the links between Cambridge's Emmanuel College and Harvard. As Morison has worded it, "If we would know upon what model Harvard College was established, what were the ideals of her founders and the purposes of her first governors, we need seek no further than the University of Cambridge" (1935, p. 40). The largest number of college-educated settlers in the Massachusetts Bay Colony in the 1630s had obtained their education at Cambridge, and among this Cambridge group the largest number—thirty-five—had attended Emmanuel College (Ibid., p. 92).

Established at a time (1584) when the English Crown was more than suspicious of the Puritan movement, Emmanuel nevertheless emerged under the guidance of its first benefactor, Sir Walter Mildmay, and its first master, Laurence Chaderton, as a first-rate, Puritan college dedicated primarily to the preparation of an educated ministry. By 1617 it had become, next to Trinity, the second largest college at Cambridge University, a college alive to its times, vigorous and productive of "stiff-backed Christians who had the moral courage to withstand social pressure" (Ibid., p. 97). Its graduates who came to Massachusetts thought well of their alma mater and sought partially to reconstruct it in the new land.

In governance, however, the founders of Harvard and of the other eight colonial colleges did not follow Emmanuel as closely as they followed other Reformation institutions. Being a part of the Oxbridge group, Emmanuel's faculty operated more independently and without the restraints of a lay board. Only the position of the master, as a precursor of the president's position in American academic governance, can be said to relate to Emmanuel's approach to governance.

Summary

The colleges that emerged in colonial America in the seventeenth and eighteenth centuries and those institutions that appeared in later centuries did not arise *de novo* from the imaginations of the colonial founders and their successors. The dominant functions of teaching and research were performed in earliest Greek times; the curriculum evolved over centuries starting with the Greeks; the corporate identity of the institutions performing these activities derives from the medieval period; and much of the organizational patterning by which these institutions are governed appears to come largely from principles introduced by Calvin as part of the Protestant Reformation. The chapters that follow show how the institutional forms of the nineteenth and twentieth centuries reflected the pressures of their own times.

Bibliographic Notes

Historians looking for a period needing more study in the context of higher education might well consider the Reformation. Recent publications on the period include Kimball's (1986) Chapter IV on "Renaissance Humanists and Reformation Preachers." In it he shows how the humanists united around the writings of Cicero and Quintilian, thus emphasizing oratory over philosophy. The "preachers" also sided with oratory, their attention to philosophy being limited largely to moral issues. Kimball's fifth chapter shows how Reformation influences came to bear on the colonial American colleges. O'Malley (1989) describes nicely the conflict that arose during the late Middle Ages and the Reformation between humanists and scholastics and the role Jesuits played in that conflict.

Rowse (1975) writes about Oxford during the Reformation and discussed briefly the rise of Puritanism both at Cambridge and at Oxford. Feingold also writes about Oxbridge, showing evidences of scientific research between 1560 and 1640, a period usually considered relatively barren of such activity. Rudy's (1984) Chapter 3 focuses specifically on the Reformation, starting with Professor Martin Luther's nailing his theses to the church door and continuing with Calvin's work in Switzerland and France, with efforts to bring Oxbridge under closer control, and with academic freedom issues in Italy, France, and Spain.

Karp (1985) will prove extremely helpful to readers seeking an understanding of the role Calvin's Geneva Academy played in the emergence of boards of trustees in Reformation and later in the American institutions of higher education. Karp shows how the plan for governing the Academy involved both church and city government participants. Herbst (1974) has also explained the Reformation influence on American colonial college governance.

CHAPTER FIVE

Germination: 1636–1776

> Now for your selfe to come, I doe earnestly desire it, if
> God so move your heart, & not only for the common
> wealth sake; but also for Larnings sake, which I know
> you love, & will be ready to furder, & indeede we want
> store of such men, as will furder that, for if we norish not
> Larning both church & common wealth will sinke: &
> because I am upon this poynt I beseech you let me be
> bould to make one motion, for the furtheranc of Larning
> among us: . . . .
>
> (Eliot, 1633, p. 5)

The colonization of the Western Hemisphere by Europeans must be
numbered among the most consequential social movements of human
history. To the immense new continents already populated by
aboriginal civilizations and nomads sailed the Portuguese explorers,
Spanish armies, French missionaries and trappers, and English
privateers and settlers. With them they brought European artifacts and
institutions and European beliefs, law, and customs. In the wilderness
of New Spain, New France, and New England they reproduced the life
they knew at home.

The institutions Europeans created on American soil included
colleges and universities. The Spanish founded a university at Santo
Domingo in the Dominican Republic in 1538, in Mexico City and in
Lima in 1551, and in Cordoba in 1613. In the colonies that eventually
formed the United States nine colleges came upon the scene before the
American Revolution. All nine were direct or indirect products of the
Calvinist sector of the Reformation.

Like their British antecedents, the colonial colleges for the most part aggrandized the classical languages, offered only "literary" or non-experimental science, and gave no occupational instruction.

Those in control of the colonial colleges and their offshoots fervently maintained the classical-theocentric predilections that had dominated education since the beginning of the Middle Ages. Nothing better illustrates this deeply grounded partnership of religion and education than the Great Awakening that inflamed colonial life during the generation antecedent to the outbreak of the Revolution.

The high earnestness that had brought the Puritans to New England and inspired the numerous German and Pietist sects in the Middle Colonies had begun to wane after the death of the pioneers who had suffered the privations of the American wilderness. As trade in flour, indigo, rice, rum, and tobacco multiplied together with the home-built ships to export them, commerce, industry, land speculation, and their material products began to become more absorbing than religion. Church attendance, in fact, fell off so noticeably in New England that in 1662 the adoption of the Half-Way Covenant made it possible for people to become members without going through the spiritual rigors of conversion. Then in 1680 many New England churches accepted the Savoy Declaration of the English Congregationalists, which made it possible for them to admit members who made no public confession of faith and regeneration. The rise of Arminianism had much to do with the spread of these Latitudinarian attitudes, since its followers opposed the grim predestinationism of Calvin's theology with a doctrine of free will and maintained that faith *and* good works and not faith alone brought salvation.

While a student at Yale Jonathan Edwards grew alarmed at these heterodox tendencies, and in 1734 he conducted a series of revival meetings in his church in Northampton, Massachusetts. In them he eloquently described to lukewarm church members and unrepentant sinners how God "will crush you under his feet without mercy; he will crush out your blood and let it fly" (quoted by Johnson and Malone, 1930, Vol. 6, p. 33). He also painted horrendous word pictures of the huge liquid mountains of fire and brimstone that would flow upon them through all eternity. Thus opened the New England sector of the Great Awakening.

Meanwhile the same fervor that gripped Edwards had been on the rampage in the Middle Colonies among the German and Dutch Pietists.

From them it spread to the Presbyterians in the Middle Colonies and the South. Then in 1738 the most inspired Awakener of all, twenty-four-year-old George Whitefield, arrived in the colonies from England. Undertaking seven American tours during the next several years, he gathered in thousands of converts and hundreds of pounds sterling. Possessed of a voice that could be heard by an outdoor audience of twenty thousand people and sometimes accompanied by an entourage of as many as 150 horsemen, Whitefield preached from Georgia to Maine and made the Great Awakening an intercolonial and interdenominational movement that ignited the entire colonial population.

Politically the revival helped prepare the way for the Revolution by aligning most of the poor and uneducated against the Church of England and hence against the Crown, and it also promoted democratic equalitarian sentiments by giving laymen a greater voice in church government. Socially it advanced humanitarian sympathy, Whitefield using some of the money he raised, for example, to establish and support orphanages and charity schools. Religiously it promoted toleration and helped forge American religious pluralism by splitting existing denominations into numerous new groupings. It prepared the way for Unitarianism on the one hand and on the other for such hot-gospeling sects as the Holy Rollers, Hillerites, and Shakers. Educationally it energized secondary education by promoting the establishment of a large number of academies or secondary schools, and in particular it quickened higher education by leading directly or indirectly to the founding of six of the nine colonial colleges that have survived to this day.

Of the nine colleges, four arose in New England, four in the Middle Colonies, and one in Virginia. All but a very few colleges established until the Civil War mirrored them. They came upon the scene in the following order.

Harvard: The first higher educational institution successfully established within the boundaries of what later became the United States, Harvard began its remarkable history in 1636. Of the approximately one hundred and thirty English university men who migrated to New England before or during 1645, thirty-five had attended Emmanuel College, Cambridge (Morison, 1935, p. 95), and when the Massachusetts Bay colony established a college in the vicinity of Boston, it largely followed the curricular Emmanuel pattern. Emmanuel had itself been founded but fifty-two years earlier under Puritan auspices and by 1617 had become one of the largest Puritan colleges in the two English universities. The Puritan movement and its collegiate stronghold, however, ran into difficulty under the early Stuarts, whose Arminianism impelled Puritans to seek new homes in the New World. In 1629, therefore, a group of Cambridge and East Anglian Puritans came to the conclusion that "the time had come to establish a new England overseas; and New England must include a new Emmanuel" (Ibid., p. 107).

Late the next spring a Massachusetts Bay Company fleet of eleven ships anchored near Boston and landed 840 passengers and their 240 cows and 60 horses. The colonists had left England chiefly to seek, as had the Plymouth Pilgrims a decade earlier, religious freedom. Other Englishmen, little interested in the abounding theological disputes, had migrated to Barbados and Virginia in search of fortunes and freedom in the New World; but the New England colonists sought a new home chiefly for religious reasons. For these reasons and also "to advance *Learning* and perpetuate it to Posterity ("New England's First Fruits," 1642 Col. 1, p. 1), the governing body of the Colony six years later voted four hundred pounds "towards a schoale or colledge" (Morison, 1935, p. 168). In 1638 it became Harvard College, thus honoring the name of the young Puritan who a week after the meeting of the first class died and bequeathed it about four hundred pounds and approximately the same number of books. In 1642 it graduated its first bachelors of arts—nine of them. Four became ministers, two physicians, one a ministering physician-school master, and one a British diplomat. No record has survived of the ninth (Morison, 1935, p. 261ff). Seven of the nine eventually left Massachusetts, most of them returning to England (Morgan, 1958, p. 178).

To oversee the operations of the new institution the General Court of the colony named a six-member committee consisting of Court officials. In 1642 this group, enlarged to twenty-one, became an autonomous body named the Board of Overseers. To this was added in 1650 a second governing board, The Harvard Corporation, which consisted of the President and Fellows of the College.

William and Mary: No less earnestly than their fellow Englishmen in New England, educated Virginians also fostered learning. The Renaissance and Reformation had led to a generally accepted conception of personal cultivation, and through all the colonies aspiring gentlemen sought to be broadly educated in the classics if not also in the Scriptures. Thus in mid-life William Byrd, an eminent early eighteenth-century Virginia aristocrat, made this entry in his diary: "I rose at 5 o'clock and read two chapters in Hebrew and some Greek in Thucydides: (Byrd, 1941, p. 211). Concerning the intellectual interests of Virginia gentlemen in general, a leading authority on the colonial South has written:

> From London booksellers, planters imported works of learning and utility to the education and training of gentlemen. Indeed, their libraries are significant of a desire to duplicate the traditional learning and cultures of England. Like the New Englanders, Virginians were determined not to grow barbaric in the wilderness (Wright, 1940, p. 94).

Three attempts to found a college in Virginia failed before success finally came in 1693. Had it not been for baneful circumstances, the initial effort, Henrico College, begun in 1619 by George Thorpe with a land grant from the Virginia Company of ten thousand acres, would have been the first American institution of higher education. But Thorpe failed because in 1622 "the Indians soon put an end to this ambitious enterprise by scalping him and sixteen of his tenants" (Slosson, 1921, p. 81). The massacre together with the revocation in 1624 of the Virginia charter wrecked the venture, and two later ones never took root. Then in 1693 James Blair, a Scottish Anglican clergyman and Master of Arts of the University of Edinburgh, brought back from London the Crown's charter of the College of William and Mary.

The "able, energetic, and irascible" Mr. Blair (Humelsine, 1965, p. 5) arrived in the area ten years before the present community of Williamsburg was founded, and he maintained a firm control over church, community, and college during the remaining fifty years of his life. The charter he brought with him proved in itself a remarkable document in that it guaranteed the College an income from revenue collected in Virginia from taxes on tobacco and from 20,000 acres of tidewater. To this income the resourceful Blair added a part of the loot of three convicted Virginia pirates, in return for which he aided the pirates in their court battles.

Blair's new institution consisted of "three schools, viz, a Grammar School, for teaching the *Latin* and *Greek* tongues: A Philosophical School, for Philosophy and Mathematicks; and a

Divinity School, for the Oriental Tongues and Divinity" (Hartwell et al., 1940, p. 68), the divinity school admitting only holders of the bachelor's degree. As nearly as can be determined Blair, while he did indeed operate under a dual board arrangement similar to Harvard's, did not openly copy that of the earlier institution. Indeed a year before the William and Mary Charter a new charter was proposed for Harvard which would have given it a single board. The newly installed English government, however, later rejected the Harvard charter. William and Mary, like Harvard, began with a single board, but this board, like Harvard's, soon became two, one consisting of the president and masters of the College, the other of eighteen Virginia laymen.

Unfortunately a series of fires have destroyed most of the older records of William and Mary, but its towering alumni of the colonial and early post-colonial period formidably influenced the history of both the nation and its education. Even before the end of its first century, however, it reached its apex. The breaking of ties with the English government during the Revolution, for instance, cost the College its access to tobacco revenues given it in its original charter. It met with such continuous difficulties as a private institution during the nineteenth century that in 1906 Virginia converted it into a coeducational state college.

Yale: As did the Virginians, the New Englanders to the south of the Massachusetts Bay and Plymouth Colonies also made several unsuccessful efforts to establish a college. Indeed, even before leaving England in 1637, John Davenport, the chief founder of the New Haven Colony, envisioned a college for the Ideal Christian State that he planned to develop in the new land. Economic and political conditions did not prove favorable, however, until the last years of the seventeenth century, and meanwhile approximately an eighth of the graduates of Harvard had come from the New Haven and Connecticut Colonies.

Discussions begun in 1698 led the General Assembly of Connecticut in 1701 (New Haven and Connecticut had been joined in 1664) to empower ten ministers—nine of them graduates of Harvard— to establish a "collegiate school" at Saybrook. The Assembly apparently chose this lowly designation because of the considerable trouble Harvard had been encountering with the Crown over its charter. In 1716, however, the governing board changed the name of the school to "college" and also moved it to New Haven. Two years later a gift from Elihu Yale of some books and of some merchandise worth about six hundred pounds induced the governors to adopt the name of Yale College.

But the story of the early college in New Haven is not that of Elihu Yale but of a group of Congregational clergymen, among them Increase and Cotton Mather. While President of Harvard Increase Mather had become concerned over the weakening position of Calvinistic Protestantism in Europe and the inroads being made in New England by Episcopalians, Baptists, and latitudinarian Congregationalists. He strove to check these trends, and he also counselled the founders of Yale to make plans consonant with his. Sharing his views, they did.

Yale thus emerged as a college administered tightly by a single governing board, all of whose members were sound-in-the-faith ministers. These men strove especially to protect the new college from the infidelities occurring at Harvard, where John Leverett, who had become president in 1708, espoused advocacy of the newer, more liberal concepts of religion. Imagine their dismay, therefore, when in the Fall of 1722 the Rector (President) of Yale, Timothy Cutler, one of the tutors, Daniel Brown, and former tutor Samuel Johnson announced their conversion to Episcopalianism. The continued defection of Yale people to Episcopalianism finally led Jonathan Edwards to the series of "fire and brimstone" revival meetings mentioned above. The efforts of the Yale board and Edwards notwithstanding, however, the New Haven college could not entirely resist the forces of change. Before the close of the eighteenth century, for example, the Connecticut authorities forced the institution to add eight public officials to its governing board.

Throughout most of its history Yale has been the strongest conservative force in American higher education. From 1795 to 1817, during the presidency of Timothy Dwight the Elder, it did substantial pioneering and for a period thereafter surpassed Harvard in size and in general esteem. In 1871, however, Noah Porter, a sixty-year-old minister who resolutely looked to the past, became president; and since then it has only in recent decades begun regaining some of the initiative and national leadership it lost during the course of the nineteenth century.

Princeton: Among the almost innumerable facets of the Great Awakening, one in particular relates to higher education, namely the question of whether religion stood to gain or lose from such advanced schooling. One group held that spiritual illumination sufficed and that anything beyond rudimentary education would turn people from God to worldly concerns. The other group repudiated this position and urged the vital necessity of both zeal and the higher learning. Men of this persuasion set to work to organize colleges sympathetic to their views.

The founders of the College of New Jersey (renamed Princeton University in 1896) belonged, of course, to the pro-education group. Its chief founder and first president, Jonathan Dickinson, a Yale graduate, had not participated in the revivals of the evangelists, but he approved of them and defended them against their critics. The twelve ministers among the twenty-three charter trustees of the College included six graduates of Harvard, three of Yale, and three—including Gilbert Tennent, one of the leading evangelists—from an antecedent school known derisively as the Log College. Tennent's father, a graduate of the University of Edinburgh, operated it halfway between New York and Philadelphia and gave its handful of students an excellent classical and theological education. From his teaching issued some of the most eloquent and also the most explosive of the revivalists. This fact led the Presbyterian Synod of Philadelphia, which disapproved of the revivalists, to refuse to accredit the Log College's work toward ordination. The Synod would ordain only those who had degrees from Harvard, Yale, or one of the Protestant universities of Europe. This action impelled leading ministers of the Middle States to begin negotiations with a succession of royal governors of New Jersey for a college charter. They acquired it in final form late in 1748, the same year that the first class of six bachelors of arts took their degrees.

Two facts about the new college need accenting, one relating to the training of ministers and the other to the composition of the board of trustees. Its founders did not organize the College for the exclusive education of ministers. The Princeton charter describes the College as a place "wherein Youth may be instructed in the learned Languages, and in the Liberal Arts and Sciences" and where "every Religious Denomination may have free and Equal Liberty and Advantage of Education" (Wertenbaker, 1946, pp. 396,397). From the beginning Princeton committed itself not only to the education of ministers but also to "raising up men that will be useful in other learned professions—ornaments of the State as well as the Church" (ibid., p. 19).

The composition of the board of trustees has unusual significance because it prevented attacks upon the College by proponents of public control of higher education such as those which harried six of the colonial colleges. These aggressions led to the monumental Dartmouth College Case, which will be discussed in the next chapter. Princeton experienced no such troubles because from the beginning representatives of both civil government and of private groups had places on its board of trustees. The eleven laymen on the board which took office in 1748 included the governor and the president, four members of the Council of the Colony, three Pennsylvanians, and three New Yorkers. None but the president were ex officio. Three of the thirteen had graduated from Yale, the governor from Harvard. Presbyterians predominated, but Governor Belcher (who signed the charter) and President Jonathan Dickinson (who had much to do with its original drafting) reached out for members of other denominations. The board therefore numbered among its members two Quakers, an Episcopalian, and at least one Congregationalist. This sagacious commingling of diverse interests on Princeton's self-perpetuating governing board saved it from being held in thrall during its formative years by religious doctrinaires and also shielded it from the attacks of those who favored civil control of higher education. Almost a half century had elapsed between the founding of Yale and of Princeton, but five colleges came upon the scene in the twenty-one years following the granting of the Princeton charter, two of them in less than a decade— Kings College in 1754 (Columbia since 1784) and the College of Philadelphia (the University of Pennsylvania since 1791). Because the latter had institutional roots reaching back to 1740, it will be considered next.

Pennsylvania: As earlier observed, George Whitefield had humanitarian as well as religious motivations, and these led him and some of his Philadelphia adherents to establish a charity school there in 1740. Though an Episcopal clergyman, Whitefield's ebullient preaching of redemption closed to him the pulpits of the Church of England in Philadelphia as elsewhere in America and also in England. As with the Methodists John and Charles Wesley, with whom he had been associated since their days together at Oxford, he preached in the churches of other denominations, in barns, and in the open air. Whitefield's Philadelphia supporters decided, however, that they should build a "House of Public Worship," for him, and he insisted that it should also be a "Charity School for the instructing of Poor Children gratis in useful Literature and the Knowledge of the Christian

Religion." The school did not prosper after Whitefield's departure, and so in 1740 Benjamin Franklin and a group of other leading citizens of the city took it over as the "Publick Academy in the City of Philadelphia." In 1755 it became the College and Academy of Philadelphia and in 1791 the University of Pennsylvania.

At this point the church ties of the new institution and also of the four colleges already established must be briefly discussed. Contrary to what appears to be the common belief, religious bodies in and of themselves did not formally establish Harvard, William and Mary, Yale, or Princeton, and none organized the University of Pennsylvania or its precursors. Harvard and Yale arose in colonies that recognized Congregationalism as their official religion, and hence Congregational ministers had legal places on their governing boards. In Virginia the Church of England had privileged status, but nothing in the William and Mary charter required that its trustees be either clerical or lay votaries of the established church. These colleges, therefore, were not church connected in the meaning of that term today. Church synods did not finance them, determine their policy, or elect their ministerial or other trustees.

Because they occasionally helped the colleges financially, the colonial legislatures controlled them to a degree indirectly; but the governing boards had considerable autonomy and essentially functioned as private enterprises. Princeton enjoyed even greater autonomy than its three predecessors because New Jersey never had an established church; Presbyterians organized the College, but the Presbyterian church could not exercise authority over it and possessed no power to ensure the membership of a single one of its communicants on the governing board. The College charter included only two stipulations concerning board membership—that the president must be a member and that twelve of the maximum of twenty-three trustees must be residents of New Jersey.

Pennsylvania, like New Jersey, did not have an established church, and thus the University of Pennsylvania and its forerunners had no official ties with a religious body. The colony, established by Quakers, practiced religious toleration through all its history, and its leading citizens, Benjamin Franklin prominently included, fostered it. When in 1740 a group of Philadelphians built Whitefield's House of Public Worship, the four trustees of its funds included a Baptist, an Episcopalian, a Moravian, and a Presbyterian. Similarly, the trustees of the College and Academy who bought the building represented a diversity of religious as well as of political allegiances. Shortly it developed, however, that the defection to the Church of England of numerous leading Quakers made the majority of its new board members of that denomination. Further, its politically meddlesome administrative head, Dr. William Smith, had abandoned the Presbyterian beliefs of his Scottish youth and had been ordained an Anglican clergyman. Thus it came about that extralegally but not legally the College "fell under the taint of Episcopacy." So it continued until the General Assembly of the newly organized State of Pennsylvania abrogated its charter in 1779.

The Pennsylvania constitution, adopted in September 1776, provided for the establishment of "one or more universities," and in 1779 the legislature commandeered the "powers, authorities, and estates" of the college and assigned them to a new corporation which it chartered as The Trustees of the University of the State of Pennsylvania. Meanwhile it had revoked the college charter on the grounds that former trustees had proven hostile to the new government and that all denominations had not received equal treatment.

The very great importance of these maneuvers in the subsequent history of American higher education will be discussed later in the consideration of the Dartmouth College Case. Here only two points need be made. First, that the controversies caused by these actions led to the abandonment of the projected state university and to the creation in 1791 of the present University of Pennsylvania. On the board of this corporation only the governor sits as an ex officio representative of the state. Second, had the University of the State of Pennsylvania survived, it would have been the first American state university and would have both greatly accelerated the state university movement but drastically interfered with the development of private colleges and universities.

Aside from the topic of state control, the College of Philadelphia has continuing significance because of its concepts of curricular content and structuring, its establishment of one of the first enduring professional schools, one of the first American uses of the word "faculty" to designate the teaching staff, and its formalization of faculty participation in academic government.

Benjamin Franklin had extraordinarily progressive ideas about education both in schools and colleges as witness his writings on the subject and especially his 1749 pamphlet "Proposals Relating to the Education of Youth in Pennsylvania." Because he believed that young

William Smith had similar and supplementary ideas, Franklin, as president of the board of trustees, personally chose him to organize and head the College. It soon developed, however, that Smith preferred established ways, and thus an antagonism developed between the two men that led to problems. Nonetheless, the College progressed curricularly somewhat further than Harvard, Yale, and Princeton in part because Smith introduced to American higher education the rudimentary departmental system of instruction under which he had studied at Aberdeen. Thus Smith organized two schools or departments which he called the Latin and Greek Schools and "the Philosophy Schools," the latter including natural philosophy or science.

In professional education the College pioneered by establishing in 1765 one of the first American medical schools. Columbia followed in 1767, Harvard in 1785. The College also pioneered in calling its body of teachers the "faculty," a step not taken by Harvard until 1825. Some of the first "Rules and Statutes" of the institution, moreover, opened with a section devoted to the "powers of the Faculty," which stipulated that "the Provost, Vice-Provost and professors" shall "meet at least once a Fortnight" and as a body, subject to the approval of the trustees, "shall have an immediate and general Regard to the Manners and Education of all the Youth, belonging to this College."

Columbia: Eight months before Pennsylvania chartered the College of Philadelphia, George the Second by letters patent created "Kings College, for the Instruction and Education of youth in the Learned Languages, and Liberal Arts and Sciences" in the "Province of New-York, in the City of New York, in America" (Van Amringe et al., 1904, p. 1). Its forty-one trustees or "governors" took their oaths of office a month before their twenty-four opposite numbers in Philadelphia took theirs. The College had opened on July 1, 1754, in a building belonging to Trinity Church.

The connection of Kings College with Trinity Church has led most educational historians to conclude that it began as a Church of England institution, but besides being housed for six years in a Trinity Church building and then moving to a plot of ground given the College by Trinity Church, it had only one legal connection with that denomination, namely, the requirement in the charter that the president "shall, forever, hereafter, be a Member of and in Communion with the Church of England" (Ibid., p.11). The trustees named in the charter counted a substantial number of Episcopalians, but among the seventeen ex officio members it specifically named not only the rector of Trinity Church but also the ministers of the Dutch Reformed, Lutheran, Huguenot, and Presbyterian churches of the city. Neither the charter nor the statutes of the College, moreover, prescribed religious tests for trustees, faculty members, or students, and the first public announcement of the College included the following interpretation of the charter:

> . . . [T]here is no intention to impose on the Scholars, the peculiar Tenets of any particular Sect of Christians; but to inculcate upon their Minds the great Principles of Christianity and Morality, in which true Christians of each Denomination are generally agreed. And as to daily Worship in the College Morning and Evening, it is proposed that it should ordinarily, consist of such a Collection of Lessons, Prayers and Praises of the Liturgy of the Church, as are, for the most Part, taken out of the Holy Scriptures, and . . . expressive of our common Christianity; and as to any particular Tenets, everyone is left to judge freely for himself. . . . (ibid., p. 444ff).

The author of this statement, President Samuel Johnson, who thirty-two years earlier had plagued Jonathan Edwards by becoming an Episcopalian, undoubtedly wrote it in part to calm those who feared control of the College by Anglicans. Led by the peppery pamphleteer, William Livingston, these critics desired to create a college which would be entirely "in the Hands of the People," that is, what would today be a state or municipal institution (Ibid., p. 7). They failed in their efforts, but thirty years later another like-minded group of New Yorkers would succeed in scuttling the College and in having its property assigned to the University of the State of New York. The gambit, like that made about the same time in Pennsylvania, did not succeed.

The College adopted the curricular pattern of Princeton, which had been built upon that of Harvard and Yale (Burnaby, 1760, p. 112). It did not, therefore, follow the broader educational ideas of Benjamin Franklin, who had invited Samuel Johnson to be president of the College of Philadelphia before the choice of William Smith. Franklin's influence can be seen, however, in the first announcement of the King's curriculum:

... [I]t is further the Design of the College, to instruct and perfect
the Youth in the Learned Languages, and in the Arts of *reasoning*
exactly, or *writing* correctly, and *speaking* eloquently; and in the
Arts of *numbering* and *measuring*; of *Surveying* and *Navigation*, of
Geography and *History*, of *Husbandry*, *Commerce* and
Government, and in the Knowledge of *all Nature* in the *Heavens*
above us, and in the *Air, Water and Earth* around us, and the various
kind of *Meteor, Stones, Mines,* and *Minerals, Plants,* and
Animals, and everything useful for the Comfort, the Convenience
and Elegance of Life, in the *Manufactures* relating to any of these
Things: And, finally, to lead them from the Study of Nature to the
Knowledge of themselves, and of the God of Nature, and their Duty
to him, themselves and one another. . . . (Van Amringe et al.,
1904, p. 11).

As with all the earlier established colleges except Philadelphia,
Kings operated without benefit of instructional departments. Then in
1767 it organized a medical school, which, as usual everywhere until
late in the nineteenth century, did not require any previous college work
for admission. In 1758 the College graduated its first class of five
young men, four of whom had unmistakably Dutch, that is, non-
Anglican names. Between then and 1776 it graduated a total of 116,
only twelve of whom are known to have been ministers. Then, as also
until after the beginning of the twentieth century, the majority of its
alumni entered law and medicine in about equal numbers (Burritt, 1912,
p. 39).

Brown, Rutgers, and Dartmouth: Two decades after the launching
of the predecessors of Columbia and Pennsylvania, the last three pre-
Revolutionary colleges appeared in rapid succession over a period of six
years: The College of Rhode Island in 1764 (Brown University since
1804), Queens College in 1766 (Rutgers since 1825), and Dartmouth in
1769. Brown and Rutgers, organized respectively by Baptists and Dutch
Reformed, opened as the nation's first church-connected colleges in any
sense akin to the current meaning of that term, but Dartmouth,
although initiated by Congregationalists, followed the legally
independent plan of the other six colonial colleges. Thus the charters of
Brown and Rutgers required that trustees be predominantly members of
the churches whose adherents inaugurated them and also that the
president and faculty members be their communicants. Like the
Dartmouth charter, however, they interdicted religious tests of students.

Brown and Rutgers resulted indirectly from the Great Awakening. That massive religious upheaval had been chiefly responsible for the number of Baptist churches in New England increasing from a meager half dozen in 1740 to about three hundred and twenty-five late in the century, and Brown's first president, an emphatic anti-Arminian, had graduated from Princeton while revivalist doctrines still burned briskly there. Rutgers had similar tangential ties to the evangelism of a quarter of a century before its founding, the son of Theodore Frelinghuysen being the pivotal figure in the long campaign to create it.

Dartmouth, even more than Princeton, emanated directly from the Great Awakening. Its chief founder, Eleazor Wheelock, had been one of its itinerant revivalists, preaching some five hundred sermons throughout New England during the year 1741. When the heat of evangelism subsided, Wheelock turned his zeal to one of its humanitarian projects, namely, the education of Indians. He established a school for that purpose in Connecticut and moved it to New Hampshire some twenty years later upon the promise of a better site for organizing a college with the funds that his agents in Britain had collected. Thus Dartmouth's charter names the education of Indians as its prime purpose, the words "and also of English Youth and others" being attached at the end of a long sentence about "civilizing and Christianizing Children of Pagans" (Dartmouth College Charter). Harvard and William and Mary also made provision for the education of native Americans, the intention in all three cases being primarily to provide literacy training to the point where the native students could participate in evangelizing other members of their tribes.

The Two Foci of Colonial Education

On the one hand the colonial colleges passionately venerated Christian concepts, and on the other they zealously honored and taught the languages and literature of the pagan Greeks and Romans. That is to say, the faith of Protestant Christianity determined their social life, but the spirit of the Renaissance dominated their curricula. During the nineteenth and twentieth centuries these rival loyalties would create complex problems for American higher education, but during the colonial period they did not conflict: the curriculum sustained a Graeco-

Roman heritage and an extracurriculum rigidly geared to religion manifested Christian convictions.

The original Harvard curriculum, the most theocentric of any, required students to give only a sixth of their time to religious courses—one hour a week to studying the Bible and another to "Divinity Catecheticall." Counting the time they devoted to the "sacred tongues" of Hebrew, Chaldee, and Syriac, students gave a quarter of their attention to studies concerned with the Judeao-Christian tradition. The other 75 percent of the curriculum related to pagan antiquity—to several of the liberal arts of ancient Athens, to parts of the Three Philosophies of Aristotle, and to the study of Greek. Greek was most important since it took up two daily instructional hours throughout the length of the college course. In sum, the curriculum of the early American colleges pivoted primarily on studies that originated in the pre-Christian world.

The extracurriculum, however, pivoted on strongly held religious convictions and practices. In varying degrees all the colleges gave allegiance to the stipulation in Harvard's original Laws that "Every one shall consider the mayne End of his life and studyes, to know God and Jesus Christ which is eternal life" (Morison, 1935, p. 434).

The colleges maintained their emphasis upon religion by means of the extracurricular devices of compulsory chapel, the domiciling of students in college residences, and the constant surveillance of devout and often severely pious teachers. Every weekday included two chapel exercises, one at sunrise and the other at five o'clock in the afternoon. These sessions in no way resembled the brief, perfunctory chapels known to modern students at these colleges. The sessions continued for a full hour during which the president prayed at least twice and read and expounded a chapter of the Bible. Student participation fortified the emphasis upon Greek, since during the morning service they translated a portion of the Old Testament from Hebrew into Greek and during the afternoon a passage of the New Testament from English into Greek.

The president also administered corporal punishment (whippings) in chapel. "This relic of barbarism," preceded and followed by a presidential prayer, continued until at least the mid-eighteenth century. Concerning it a Harvard historian of the nineteenth century wrote:

> The late venerable Dr. Holyoke, who was of the class of 1746, observed, that in his day "corporal punishment was going out of

use"; and at length it was expunged from the code, never we trust, to be recalled from the rubbish of past absurdities (Peirce, 1833, p. 228).

Besides twelve compulsory weekly chapels, students were required to attend at least two Sunday church services and at some colleges as many as four. Now and then, also, college authorities called off classes so that students could attend special services.

The president and his fellow teachers also prayed privately with errant students whose rooms they policed to check on their Bible reading, their personal devotions, and their behavior in general. Students reacted to the theocentric paternalism of their teachers sullenly and often violently, especially toward the end of the Colonial Period and thereafter. When Ezra Stiles became President of Yale in 1777, for example, he likened the "Young Gentlemen" there to "a bundle of Wild Fire not easily controlled and governed" (Stiles, 1777, Vol. 2, p. 209). And well he might, since "students were wont to express their displeasure with their tutors by stoning their windows and attacking them with clubs if they chanced out after dark" (Fulton and Thomson, 1947, p. 9).

The two-pivoted educational pattern of the colonial college continued to control almost all of American higher education until after the Civil War, and in some colleges it remained in force well into the twentieth century. The curricular pivot, largely devoted to the study and exaltation of pagan antiquity, changed slowly and obstinately under the impact of the torrents of new knowledge cascading upon society. Meanwhile the extracurricular pivot, zealously concentrated upon promoting piety, became humanized only after student riots and rebellions and declining enrollments led college authorities to approve of athletics and other outlets for the excess energies of students. More about these changes in due course. The point to be stressed here is that the colonial colleges had two foci of loyalty, two allegiances—pagan antiquity and the Judeao-Christian tradition. Each continued to be vital during most of the subsequent history of American higher education, and the latter in particular still has ardent advocates.

Other Common Characteristics of the Colonial Colleges

Beyond these two foci the colonial colleges had a number of other characteristics in common, including the following: (1) they educated widely for fields outside the clergy, (2) they tended (except for Philadelphia and Kings, which established medical schools just before the outbreak of the Revolution and William and Mary, which operated a graduate divinity school) to give instruction only to undergraduates seeking a broad education, (3) they consisted, with the exception of Philadelphia (which pioneered with a rudimentary departmental system) of unitary instructional units, (4) they and their successors had extremely small student bodies, (5) their students represented largely the middle economic classes, (6) they emphasized teaching over research, (7) at the head sat an administrator typically called the president, (8) all operated under external boards of control, and (9) none, aside from an occasional gift from individual congregations (such as the five or six acres given by Trinity Church, New York to help Kings College get started), received financial aid from religious bodies. Certain of these characteristics require further discussion.

The Careers of Colonial College Graduates: No myth about American higher educational history persists more tenaciously than the fable that the organizers of the colonial colleges founded them primarily if not solely for the education of prospective ministers. It has scant basis in fact. Harvard's charter, issued in 1650, for example, opens with the following statement of purpose:

> Whereas through the good hand of God many well devoted persons have been and daily are moved and stirred up to give and bestow sundry gifts, legacies, lands, and revenues for the advancement of all good literature, arts and sciences in Harvard College. . . . ("The Harvard Charter of 1650," in Hofstadter and Smith, 1961, Vol. 1, p. 10).

Nowhere does the charter or any other legal instrument relating to Harvard mention the education of ministers. The same statement applies to the founding documents of six of the other eight colonial colleges, the two exceptions being William and Mary and Queens College, the

Rutgers of today. Ministerial training at both these institutions, however, took second place from their earliest days to what the Queens College charter called "the education of youth in the learned tongues, the liberal and useful arts and sciences." Further, at William and Mary the Divinity School gave future clerics their professional preparation. It required the bachelor of arts degree for admission and never included more than a handful of students.

Had the colleges been established primarily to educate ministers, moreover, one would expect that most if not all of their graduates would have become preachers. Not so, however. Harvard during its first century (1636–1740) sent only 41.6 percent of its alumni into the ministry, Yale during its first hundred years (1701–1802) 41.5 percent, and Princeton (1748–1850) 26.6 percent (Burritt, 1912). For all nine of the colleges the percentage of graduates entering the ministry declined to approximately 22 percent at the time of the outbreak of the Revolution. It rose to 30 percent in 1836 for thirty-seven leading colleges in the East and Middle West, but by the opening of the twentieth century it had dropped to 6 percent (Ibid.)

The graduates of the early colleges entered upon all the careers then considered appropriate for educated men. Thus in his catalogue of Harvard alumni Cotton Mather wrote in 1702:

> In the perusal of this Catalogue, it will be found that, besides a supply of MINISTERS for our churches from this happy *Seminary*, we have hence had Supply of *Magistrates*, as well as *Physicians*, and other *Gentlemen*, to serve the Commonwealth with their Capacities (p. 127).

The steady decline over the decades of ministerial alumni brought few protests, because the colonial colleges and those modelled upon them had been established not for theological education *per se* but, instead, in the words of the Princeton charter, "for encouraging and promoting a learned Education of Our Youth" (Wertenberger, 1946, p. 396). What Morison has written about Harvard on this score applies to all the early colleges, including Rutgers, which never sent more than a third of its graduates into pulpits:

> Harvard was a religious college, but emphatically not a "divinity school" or a seminary for the propagation of puritan theology. . . . The difference was very nearly like that between a Catholic

university today and a Catholic diocesan seminary. . . . President
Oakes addressed a graduation class in 1677 as *liberi liberaliter
educati*, "gentlemen, educated like gentlemen." And in 1721 the
resident fellow declared, "Now the great End for which the College
was founded, was a Learned, and pious Education of Youth, the
Instruction in Languages, Arts, and Sciences, and having their
minds and manners form'd aright" (Morison, 1935, p. 22ff).

Small Student Bodies: The colonial colleges and their successors
had extremely small student bodies, and smallness continued to be a
trait of all American colleges and universities until late in the
nineteenth century. For example, John Adams's Harvard graduating
class (1755) had 24 members, Ralph Waldo Emerson's (1821) 59, and
Theodore Roosevelt's 166. Yale, which during the nineteenth century
had more students than Harvard, graduated its first class of more than a
hundred in 1826, but Harvard passed it in the eighties and for the first
time graduated a class of more than five hundred in 1899. Michigan, the
largest of the state universities during that period, did not surpass
Harvard in total enrollment until about 1910.

Middle-Class Clienteles: Their students came chiefly from
families of the middle economic brackets, but they included a
proportion of sons of artisans and laborers. Harvard during the colonial
period and long thereafter, according to Morison, "was largely composed
of boys from New England families of middling fortune, and the swells
were outnumbered by the horny-handed lads from the country districts
'fitted for college' and provided with a scholarship through efforts of the
local minister" (1936, p. 199). Harvard students of meager means
included, among many others, Isaac Parker, who became Chief Justice
of Massachusetts, Jared Sparks, who had been a journeyman carpenter
before entering as a freshman at the age of twenty-two and who later
became President of the College, and Ralph Waldo Emerson, who
earned his way entirely. Yale students from poor families included Eli
Whitney, the son of an unsuccessful farmer, and Lyman Beecher, the
grandson and son of blacksmiths.

Teaching Emphasized over Research: Although during the
colonial period a handful of men such as Isaac Greenwood and John
Winthrop of Harvard undertook scientific investigations, the research
function had little status and would not be generally recognized until the
opening of the Johns Hopkins University in 1876. Some presidents and

professors wrote scholarly articles and now and then a book, and the mid-eighteenth century saw the beginnings of greater research activity, but the American colleges of this period remained primarily teaching institutions.

The Presidency: The colleges all operated under the immediate direction of an administrative head typically called the president. The office originated as an American adaptation of the headship of Oxford and Cambridge colleges, and hence its roots reach back to the thirteenth century. It is not, as frequently alleged, an American invention patterned on the presidency of business corporations, which, it must be observed, did not become either numerous or important in American life until late in the nineteenth century.

External Boards: All nine of the colleges functioned from their establishment under the government, in whole or in part, of external (non-professorial) boards of control, a form of academic government that had its origins in fourteenth-century Italy. As developed in the previous chapter, John Calvin adapted the plan to his purposes upon his founding of the Geneva Academy in 1559; and from there it spread through Calvinistic channels to the University of Leyden, to the four Scottish universities, to Puritan-initiated Trinity College, Dublin, and from these sources to America. Three facts about this enormously important factor in the history and present operation of American colleges and universities need accenting: first, the concept is post-medieval and did not take hold at Oxford and Cambridge, second, external governing boards perform the function of trusteeship, thus distinguishing the managers of trust funds from their beneficiaries, and third, the oft-made statement that American academic boards of trustees have been modelled after the boards of directors of business corporations is mythical.

Financial Support from the Churches: Aside from an occasional gift from individual congregations, none of the colleges during the colonial period received financial aid from religious bodies. Their funds came from half a dozen other sources: land and money grants from civil legislatures to help them begin operations but only paid irregularly thereafter, continuing subsidies in the form of a percentage of some kinds of tax returns such as that on tobacco paid to William and Mary, lotteries licensed by civil authorities, student fees, private gifts and legacies made spontaneously, and funds raised by vigorous solicitation at home and abroad. All the colleges except Rutgers received aid from colonial legislatures; but the amounts and continuity of such help differed greatly, the older six colleges (Princeton excepted) being provided for far better than the three younger ones. Although eight of the nine institutions derived funds from public treasuries, no one thought of them as state colleges in the sense of that term today. The public-private dichotomy as applied to education had not yet been schematized.

The Immediate and Continuing Importance of the Colonial Colleges

The colonial colleges served their times brilliantly and, moreover, laid down foundations which would powerfully influence the future. Consider these two generalizations in turn.

The American population of two and a half million people in 1776 included only about two thousand alumni of the nine colleges, but the fifty-six signers of the Declaration of Independence numbered twenty-one of them from five of the nine: Harvard eight, Yale five, William and Mary four, Pennsylvania two, Princeton two. Of the committee of five appointed by the Continental Congress to draft the Declaration, three had attended colonial colleges: Jefferson from William and Mary, John Adams from Harvard, and Robert T. Livingston from Columbia. The other two had not attended college— Franklin, who had been the chief founder of the University of Pennsylvania, and Roger Sherman, a treasurer of Yale.

The colonial colleges graduated 102 of 349 members of the Continental Congress—Princeton twenty-nine, Yale twenty-four, Harvard twenty-three, William and Mary twelve, Pennsylvania eight, Columbia four, and Brown and Rutgers one each. Only Dartmouth contributed no members, but it had been established just a few years before the outbreak of the Revolution in out-of-the-way New Hampshire and did not graduate its first class until 1771.

Of the four members of Washington's first cabinet, the colonial colleges produced three: Jefferson and Randolph of William and Mary and Hamilton of Columbia. The three young men who persuaded New York through the Federalist papers to ratify the Constitution, thus saving it from defeat nationally, had all been educated in the colonial colleges: Hamilton and Jay at Columbia and Madison at Princeton.

These are but a few of the facts that can be cited to illustrate the importance of the colonial colleges in the early life of the nation. Their classical education became outmoded during the nineteenth century, but it gave the men of the colonial period both the knowledge and the impetus they needed to be equal to the problems of their pivotal era.

Not all the operational arrangements of the colonial colleges remained in force during later periods, but several of them have been enduring. These include external governing boards, the office of president, and support from both public and private sources. Faculty members ceased being predominately clergymen about the time of the Civil War, and soon thereafter the clienteles and products of American higher education shifted conspicuously.

The classical curriculum monopolized American higher education until after the passage of the Land Grant College Act in 1862; but even after that legislation phenomenally changed American educational directions, the emphasis that the old time college put upon liberal or general education remained potent. Indeed, the advocates of education for humane breadth and depth have continued from colonial times to be a vital although often, unfortunately, a reactionary force in American colleges and universities.

Finally, and significantly, the great majority of the alumni of the colleges held them in high regard and helped convince the American people of their vital importance in the life of the nation. Although Daniel Webster probably never said about Dartmouth as it has been so often written that "It is a small college, but there are those who love it," the epigram nonetheless bespeaks the robust and influential affection of the alumni of colonial colleges.

Bibliographic Notes

The reader looking for recent materials on the colonial American college will find a number of helpful sources. Robson (1980) provides, for instance, an excellent review of books written in the 1970s about the pre- and post-Revolution colleges. He explored the extent to which these histories offer insights into the American culture of that time. Oscar and Mary Handlin (1970) have a somewhat similar motive in their Chapter 2, which discussed the value of the degrees offered in colonial times, the approach Harvard took to disciplining its students, and the utility of the colonial curriculum. Moore (1974) also studies student discipline at Harvard, showing how presidents and faculty differed on the use of corporal punishment. In a later paper (1978) she focuses on the conflict between students and their tutors at Harvard and Yale during 1745–1771. At Yale, for instance, Moore attributed these "wars" to a distinct difference in the backgrounds of the two groups, students most often in trouble coming from traders' families and tutors from the families of clergy.

Finkelstein (1983 and 1984) deals with characteristics of the faculty. Instructional staffs through the mid-eighteenth century, he points out, consisted almost entirely of the president and of tutors— recent graduates of the colleges serving in their positions temporarily while awaiting a ministerial position. This pattern began to change with the endowing of professorships at Harvard in the 1720s and later at Yale. As a result a more permanent professorship began to emerge.

Cremin's (1970) Chapter 7 covers the emergence of the American college during colonial times. He starts with some general history of the medieval universities, especially Oxbridge, and proceeds from there to show the role of university-educated people in the establishment of new institutions, especially Harvard, in the New World.

Rudolph (1977) shows in good detail the impact of the English universities on the curriculum of the early American colleges. There follows attention to the changes occurring in the curriculum as the colonies began to assert their independence. Kimball (1986) covers much of this same ground, albeit more briefly, in his Chapter V. Bailyn (1986) deals with the colonial beginnings of Harvard, especially as various Harvard historians treated that event. Did the founders have in mind a theological seminary, he asks, or one that focused on the liberal arts education of young gentlemen? When did people actually start calling it "Harvard"? Why was it that Harvard did not follow English university governance practices when it copied most everything else English in its founding?

Robson (1985) looks at the role the colonial colleges played in educating the people who would participate in the American Revolution and the beginnings of the new nation. This richly-detailed book, covering the half-century between 1750 and 1800, deals both with curricular changes and with the roles various individuals within the colleges played in the Revolution and its aftermath. In this same context Tucker (1974) writes about the role of Yale as a "Seminary of Sedition" during the period of the American Revolution.

Warch (1973) also deals with Yale and provides excellent background on the period 1701–1740. Yale was a symbol during this period of Congregational orthodoxy, but this did not mean that its religious orientation remained static. Another excellent source on the beginnings and later development of Yale appears in Pierson's (1988) study, which includes exploration of the use a later president, Thomas Clap, made of a gift of forty folios possibly given the College at its founding.

Dunn (1983) has prepared a detailed account of the impact of the Great Awakening on Harvard during 1741–44. Vine (1976) studies the expectations of parents and college leaders at about this same time, especially as these expectations included both moral/religious factors as well as the positions graduates would eventually assume in society.

Herbst has written extensively about governance of the colleges of this period. His 1974 paper provides useful detail on the beginnings of Harvard, William and Mary, and Yale, pointing to their roots, especially as relates to governance, not in the medieval universities but in various institutions connected with the Reformation. In 1975 Herbst turns to the eighteenth-century split between public and private higher education in America. Several patterns appeared, ranging from the germ of an idea in New York for a state university to a multi-denominational approach in Rhode Island to a one-denominational approach in New Jersey. From these patterns there emerged after the Revolution the distinction between public and private higher education in the United States. Herbst's 1976 and 1981 papers look at governance changes toward the end of the colonial period, especially as ethnic and religious diversity within the colonies and changes in the political climate led away from the more sectarian character of earlier governance patterns. His 1982 book expands on his earlier work and provides a most helpful analysis of governance in the American colleges during the period 1636 through 1819. His first two chapters deal with the colonial period.

Sloan (1971) studies Scottish influences on eighteenth century American higher education. Following a chapter on "The Scottish Universities in the Enlightenment," he identifies the adaptations made by colonial college leaders, especially at Princeton, based on the

Scottish patterns. Miller (1976) also gives attention to Princeton in the broader context of the Presbyterian influence on colonial higher education. Princeton also enters Humphrey's (1972) discussion of the impact of the English dissenting academies on curricular and other matters in the colonial colleges. Outside of the New Jersey institution, Humphrey can find little evidence that the academies had that much influence.

CHAPTER SIX

Exploration: 1776–1862

> The business of education has acquired a new complexion by the independence of our country. The form of government we have assumed, has created a new class of duties to every American. It becomes us, therefore, to examine our former habits upon this subject, and in laying the foundations for nurseries of wise and good men, to adapt our modes of teaching to the peculiar form of our government.
>
> (Benjamin Rush, 1798)

In England soon after the American Revolution a prominent member of the rearguard of one age met and briefly conversed, so it has been reported, with a humble but prodigious member of the oncoming age. One was King George III, the other James Watt, the inventor of the steam engine. When the King asked Watt the nature of his work, he replied that he was engaged in producing a commodity that kings greatly desired. The monarch queried what that might be, and Watt answered, "Power, your Majesty, Power!!" (Garbedian, 1936, p. 242)

In 1776 Watt's steam engine had gone into successful operation for the first time—one in a coal mine in Staffordshire, the other in an ironworks in Shropshire. These new engines symbolized the passing of the age of muscle power and the dawning of the age of machine power—an age that would require new educational institutions to serve new social needs, an age in which the insistent problem of existing educational institutions would be not *whether* they should adapt to change but, rather, *how.*

The advent of the age of machine power inescapably forced an era of exploration upon American colleges. Their search for new patterns, triggered by the Revolution, turned them from their English traditions, and they sought new models first in France and then in Germany. The most far-sighted educators, however, sought to break away from the academic molds of Europe and to build institutions peculiarly American. Their efforts came to fruition on July 2, 1862, when President Lincoln signed into law the most important higher educational legislation enacted in America in the nineteenth century: the Land Grant College Act. With this event the eighty-six-year era of exploration reached its culmination.

Although the period of exploration in American higher education can be said to have begun in 1776 with the Declaration of Independence, no definite date can be assigned to the beginning of the age of machine power that underlay the exploration. The change came gradually, and it spread to different countries at different times. England as a coal-producing, iron-manufacturing, and trading nation confronted the new day first; its full impact reached the United States about the time of the Civil War; it moved into Russia with great force only after the October Revolution of 1917; it now advances through Asia, Latin America, and Africa. Yet during the last half of the eighteenth century the graph representing power available to humans took a more spectacular leap than ever before. Historians have generally labelled this leap as "the Industrial Revolution"; Ralph Linton called it "the third great mutation in human culture" (1955, p. 663); but I prefer to call it the beginning of the modern power saltation. Not simply an industrial revolution, it changed the technological, economic, and social foundations of society and has affected the lives of all peoples everywhere. Consider, for example, the saltatory events of the year that opened the age of exploration—1776:

- In science and technology, not only did Watt's steam engine begin successful operation in 1776, but in France Lavoisier reported one of his most significant studies leading to his enunciation of the law of combustion. His work killed off the phlogiston theory which had hobbled chemistry for almost two centuries, led to the complete reorganization of chemical knowledge and procedures, and stimulated new approaches to physics. In solving the problem of heat, Lavoisier made it possible for both the physical and biological sciences spectacularly to accelerate their pace in the nineteenth century.

• In economics, Adam Smith in 1776 published *The Wealth of Nations*, the source of the intellectual and spiritual power of capitalism over the next century. His economic theories gave the death blow to mercantilism and stated the economic principles that made it possible for entrepreneurs to exploit the steam engine and the myriad of other new machines being produced by inventors and engineers.

• In politics, the Declaration of Independence constituted but one development of 1776. On January 10 of that year appeared Thomas Paine's *Common Sense*, a forty-seven page pamphlet that probably did more than any other publication to arouse Americans to support their leaders in their crusade for freedom from English rule. During the same month in France, Turgot, the Controller General of Finance, presented his "Six Edicts" to the *Conseil du Roi*—a document that forced his resignation and which helped prepare the way for the French Revolution. In England, young Jeremy Bentham wrote his *Fragment on Government*, a statement on the utilitarian philosophy that would become so influential during the nineteenth century.

• In terms of social democracy, a committee chaired by Jefferson presented a series of bills to the Virginia House of Burgesses in 1776 calling for the end of primogeniture and entails, thus making hereditary aristocracy or a "landocracy" impossible in Virginia. The adoption of similar legislation in other states confirmed equalitarianism as a permanent characteristic of American social and political life.

• Jefferson also conceived his Bill for Religious Freedom in 1776: a bill which separated church and state in Virginia and which led to their separation in the United States Constitution and the constitutions of all the states.

• One of the first volumes of history written in the modern spirit appeared in 1776: Edward Gibbon's *The Decline and Fall of the Roman Empire*. Some have considered it the greatest historical study ever published, and certainly it began a new era in historiography.

- Humanitarian sentiments intensified, and new conceptions of the dignity of man appeared. In 1776 the Quakers of Philadelphia, for example, voted to excommunicate any of their number who owned slaves.

- International educational conceptions had burgeoned during this period. In 1776 Pestalozzi was at work at Heuhof, Switzerland, putting Rousseau's educational theories into practice; Basedow had opened his Philanthropium at Dessau near Leipsig; and Behrdt was organizing one at Heideshein. These educational reformers planted the seeds which later flowered in American elementary education. In 1776, too, occurred a significant event for higher education: Diderot's description for Catherine the Great of Russia of a plan for the University of St. Petersburg that she hoped to found. An amazing document, it blueprints the comprehensive American university of today.

These and other portentous developments of 1776 and surrounding years commingled to sound taps on the age of muscle power and reveille for the age of machine power. They also challenged the value of the literary education given by the colonial colleges. The new age required educational conceptions and processes that could produce the manpower needed to direct and use the new energies—social as well as physical—becoming available with fantastic rapidity to men and nations. It also required massive quantities of new knowledge and large numbers of specialists to develop and to disseminate it among the managers and workers of the fast developing new-type agricultural, commercial, industrial, political, and social institutions spawned by the new forces in the world.

A few discerning people such as Benjamin Franklin foresaw the coming of the new era and recognized its intellectual and educational implications. Some others in the American colleges sensed it, too, and after 1750 began offering courses, for instance, in natural science— astronomy, physics, and chemistry particularly. Add to these courses instruction in technical subjects such as surveying and navigation, early professorships in mathematics and natural philosophy, and the general (but not consistent) support of the ministry for scientific endeavors, and one begins to recognize the changing mood among certain American academics.

Strangely enough, however, the great bulk of Americans gave little thought to the possibilities of the extraordinary changes that the modern power saltation would bring, and practically no one had any inkling of the speed which change would soon attain. Even such a wide-ranging, far-seeing thinker as Jefferson observed when he negotiated the Louisiana Purchase in 1803 that it would probably take a thousand years for Americans to settle all the land east of Mississippi. The average citizen, meanwhile, continued to believe that the future would continue to be much like the past; and most professors resisted the facts of the power saltation even more obstinately than the person on the street. Within higher education colleges made enough incremental changes to satisfy their publics, but those that limited their changes enjoyed higher enrollments than those that changed too willingly. Local support remained with those institutions, such as Yale, that kept close to the tried and true ways. (Potts, 1977, 1981). The English philosopher, C.E.M. Joad, has epigrammatically described the changes of attitude that followed the technological advances. Modern man, he suggested, has said "first, 'It is absurd,' second, 'It is contrary to Scriptures,' and third 'Of course, I knew it all the time'" (1925, p. 49). Before the Civil War few academics adopted this third attitude, and as a result they did little to prepare their students for the momentous years ahead. In the meantime, however, two other developments in American life would formidably affect the nation's colleges: the influence of France and the meteoric rise and fall of deism.

The Impact of French Culture and of Deism

Even before the birth of the nation, influences from France contributed to American Protestant, Roman Catholic, and secular developments. Huguenot refugees, seeking religious liberty in the middle colonies, had been a leaven for French culture along the Atlantic seaboard; and French Roman Catholic traders and missionaries, penetrating the Ohio and Mississippi valleys, had left a marked French stamp on the Middle West. Then in 1778 the political *entente* between France and the beleaguered colonies facilitated the spread of French secular culture. Things French became *comme il faut*, and for the first time American colleges offered instruction in the French language. Columbia began such instruction in 1779; Harvard gave it a fairly permanent place in its curriculum in 1780, William and Mary in 1793, and Union in 1806.

During this same period Americans organized academies similar to those of France. In 1780 the American Academy of Arts and Sciences got under way in Boston, partly inspired by John Adams, then American envoy in Paris. Its founders placed on record their intention "to give it the air of France rather than that of England, and to follow the Royal Academy rather than the Royal Society." It therefore published *Memoirs* to contrast with the British-dominated American Philosophical Society at Philadelphia, which issued *Philosophical Transactions*. During these same years Quesnay du Beaurepaire, grandson of the famous physiocrat and himself a French officer in America during the Revolution, inspired the Academy of Sciences and Fine Arts in Richmond.

Similarly, French educational views, which had been nurtured by the eighteenth century Enlightenment, affected the plans for the establishment of American universities. In 1784 French influences stimulated Alexander Hamilton and others to organize the University of the State of New York as a non-teaching and non-degree-granting institution to supervise the statewide system of education on all levels. Likewise, when Michigan, long within the orbit of French missionaries and traders, projected its state university in 1817, French ideas intertwined with those of Americans educated in the colonial colleges. Most important of all, when Thomas Jefferson conceived the University of Virginia, his insistence that it be independent of organized religion came in large measure from his first-hand knowledge of the movement of French thought.

French influences began to wane early in the nineteenth century for a number of reasons: the political liberalism let loose by the French Revolution, the rise to pre-eminence of the German universities, and— most immediately—the ebbing of the deistic tide that had spread from the French rationalists to the American revolutionists.

The deistic meteor fell to earth during the first decades of the nineteenth century. Immorality and lawlessness brought protests against it from the church, the state, and leading citizens. Deism, an intellectual religion, failed as an ethical system for most citizens because they found it cold and impersonal and because it made no provision for satisfying the craving for emotional excitement and promised nothing after death. Religionists recognized these weaknesses and soon initiated the Second Awakening—a series of vigorous and continuous revivals across the country comparable to the Great Awakening of the previous century. So fervid were their missionary efforts that in time all but a small fraction of the people penitently returned to the churches. More important for the future of American higher education, these religious leaders established hundreds of denominational colleges across the length and breadth of the new nation—throughout the original thirteen states, over the Appalachians into the Ohio and Mississippi valleys, and out onto the Great Plains. Also contributing mightily to the spread of these institutions was the spirit of localism. Local communities welcomed the cultural and social benefits associated with having a college within their borders (Potts, 1971).

This period of growth also marks the beginnings of black higher education in the United States. Prior to 1827, for example, American colleges awarded degrees to at least three blacks—Lemuel Haynes at Middlebury, Edward Jones at Amherst, and John Brown Russworm at Bowdoin. Jones and Russworm later became educational leaders in the African colonies—Jones playing a leading role in founding what is today the Federal University of Sierra Leone, Russworm becoming the superintendent of schools in Liberia. Other black students prior to the Civil War are known to have attended Antioch, Oberlin, Franklin, Rutland, and the Harvard Medical School (Brubacher and Rudy, 1976). In addition a few institutions opened specifically for black students during this time, namely, Cheyney State (known then as the Institute for Colored Youth), Ashmun Institute in Pennsylvania, and Wilberforce in Ohio. The opportunities offered by these colleges contrasted sharply, however, with laws in other parts of the nation at the time which forbad even the teaching of reading and writing to blacks. Colleges such as Antioch and Oberlin, in turn, played active roles, not only in helping blacks escape from areas having these restrictions but also by opening their doors both to white and black students.

For Native Americans the educational picture during the nineteenth century turned bleak. The Five Civilized Tribes in 1815 began their own educational system, but for most others any education received was rarely at the postsecondary level and required youth to live in special schools far from their families. A few Native Americans found their way into the black schools during the nineteenth century.

Life in the Traditional Colleges

Colleges of this time followed the colonial college pattern. Called "academical" or "classical" colleges, liberal arts colleges are their present-day counterparts. The name of "liberal arts college" did not come into use until about 1890, however, and because the so-called liberal education they offered chiefly meant *literary* education, they ought properly to be called "literary colleges." They gave major attention to the heritage of the race as expressed in classical literature, and thus the classical languages continued to stand high above all other subjects. For example, students read the historians Herodotus and Thucydides in the original Greek, the physician Galen in both Latin and Greek, the essays of Cicero and the natural science letters of Pliny the Younger in Latin. They did not, however, read much imaginative literature, drama, or poetry, and what they did read their puritanical professors expurgated.

Two additions to the prescribed curriculum occurred before the end of the eighteenth century—both as the result of the social changes mentioned above. French became the first modern language to be offered in American colleges, but students usually studied it outside the regular curriculum and for extra fees. And to counteract the spread of "French and English infidelity," students were required to take either or both of two new courses to fortify their religious convictions: one called "Evidences of Christianity" and the other "Moral Philosophy." The president usually taught them, and through them he attempted to harmonize everything that students had learned earlier with Christian concepts.

The colleges relied not only on these new religious courses and on their traditional devices of compulsory chapel and faculty surveillance to maintain the purity of their students, but they also adopted the revival meeting as an almost annual event for cleansing the more tarnished souls. Between 1802 and 1837, for example, Yale experienced seventeen "distinct effusions of the Holy Spirit."

Interestingly enough, colleges adopted the religious revival at the same time that they became centers of student riot and rebellion. Outbreaks of large proportions took place at Harvard, for example, in 1766, 1768, 1790, 1805, 1807, 1818, 1823, 1834, and 1841. Some of them related to food—as did the Great Butter Rebellion of 1766, which took more than a month to quell, the Bread and Butter Rebellion of

1805, and the Rotten Cabbage Rebellion of 1807. Others, however, resulted from dissatisfaction with the prevailing methods of teaching and discipline, and the Great Rebellion of 1823 helped prepare for the crucial Harvard reforms of 1825. Samuel Eliot Morison reports the Great Rebellion as follows:

> The class of 1823 was uncommonly rowdy. A class history kept by a member chronicles class meetings and forbidden dinners, battles in commons, bonfires and explosions in the Yard, cannon balls dropped from upper windows, choruses of "scraping" that drowned Tutors' voices in classroom and chapel, and plots that resulted in drenching their persons with buckets of ink-and-water. A schism developed between the "high-fellows" of the class and the obedient "blacks." . . . The climax came in the spring of the senior year when a "black" played informer against a "high-fellow," who was expelled; and the rebels swore on oath under the Rebellion Tree that they would leave College until the departed hero was reinstated and the informer deprived of his Commencement part. The Faculty, determined to rule, expelled forty-three students out of a class of seventy, almost on commencement eve; and although John Quincy Adams, the parent of a rebel, protested vigorously, President and Fellows were inflexible (1936b, p. 230).

At Yale a bread and butter rebellion took place in 1828, and two years later the sophomore class none too politely declined to recite their mathematics as the rules required. The riots that ensued have come down in history as the Conic Section Rebellion.

Along with these faculty-student clashes went town and gown riots, a pastime in which Yale students particularly specialized. In 1841 they staged what has since been known as the First Firemen's Riot, a street fight in which the students reportedly cut the fire hose into small pieces, overturned the engine, and strewed fire-fighting apparatus about the town and college yard. Compared to two subsequent tilts, however, this 1841 riot seems as mild as a May-pole dance. In 1854 a group of "townies" objected to the conduct of a number of undergraduates at a New Haven theater. The fight that followed brought death to a local bartender whom a student struck with a dagger, and four years later, on the occasion of the Second Firemen's Riot, a student shot and killed one of the firemen.

Townies, however, were not the only people damaged in these pitched battles. William Hickling Prescott, the eminent historian, lost an eye when, as a Harvard junior departing from the dining room, he furnished the target for a piece of stale bread. Describing these uprisings as they occurred at Harvard, Morison wrote that President Josiah Quincy, upon retiring and moving to Boston, "humorously complained that the 'unearthly quiet' kept him awake, after the nocturnal clamor of the Harvard Yard" (1937, p. 275).

Reasons for such wanton behavior abound: college authorities prohibited athletics, even such innocent physical activities as ball-tossing; co-eds to tame students had not yet been admitted; and the sobering tie between a college degree and a career had as yet little potency. Moreover, the curriculum had lost its appeal, and the college faculties seemed unable to communicate their own intellectual interests to their students. Some professors were undoubtedly inept, having entered teaching after failing as preachers; but even the competent bored students because of their drillmaster conception of teaching. Andrew Dickson White has described how it functioned at Yale:

> The worst feature of the junior year was the fact that through two terms, during five hours each week, "recitations" were heard by a tutor in "Olmstead's Natural Philosophy." The text-book was simply repeated by rote. Not one student in fifty took the least interest in it; and the man who could give the words of the text most glibly secured the best marks. . . . Almost as bad was the historical instruction given by Professor James Hadley. It consisted simply of hearing the student repeat from memory from "Putz's Ancient History." How a man so gifted as Hadley could have allowed any part of his work to be so worthless, it is hard to understand. . . . In the senior year the influence of President Woolsey and Professor Porter was strong for good. . . . Yet it amazes me to remember that during a considerable portion of our senior year no less a man than Woolsey gave instruction in history by hearing men recite the words of a textbook. . . . (1906, Vol. 1, p. 27).

A Yale sophomore who became a great publisher, Henry Holt, observed about such teaching methods that "the most diabolical ingenuity could hardly have done more to make . . . scholarship repulsive" (1923, p. 36); and a Harvard historian has reported that "almost every graduate of the period 1825–60 has left on record his detestation of the system of instruction" (1937, p. 260). "The Faculty," he states, "were not there to teach, but to see that boys got their lessons."

Students rioted and rebelled not only because of the recitation method, the stale curriculum, and the bad food but also because of the constant snooping of faculty members into their personal lives. Concerning the latter a Dartmouth historian has written:

> Teaching was not the only duty of the professor. He was also expected to be a detective, sheriff, prosecuting attorney, and judge. . . . At the beginning of the year, the village was divided geographically, and each professor was assigned a section of it. It was his duty to visit the rooms of all students located in his area at least once a term, acting partly as spy, partly as inspiration to good (Richardson, 1932, Vol. 2, p. 461).

During an academic year not long before the beginning of the Civil War the Dartmouth faculty held sixty-eight meetings and "cases of discipline occupied the greater part of the time." When no disciplinary problems appeared on the agendum, the faculty created them by the device of "reading the catalogue." The President would name students in alphabetical order "with a call for comments by any professor who had information concerning 'moral delinquencies.'" Small wonder, as Professor Andrew P. Peabody of Harvard wrote, that students "considered the Faculty as their natural enemies" and proceeded to make their lives as miserable as possible. Peabody also wrote:

> There existed between the two parties very little of kindly intercourse, and that little generally secret. If a student went unsummoned to a teacher's room, it was almost always at night. It was regarded as a high crime by his class for a student to enter a recitation-room before the ringing of the bell, or to remain to ask a question of the instructor. . . . The professors, as well as the parietal officers, performed police duty as occasion seemed to demand; and in case of general disturbance, which was not infrequent, the entire Faculty were on the chase for offenders—a chase seldom successful (1888, p. 13).

Such were the conditions under which "Christian gentlemen and scholars" were educated in the nineteenth century. The educational philosophy that permeated the colleges emanated from the beliefs that their graduates should be helped to godliness, that all utilitarian knowledge was servile and beneath the dignity of gentlemen, and that the college curriculum should above all provide "mental discipline." No clearer statement of this philosophy in American higher education has been published than that by the president of Yale, Jeremiah Day, and a Yale professor of classics, James L. Kingsley, who in August 1828, issued the famous Yale "Report on a Course of Liberal Education." Perhaps the most conservative, if not reactionary, document in the history of American education, it flayed any tampering with the "god-given" prescribed classical curriculum and specifically precluded the introduction of the modern languages and the experimental sciences.

Needing a weapon to defend the classical curriculum against the radical curricular adventures of Harvard, Amherst, Virginia, and Union, the Yale writers appealed to the venerable doctrine of mental discipline. This concept, stemming from the psychological theories of the Greek philosophers, the theologians of the late Middle Ages, and the "faculty psychology" of John Locke, postulated the existence of an unstated number of mental faculties by means of which people think and act: cognition, perception, memory, imagination, will, and so forth. These, so the theory ran, could each be developed through exercise. Schools and colleges existed, its adherents maintained, to furnish opportunities for such exercise. Thus the Yale Report defended the classical curriculum in terms of Faculty Psychology:

> A commanding object, therefore, in a collegiate course, should be to call into daily and vigorous exercise the *faculties* of the student. Those branches of study should be prescribed, and those modes of instruction adopted, which are best calculated to teach the art of fixing the *attention*, directing the train of *thought*, analyzing a subject proposed for investigation; following, with accurate *discrimination*, the course of argument; balancing nicely the evidence presented to the *judgment*; awakening, elevating, and controlling the *imagination*; arranging, with skill, the treasures which *memory* gathers; rousing and guiding the powers of genius (Hofstadter & Smith, 1961, Vol. 1, p. 278). (Emphasis added.)

Perhaps not surprising, President Day, a mathematician, and Professor Kingsley, a classicist, considered two subjects to have super-disciplinary worth: mathematics and the classical languages. The classics had had superior status in higher education since the late

Renaissance, but mathematics did not come into the curriculum of the American colleges until the time of the Revolution. By 1828, however, it extended through calculus and had become firmly established. These two subjects together lorded over all others; and when the advocates of modern languages and experimental science increased their demands for places in the curriculum, the defenders of the status quo appealed to their disciplinary worth to save the existing pattern.

Few questioned the hoary theory of mental discipline until early in the nineteenth century, when the German philosopher, Johann Friedrich Herbart, smote it mightily. Americans did not hear much about Herbart's work for another fifty years, however, and when they learned of him, only the radical educators took him seriously. Meanwhile the classicists stood behind the fortifications of faculty psychology. From that vantage point they fought off all unwelcome curricular intruders, brandishing the concept of mental discipline to good effect in every educational discussion and controversy from admission requirements to graduation "standards." Most important, they succeeded in identifying the curriculum of classical languages and mathematics with the term, *liberal education*, despite the fact that the adored seven liberal arts had contained no Greek, no Latin, no literature of any sort, and only the rudiments of arithmetic and geometry. Thus a wide and deep breach developed in American higher education during the first half of the nineteenth century between the upholders of "liberal education," so defined, and the promoters of what in the 1860s came to be known as "the New Education"; that is, the education which admitted the modern languages, the natural sciences, the social sciences, the imaginative arts, and vocational studies. For the time being the old curriculum dominated, and institutions that stayed with that curriculum maintained their status and health throughout the nineteenth century.

Machine Technology and Equalitarianism

Massive new technological forces and such novel social concepts as progress, evolution, nationalism, equality, and democracy overspread the new era; change was in the wind. Above all the railroads dramatically symbolized the transition from the old age to the new. Charles Carroll, the last living signer of the Declaration of Independence, drove the first spike for the Baltimore and Ohio the

Fourth of July, 1829, and two years later a locomotive named Tom Thumb raced a man on horseback over the thirteen miles of its track. The spectators hooted the iron horse when the rider won, but nonetheless the technological saltation had begun.

One incident involving the new railroads epitomizes their effect upon education. It occurred during the 1850s, when the Chicago, Burlington, and Quincy Railroad arrived in Galesburg, Illinois, the home of Knox College. Jonathan Blanchard, president of the College and a Congregational minister, had supported the building of the railroad; but he was shocked to discover that on the first Sunday morning following its opening the train arrived and departed just as on an ordinary weekday. Blanchard resolved to stop this Sabbath-breaking, and so the following Sunday morning, according to Earnest Elmo Calkins, "among the goodly crowd assembled at the station was a tall commanding figure in a long frock coat, distinctly clerical, and otherwise clothed with unmistakable authority." Calkins continued the tale as follows:

> There was the engine with steam up, smoke pouring from its enormous top-heavy stack, its tender full of cordwood, its sweeping cow-catcher—so necessary in a country where livestock ran loose even in the village streets—drawing a string of short, square, flat-topped boxlike cars—all as if just steamed out of a Currier & Ives print. Before the conductor could shout his "All aboard," and the engineer grab the bell rope, the tall, commanding figure stepped from the crowd, raised his hand, and bade the engineer to take the engine to the roundhouse.
>
> "Who are you to give me such orders?" asked the astonished engineer.
>
> "I am President Blanchard of Knox College, and again I order you to take that engine to the roundhouse and not run this train on Sunday."
>
> "Well, President Blanchard of Knox College, you can go to hell and mind your own business, and I'll take my train out as ordered."
>
> And that is what the engineer did. The town had asked for transportation and had got it. . . . President Blanchard was

as powerless to stem the tide of liberal ideas which came rolling in
with the advent of the railroad as old King Canute had been to halt
the inrolling breakers of the North Sea. Galesburg was never the
same again (Calkins, 1937, p. 219ff).

Nor would the nation at large ever be the same again; and hence
traditional educators and religionists such as President Blanchard found
that they could do nothing to hold back the forces swirling around and
through the colleges.

The American Revolution set up a republic and killed the
growing movement among American tories for an hereditary
aristocracy, but it moved only indirectly toward political democracy.
Jefferson, inspired by Locke, had opened the Declaration of
Independence with the eloquent pronouncement that "all men are created
equal" to engage in "Life, Liberty, and the Pursuit of Happiness"; but
the war over, many American leaders wrote off such idealistic
sentiments and organized against the onslaughts of the "rats and
vermin" of "mobocracy."

Early in his career Jefferson fought against suffrage restrictions,
and in 1778 he led the victorious fight in the Virginia legislature for
voting privileges for all white male adults. In time other states followed
Virginia's example; and by 1828 enough had liberalized their suffrage
laws to make possible the election of Jackson. Political democracy for
white men did not become a fact throughout the nation until just before
the Civil War.

Simultaneously with the campaign for suffrage a demand arose
for equality of educational opportunity. Massachusetts had established
schools partially supported by taxation as far back as 1647, but existing
schools made little provision for the children of the growing number of
industrial workers. To extend educational opportunities to all the
people, various groups of citizens began campaigns for democratic
schooling. In 1779 Jefferson had presented a bill to the Virginia
Legislature calling for the establishment of common schools and
colleges supported by the state within riding distance of every student's
home. The bill failed, but like-minded men succeeded in writing into
the contracts of land developers on the frontier provisions setting aside
land which was to be sold for the purpose of establishing educational
facilities. "Religion, morality, and knowledge being necessary to good
government and the happiness of mankind," the Northwest Ordinance of
1787 declared, "schools and the means of education shall ever be

encouraged." This great charter not only embodied the principle of political democracies, but it also established education as a fundamental responsibility of government. Four states fashioned out of the Northwest Territory promptly wrote educational articles into their constitutions. Ohio took the first steps. Michigan, Indiana, and Wisconsin followed, all promoting in their basic laws the cause of education "ascending in regular gradations," to quote the Indiana constitution of 1816, "from township schools to a State University, wherein tuition shall be gratis and equally open to all."

These legal provisions made history not only because they committed the new states to educational programs at public expense but also because they set up standards which the eastern states followed in subsequent decades. Yet perhaps even more importance should be attached to the fact that they set up a *unitary* system of state education. Predominantly the educational programs in the eastern states had been organized after the dualistic European model: an academic school system leading to college, another available to the lower classes and limited to elementary education. The frontier states in large part passed over this class-conscious plan and constructed a single educational ladder leading from the elementary school to the university and open to the children of all the people. To be sure, certain "select schools" existed and at times flourished in the West until about the end of the nineteenth century, but the more common pattern which emerged during this period was a one-track system. In time this pattern spanned the nation.

In the East the reduction of the two-track secondary school system led to new roles for the private academy, several thousands of which existed by the close of the fourth decade of the nineteenth century. After this date the academies began disappearing, some changing to become colleges. From these origins have come, for example, such present-day institutions as Hamilton College, Washington and Lee University, and Hampden-Sidney College (Eby and Arrowood, 1934).

Another group—the humanitarians led by such men as Channing, Parker, and Alcott—lent their vigorous support to democratic education. Protesting the doctrine of the natural depravity of man, and declaring a person's essential excellence when unshackled from vicious institutions, the humanitarians set out to reconstruct American life. Practically every department of social endeavor in the new nation came under their scrutiny and brought forth their proposals and plans for betterment. A group of them under the leadership of Garrison and Phillips attacked slavery and helped precipitate the Civil War. Another organized the temperance movement. Another launched the first American peace societies. Still others worked for the education of the blind and the deaf, for better treatment of the insane, for prison reform, and for a score of other social improvements too numerous to be listed.

In higher education the humanitarians took up the black cause (discussed earlier) and the feminist cause. On behalf of the latter, "a glorious phalanx of old maids" and what Hawthorne called "that damned mob of scribbling women" set about the business of getting equal rights for their sex, not only politically, legally, and economically but also educationally. Their successes have long been recorded in history. In 1833 Oberlin initiated coeducation and the "elevation of the female character" by admitting thirty-eight young women as members of its first 101 students. (It also opened its door, as already mentioned, to blacks, and a few—including black women—enrolled prior to the Civil War.) The next year a "Young Ladies College" opened its doors in Kentucky to the merry scoffing of *The New York Transcript*, which suggested that the degrees be "Mistress of Pudding Making" and "Mistress of the Scrubbing Brush" and that the honorary degrees be R.W.—"Respectable Wife," and M.W.R.F.—"Mother of a Well Regulated Family" (Boas, 1935, pp. 11ff). When Mary Lyon established the Mount Holyoke Female Seminary in 1836 the jibes continued. The newspapers called it Miss Lyon's Rib Factory, but the principle of equal educational rights for women soon conquered.

In the fight for equal educational rights for the working classes, the underprivileged laborers of the fast-growing cities played important roles. The coming of the franchise and the launching in 1827 of a partially unified American labor movement gave working people a voice in government for the first time. The movement set up two major social objectives: leisure and education. Many years of agitation were required to establish the ten-hour day, which stretched from 6 a.m. to 6 p.m. with an hour for breakfast and another for noonday dinner, but in their educational demands labor made more rapid progress. The scandalous status of children in the factories drove their parents to organized action for relief. Children seven years old and upwards were regularly employed from dawn until eight in the evening, and in 1833 it was estimated that, among the national population of about fifteen million, a million children between the ages of five and fifteen attended no school. The next year a labor publication placed the number of illiterate children throughout the nation at a million and a quarter.

These unhappy conditions drove the unions to place education, according to J.R. Commons, "distinctly and definitely at the head of the list of measures" which they urged upon state legislatures (1918, Vol. 1, p. 244). In all the industrialized centers of the East they campaigned intrepidly for free schools and for candidates who would support them. They went to the polls with their new ballots; and they contributed the chief strength toward passage of the 1834 public school law in Pennsylvania, the 1842 ordinance in New York City, the 1849 legislation in New York State, and similar laws in other states. At the higher education level they worked for the creation of new types of colleges, less strongly tied to the literary traditions of the existing institutions and devoted to practical occupational training.

During the first half of the nineteenth century, in summary, changes in American social life stimulated criticism of the limited classical curriculum. Despite these calls for change, most institutions held the line and adjusted slowly to the changes occurring around them. Those institutions that moved more quickly walked a more difficult road. New institutions offered the best setting for these changes, and eventually these institutions would lead the way in directions that American higher education needed to take.

Colleges over time could not avoid change, and three courses of action lay open to them: they could remain as they were and allow new educational institutions to accept responsibility for meeting the practical needs of the nation; they could throw open their curricula to the new subjects and permit their students to choose or elect their courses from among the total list; or they could create a parallel but separate curriculum for the new practical knowledge and permit their freshmen to choose either of the two programs. Each of these three courses of action would be followed, and combinations of them would in time become standard.

The Dawn of Curricular Innovation

The American literary colleges of the nineteenth century adjusted to change at their own pace and on their own terms. In the process they held their own against the newer institutions with newer ideas.

Among the newer structures, West Point, opened in 1802, followed by Rensselaer Polytechnic Institute in 1826. West Point patterned itself after the French *ecoles*, and its graduates designed many of the bridges constructed in the United States during the first half of the nineteenth century. The large-minded *patroon*, Stephen Van Rensselaer, financed and organized RPI, drawing upon the ideas of Union College Professor Amos Eaton. RPI sought primarily "to qualify teachers . . . in the application of experimental chemistry, philosophy, and natural history to agriculture, domestic economy, the arts and manufactures" (Rensselaer, 1940, p.7). As an example of the emphasis on applications, students visited a bleaching factory before undertaking the laboratory study of chlorine. In its purposes Rensselaer succeeded spectacularly, the majority of naturalists and engineers who became teachers of civilian practitioners in the United States in 1850 being its alumni. Many of them had previously graduated from Harvard, Yale, Princeton, and other "literary seminaries." This in a sense made Rensselaer in fact if not in name the nation's first graduate school outside the traditional professions.

The other great unitary school of science and engineering that opened during this period, Massachusetts Institute of Technology, got its charter the year before the passage of the Land Grant College Act. Between the founding of MIT and RPI a second type of occupational college appeared: the agricultural school. In 1791 the New York Society for the Promotion of Agriculture, Arts, and Manufactures had been established, and counterparts grew up in other states. These societies became earnest advocates of manual-labor schools and colleges in which students would both study and do farm labor, and they attracted much support.

While men such as Van Rensselaer strove to create new educational institutions entirely divorced from the traditional literary colleges, others began to remodel the prescribed curriculum of the latter institutions. Until this time the colleges had required all of their students to take all courses taught, but their fixed curriculum offered no provision for adding the new knowledge which gushed forth in the sciences, the social sciences, and the practical arts as a result of the modern power saltation. After this time colleges joined with educational reformers in championing the device known as the *elective principle*.

Observe the word "principle." Most writers refer to the "elective system"; but dozens of elective systems developed, all of them expressions of the one principle that the student should be allowed to elect at least a portion of his or her courses. Two of the first systems utilizing this principle appeared in 1825: one, promoted by George Ticknor at Harvard, permitted students to choose among courses within the College's expanded curriculum; the other, which one might term the "selective system," Thomas Jefferson devised for the University of Virginia. It established new "parallel" curricula among which students could choose. Both plans proved so influential that they deserve brief description.

Election of Courses at Harvard: George Ticknor, after graduating from Dartmouth in 1807, studied law in Boston but abandoned this field for a professorial career. In 1815 he, George Bancroft, Edward Everett, and Joseph Cogswell went abroad for study in German universities and for general European travel. When Ticknor returned to become Smith Professor of Spanish Language and Literature at Harvard, he brought back with him a knowledge of and devotion to the German conception of *Lernfreiheit*; that is, the freedom of the student to study anything he or she pleases. Earlier he had visited Jefferson at Monticello, and he kept in touch with him by correspondence. Thus when he took up his duties at Harvard, Ticknor knew about European practices and about what would soon be afoot in Virginia. Further, he saw that his own subject could not progress at Harvard or elsewhere until the monopoly of the classical languages gave way, so in 1825 he wrote a brilliant appeal to the Harvard Board of Overseers. Meanwhile the students joined in with one of their not infrequent rebellions. As a result, Harvard made some of its offerings elective, permitting freshmen, for example, to substitute a modern language for half the required work in Greek.

From 1825 to 1882 this plan of substitution see-sawed at Harvard, until Charles W. Eliot succeeded in extending the elective principle to almost the entire curriculum, a plan that came to be called the "free elective system." Meanwhile, however, the University of Virginia pioneered in the development of the second type of elective system which permitted freshmen to select one among several curricula.

Selection among Curricula at Virginia: The University of Virginia had sprung from the head and heart of Thomas Jefferson. He had been deeply concerned with education during all his career, and he gave most of his thoughts to his university plans from the time he left the White House in 1809 until his death in 1826. He considered his founding of the University of Virginia to be such a significant accomplishment, in fact, that in his self-written epitaph he mentioned it to the neglect of his presidency of the United States.

Under Jefferson's plan the new subjects of study were organized in separate curricula running parallel with each other, each with its own student body. Thus the University of Virginia opened in 1825 as a federation of seven parallel departments called colleges: ancient languages, modern languages, mathematics, natural philosophy, moral philosophy, chemistry, and medicine. The following year an eighth substructure, the college of law, opened. Each of these eight units had its own fixed curriculum and gave its own degree. Freshmen selected the college which most appealed to them, and thereafter they followed its curriculum, but they were free to take courses in others if they so desired as long as they completed the requirements of their own college.

This University of Virginia system provided the most immediately effective method of introducing new subjects, but the literary colleges adopted it slowly. Two years after the opening of the University of Virginia, for example, the faculty members of Amherst unsuccessfully petitioned their Board of Trustees to permit the establishment of a parallel curriculum in history and the modern languages. A year later, Union College initiated a parallel curriculum in science and engineering, but two decades passed before Harvard established its Lawrence Scientific School and Yale initiated what later became the Sheffield Scientific School. Thereafter in the Middle West the colleges generally organized two curricula parallel to the classical course of study and its sacrosanct A.B. degree. One emphasized the modern languages and led to the Ph.B. degree, the second the sciences and B.S. degree. The classicists might disdain and denounce them, but they soon attracted students.

The battle to introduce the sciences, the social sciences, the modern languages, and the fine and practical arts by means of these two plans continued to rage throughout the nineteenth century. The reformers won most of the battles but suffered occasional defeats. At Harvard, for example, the Old Guard nibbled away at Ticknor's innovation until President Charles W. Eliot eventually rescued and extended it. At Brown, Francis Wayland, author of the most perceptive book about American higher education written before the Civil War— *Thoughts on the Present Collegiate System in the United States*— argued cogently for curricular reform and instituted it at Brown in 1850. Unhappily, however, he watched it fail for lack of support after his opponents forced his retirement in 1855.

Another stimulus for reform of the traditional college curriculums came ultimately from the new government-supported institutions that offered the new knowledge: the "land grant" colleges. These new institutions, along with the earlier Dartmouth College Case, helped define during this period the relationship between civil government and American higher education which still exists today. The present chapter therefore concludes with these two salient nineteenth century events.

The Dartmouth College Case

A clear-cut distinction between public and private higher education has existed legally in the United States since 1819, the year the Supreme Court handed down its decision in the Dartmouth College Case, and 1862, the year President Lincoln signed the Land Grant College Act.

Civil authorities partially controlled or attempted completely to control six of the nine colonial colleges: Harvard, Yale, Pennsylvania, Columbia, William and Mary, and Dartmouth. In no case did they succeed for long in their efforts, with the result that the advocates of state-supported universities turned to separate institutions rather than attempting to assume control over already existing private ones. The Dartmouth College Case contributed heavily to this development.

The Dartmouth trouble began in the disputes between President John Wheelock, a Presbyterian and Jeffersonian, and his board of trustees, a large majority of whom were Congregationalists and Federalists. A split within the Board had begun appearing even during the previous presidency of Wheelock's father, Eleazor, and in 1809 the anti-Wheelock faction assumed the majority. When a few years later John Wheelock published a pamphlet attacking the Board for its conduct of College affairs, the Board published its own pamphlet in response and in 1815 dismissed Wheelock from the presidency. Wheelock then appealed to the newly-elected Jeffersonian governor, William Plumer, and to the New Hampshire legislature, who rallied to his support. Plumer and the legislature revised the College charter, established a new institution called Dartmouth University, and made Wheelock its president under the direction of a reconstituted board of trustees supplemented by a board of overseers modelled on Harvard's.

When the displaced trustees unsuccessfully contested the action in the Plumer-dominated New Hampshire courts, they appealed to the United States Supreme Court, which, early in 1819 by a vote of five to one handed down its history-making decision. The official summary of the judgment reads in part as follows:

> The charter granted by the British crown to the trustees of Dartmouth College . . . is a contract within the meaning of that clause of the constitution of the United States (Art. 1, s. 10) which declares that no state shall make any law impairing the obligation of contracts. The charter was not dissolved by the Revolution.

> An act of the State of New Hampshire altering the charter without the consent of the corporation in a material respect is an act impairing the obligation of the charter, and is unconstitutional and void.

The decision in the Dartmouth College Case constituted a solid victory for those—Federalists and religionists—who believed that higher education should be kept in the hands of private enterprise, and it led to the founding before the Civil War of literally hundreds of denominational colleges throughout the expanding nation. But those who believed with Thomas Jefferson and his associates and disciples that education should be a public concern had an almost simultaneous and no less consequential victory: five days before the Supreme Court handed down its Dartmouth decision, the General Assembly of Virginia chartered the University of Virginia, which functioned under complete state control and received regular legislative appropriations for its work. Eight other present-day state universities (Georgia, North Carolina, Tennessee, Ohio University, South Carolina, Miami, and Maryland) trace their beginning to years earlier than 1819, but none of them had consistent financial support from their legislatures until late in the nineteenth century. Further, and much more important, some of them began under denominational auspices and became state universities much later, and the others operated for many years under partial or periodic church control.

During the period leading up to the Civil War the state universities of the South enjoyed unusual growth, both in terms of number of students enrolled and money spent in the universities' behalf. Leading the way were the Universities of Virginia, South Carolina, Georgia, Alabama, Mississippi, and Louisiana. But the War brought an end to their vigor, and in their place grew the new land grant colleges envisaged by Jonathan Baldwin Turner.

Turner had gone from Yale to Illinois College in 1833 as Professor of Rhetoric and Belles-lettres, but he resigned under pressure in 1847 because of his anti-slavery ideas. Immediately he began to devote his energies to the creation of institutions for the education of "the industrial classes" and for federal land grants to the states for establishing such colleges. Then during the 1860 presidential campaign he is thought by some historians to have persuaded fellow Illinoisian Abraham Lincoln to agree, if elected, to sign the Land Grant College Act that President Buchanan had recently vetoed. The Act ensured the permanence of the selective plan of election in all state colleges and universities and also in many liberal arts colleges. The majority of the latter, however, developed a third elective plan, namely the Group System. It consists of a kind of selective plan among general education courses.

The Land Grant College Act

The Land Grant College Act has frequently been called the "Morrill Act" because Representative Justin S. Morrill of Vermont sponsored it, but Morrill originally seems to have had more interest in freeing federal lands for speculation than in promoting education. Later, however, he delighted in being called the father of the resulting colleges. His thirty-two years in the United States Senate (1867 to 1898) provided many opportunities for him to play the role.

The legislation actually carried this cumbersome title: "An Act donating Public Lands to the several States and Territories which may provide Colleges for the Benefit of Agriculture and the Mechanic Arts." It apportioned to each state thirty thousand acres for each senator and representative in Congress under the census of 1860, the land to be sold and the interest from the receipts to be used as follows:

> . . . to the endowment, support, and maintenance of at least one college where the leading object shall be, without excluding other scientific and classical studies and including military tactics, to teach such branches of learning as are related to agriculture and the mechanic arts, in such manner as the legislatures of the States may respectively prescribe, in order to promote the liberal and practical education of the industrial classes in the several pursuits and professions of life (*Statutes at Large*, Vol. 12, 504).

Note well the words "to teach such branches of learning as are related to agriculture and the mechanic arts . . . without excluding other scientific and classical studies." These last seven words determined the structural future of American higher education. They successfully ended the 113-year clamor begun by Franklin in 1749 for practical education on the college level by conjoining within the same institutions training programs for agriculture and engineering with the traditional literary curriculum. American equalitarians, resentful over the snobbishness of the classical colleges and honoring the ideal of equal status for all occupations, forced American higher education to abandon the European practice of organizing separate institutions for the literary professions on the one hand and for lower-status occupations on the other. Through the Land Grant College Act they introduced the equalitarian American pattern of offering both "academic" and "technical" education side by side in the same institutions. Although still deplored by many who revere the genteel tradition and admittedly open to the dangers of occupational over-specialization, the Act and its consequences have given the United States a system of higher education remarkably adaptable to the needs of the nation for constantly expanding varieties of trained personnel.

An equally important consequence of the Land Grant College Act has been the stimulus it has given publicly-supported higher education. Until 1862 American colleges had been dominantly sectarian, the few existing state universities languishing from lack of funds and, in fact, largely operating under religious influences. With the birth of the land grant colleges, competition between civil and private higher education began in earnest. Supplementary acts extended the provision of the 1862 legislation to new states and also to black institutions, and by

1900 sixty-nine land grant institutions were in operation. Since then some of them, such as the Universities of California, Illinois, Minnesota, Ohio State, and Wisconsin have grown tremendously both in size and eminence. Indeed, they must be reckoned among the great universities of all time.

By the end of the nineteenth century, moreover, partly because of the Land Grant College Act, state legislatures began to make biennial grants to state colleges and universities, which thereupon began powerfully to influence those under private control. As President Cyrus Northrup of the University of Minnesota expressed it in 1904: "If I am not mistaken, Harvard in last 20 years has moved much farther toward Michigan than Michigan toward Harvard" (1904, p. 161).

To review, the Land Grant College Act, although it introduced ideas that required institutions several decades to implement, profoundly influenced the nature of American higher education in two vital ways: it brought to fruition the attempts to diversify the educational range of American colleges by adding practical education to their curriculums, and it promoted the benefits of competition and diversity of control by stimulating the growth of public institutions. The Act culminated the era of exploration, the long period during which American higher education searched for arrangements and methods that would most effectively serve the nation's unique educational needs.

The period had been marked by a series of notable events: the founding of West Point in 1802 and Rensselaer in 1824, leading to the teaching of new technological subjects, the opening of the University of Virginia's parallel colleges, the beginning of Harvard's elective reforms in 1825, the organization of Union College's parallel curriculum in science and engineering, the conservative Yale Report of 1828, and the commencement of higher education for women and blacks at Oberlin, Mount Holyoke, Wilberforce, and elsewhere.

During this era educational reformers primarily fought for admission to the college curriculum of the new knowledge triggered by the burgeoning technological saltation. The enormity of the social changes produced by this modern saltation were of such magnitude, however, that even the undergraduate colleges that offered the new occupational and scientific courses could no longer meet the higher educational needs of American society. The country demanded more complex and more advanced institutions to provide not only undergraduate education but also graduate instruction and to promote research. After the Civil War, therefore, the purely literary colleges faced new competition. This competition came from at least two directions: from the junior colleges below and from the research universities above.

Bibliographic Notes

Historians in recent years have paid considerable attention to higher education during the period between the American Revolution and the Civil War. They have written about changes in the curriculum and in the students enrolled in those courses. They have written about the many new colleges that appeared, about the openings of higher education to women, and about the changing relationship between higher education and civil government. Several have found fault with what earlier historians wrote about this period and have proposed the appropriate revisions.

Sloan's (1971) analysis of the impact of the Scottish enlightenment on American colleges continues into the post-Revolution period. The end of the eighteenth century, as shown by Sloan, heralded establishment of a scientific community in American higher education and the building of a new curriculum. Miller (1976) also studies some of these phenomena in his book on Presbyterian higher education, showing how the post-Revolution republican spirit stimulated interest in education. Student unrest in the early nineteenth century complicated the plan as did a schism among Presbyterians in 1837.

Allmendinger (1971) shows how the arrival in New England colleges after the Revolution of many students from poor families changed these institutions. Threatened were the residential collegiate communities, the fixed curriculum, the level of student discipline, and the concept of *en loco parentis*. Vine (1975) describes the gentlemen's education provided by five eighteenth- and nineteenth-century American colleges.

Robson (1983) identifies sixteen colleges that opened in the United States between 1776 and 1800 that were still operating in 1983. The American Revolution generated new ideas, especially those having to do with republicanism. Robson returns to this subject in 1985, describing the changes occurring in the American colleges after the

Revolution. Certain of these changes—especially those occurring in the colleges established after the Revolution—reflected pressures from frontier leaders of that time.

Thomson (1970) writes about the emergence of new colleges in the South following the American Revolution. Conditions before the war militated against the founding of these institutions, but with independence came the opportunity to start what had not been possible earlier. Dabney's (1981) history of the University of Virginia shows the high favor with which Thomas Jefferson's ideas were received in the South throughout the nineteenth century but also the problems University officials encountered at times putting those ideas into action. Wagoner (1986) also deals with this subject.

Cremin (1980) points to the evangelical movement of the early nineteenth century as a generator of numerous colleges throughout the land and a major source of influence on the curriculum. He also writes about Virginia as the "archetype of the public state university" (p. 159) and about efforts to reform American higher education at Amherst, Yale, Union, Brown, and elsewhere.

Findlay (1977) studies the role played by the Society for the Promotion of Collegiate and Theological Education in the West. The Society saw as its primary mission the Christianizing of the American culture as it moved west. A part of that mission involved encouraging the establishment of schools and colleges. In a later paper Findlay (1982) focuses on colleges in Illinois and Indiana during the period 1830–1870 as starting from the pattern of the more conservative eastern institutions such as Yale but also responding openly to calls for curricular change that developed around them during this period.

Turning to the situation in some of the colonial colleges after the Revolution, Pearson (1988) shows how the claims made during colonial times for freedom of Yale from colonial interference were echoed in periods after the Revolution. Lane (1987) also looks at Yale, especially as the Yale Report of 1828 served as a statement from its authors as to the contributions liberal education as taught at Yale might make to American society in a time of considerable change and ferment. Bailyn (1986) studies John Kirkland's presidency at Harvard between 1810 and 1828. Judged by Bailyn "the most popular, the most beloved president Harvard ever had" (p. 19), Kirkland nevertheless was forced from his position by persons upset by his efforts to change the institution, by student unrest, and loss of subsidy from the state of

Massachusetts. Story (1975) shows the role Harvard played in cultivating an elite class in Boston during the nineteenth century.

Harcleroad and Ostar (1987) show how the beginnings of today's comprehensive public state colleges and universities centered around issues relating to state vs. federal control of the institutions, religious vs. sectarian control, tax support vs. fee support, elitism vs. egalitarianism, and the classical vs. the professional/liberal education curriculum. Many of the older of these institutions, the authors show, began as academies or normal schools during the pre-Civil War period. Herbst (1989) writes in good detail about the normal schools of the antebellum period and the support they received both from the Whigs and from the workingman. A movement begun in New England, it spread during this period into the Midwest.

Ideas relating to the later emergence of the community college also appeared during this time. Diener (1986) includes some of those ideas in his documentary history of the community college.

Rudolph (1977) writes about the curricular flux that characterized the period after the Revolution. At question was the place of Latin and Greek and the efforts to bring new subject matters, including science and modern languages, more directly into the curricula of that period. Kimball (1986) also writes about curriculum during this period, a curriculum that reflected influences of the Enlightenment. Guralnick's (1975) book calls attention to the awakening during the antebellum years to science in the American college curriculum.

Church and Sedlak (1976) in their Chapter 2 treat the antebellum academies and colleges as a unit, describing the two as fundamentally similar. Their account includes episodes of student unrest, the effort to provide higher education for women, pressures to change the curriculum, the astounding number of new institutions established after the Revolution, and the role they played in diffusing culture and education in a rapidly-expanding nation. Smith (1974) offers an essay on community life in the antebellum American college town. The college and town shared a common religious orientation; and the college served, too, as an attraction for people from the denomination who hailed from other communities. "Denominational colleges," he wrote, "were designed to be the effective arm of the church in a Christian republic" (p. 132). Smith concludes with an analysis of the sense of community within the colleges themselves.

Herbst (1975, 1981, and 1982) points to the late eighteenth and early nineteenth centuries as marking higher educational change, both in Europe and in the United States. In Europe there appeared the new University of Berlin, which would set new patterns for university education throughout much of the world. In the United States distinctions between public and private higher education became more clear, and state universities and state university systems were established. In the process the relationship between the churches, civil government, the courts, and higher education changed. Whitehead (1973) concludes that the distinction between public and private higher education which Herbst places in the late eighteenth and early nineteenth century, did not actually occur until after the Civil War. An exchange between him and Herbst appears in Whitehead and Herbst (1986).

Novak (1974) brings to light some of the problems that preceded the Dartmouth College Case. Among these problems was the appointment of a new pastor at the church where students and townspeople worshiped, the evangelical pressures of religious groups concerned for the possible drift of students away from orthodox beliefs, and moments of student unrest. Stites (1972) also seeks to give full detail to events surrounding the Dartmouth College Case. Included is information about the College from its beginning to the time of the controversy, the details surrounding the controversy, its moving into the courts, and its aftermath.

This is the period when women gained a place in American higher education, and numerous publications have appeared on the subject. Conway (1974) warns her readers that women did not prosper simply because they gained a place in nineteenth century American higher education. By 1830 they had gained credibility as school teachers, but most other roles that went beyond the nurturing of the young and protecting society's moral standards were denied them. Scott (1979) studies the impact of the Troy Female Seminary on women's education between 1822 and 1872. Allmendinger (1973) describes the role of Mary Lyons at Mount Holyoke College in encouraging her students to participate in life-planning activities. Horowitz (1984) also includes a chapter on the founding of Mount Holyoke.

Rury and Harper (1986) study the Antioch experiment with coeducation during 1853 to 1860. Women students in those early years took most of the same courses as men (women were denied access to courses in which politics were discussed), and they studied alongside men in the classroom. President Horace Mann could not escape his Calvinist origins, however, in the matter of regulations controlling the students' out-of-class lives. Kerns (1986) writes about women who studied at Alfred Academy (later Alfred University) during the antebellum period and about the "Ladies Course" that emerged at Alfred late in the period. Palmieri (1987) labels the years 1820–1860 as the "Romantic Period" in the history of women's higher education. Woman, as viewed in this period, had a "capacity to be pure, moral and sentimental" (p. 51), and in that capacity found certain doors to education opened to them. Solomon (1985) in her comprehensive history of women's higher education shows the doors to higher education for women closed during the colonial period but open after the Revolution. The author identifies leaders of this movement, the institutions in which some of them worked, and the utility of the education women received. Walsh (1977) pays particular attention to the struggles of women to gain a medical education during the colonial and antebellum periods.

Perkins (1983) addresses the curricula offered women in the nineteenth century and contrasts the reasons why whites and blacks were educated. White women in the early nineteenth century were expected to become good wives and mothers, which meant becoming literate but also familiar with "needlepoint, painting, music, art, and French" (p. 18). Black women who sought education, on the other hand, were expected to play a role in the uplift of their race. Many thus took courses that would prepare them for teaching. Lawson (1984) pieces together documents and biographies of three black women—Sarah Kinson, Sara Stanley, and Sarah Woodson—who received degrees from Oberlin prior to the Civil War.

Turning to writing about the faculty, Finkelstein (1983 and 1984) shows how endowed professorships at Harvard and Yale in the eighteenth century set a pattern for a more permanent professoriate to develop throughout American higher education during the early decades of the century that followed. These more permanent faculty members also committed themselves more specifically to a discipline than had their predecessors.

This period also marks the entry of German patterns into American higher education. Thomas (1973) shows the vital role played by Wilhelm Von Humboldt in reforming Prussian education following the defeat of Prussia by Napoleon in 1806. Diehl (1976) reports on the numbers of American students who studied in German universities between 1810 and 1870.

McLachlan has written several items dealing with this period. His 1974 publication shows how student societies at nineteenth century Princeton encouraged their members to make the "choice of Hercules," which meant turning their backs on pleasure and the life of ease in favor of a life of virtue spent serving others. In 1978 he pointed to the key roles college-educated citizens played in development of the nation during the nineteenth century.

Several authors wrote about student unrest during this period. Novak (1977) provides a major study of the subject, describing these years as a time of sustained riot and rebellion in American higher education. Often at the heart of the unrest was the matter of student rights. Horowitz (1987) also writes about student unrest during the antebellum period.

The Handlins (1970) explore alternatives to attending college in the nineteenth century. Despite the attractiveness of these alternatives, colleges proliferated during this period.

Using examples from the University of Wisconsin, Johnson (1974) studies changes in legal and medical education during the nineteenth century, changes which led away from apprenticeships in favor of attendance at a professional school. This change occurred first in medicine during the pre-Civil War period. Stevens (1983) also studies the transition in legal education from apprenticeship to professional schools. He places the transition in the antebellum period.

Potts is among those who have written revisionist versions of the history of this period. In 1981 he responds to claims that curricula in antebellum colleges became unpopular and failed to attract students. He shows that enrollment at Yale, which remained relatively firm in its expectations for the classical curriculum, enjoyed popularity and relatively good enrollments, while other institutions that changed their curriculum experienced little or no growth. In 1977 Potts took to task those earlier historians who portrayed antebellum colleges as struggling to find support in American society. To the contrary, writes Potts, the institutions often had the enthusiastic support of their local communities. In a 1971 paper Potts argues that localism, rather than denominationalism, played a major role in the founding and development of American colleges before 1850. Communities sought the cultural and social benefits that a college could bring them; their denominational concerns before 1850, according to Potts, were secondary.

Another of the revisionists, Burke (1982) also finds merit in the antebellum colleges. To support his argument he gathers a host of statistics about the institutions, their enrollments, the characteristics of their students, and the careers their students pursued following graduation.

Naylor (1973) takes earlier historians to task for depending too heavily on Tewksbury's (1932) analysis of higher education in antebellum America. Tewksbury readily admitted that his was only a first study of a large topic, but those who followed him relied too heavily on his reported findings. In 1977 Naylor returns to this period, focusing this time on the theological seminaries of that time. These institutions, according to Naylor, brought formal organization to the preparation of ministers and provided a prototype for the later-developed American graduate professional school.

Blackburn and Conrad (1986) review revisionist treatments published during the previous decade on the history of American higher education. The authors warn their readers that the data bases for claims made on both sides of the controversy require further attention. "There is exciting work," they conclude, "awaiting historians of higher education" (p. 230).

CHAPTER SEVEN

Diversification: 1862–1900

> What we need is a university. Whether this is to be a new creation, or something reared on the foundations now laid at Cambridge, or New Haven, or Ann Arbor, is unimportant. Until we have it somewhere, our means of culture are still provincial.
>
> (Thomas Wentworth Higginson, 1867)

On August 31, 1837, Ralph Waldo Emerson delivered the annual Phi Beta Kappa oration at Harvard. He entitled it "The American Scholar," and for an impassioned hour he read a manuscript that immediately became one of the enduring testaments of the American spirit. "Our day of dependence," he declared during the first minute of his address, "our long apprenticeship to the learning of other lands, draws to a close. The millions, that around us are rushing into life, cannot always be fed on the sere remains of foreign harvests."

Emerson spoke prophetically, not factually. "Our long apprenticeship to the learning of other lands" persisted for not a few decades. Having begun upon British foundations and then experienced a short-lived infatuation with French patterns, the young American nation looked abroad again for new educational ideals. It found them in Germany. Throughout the nineteenth century and into the twentieth young Americans by the thousands would trek to Germany for advanced instruction and inspiration. They returned with ideas and loyalties that would further accentuate the convoluted character of American education.

The period of diversification described in this chapter begins with the passage of the Land Grant College Act and ends in 1900. All historic periodizations are, of course, no more than convenient devices employed to marshal facts and ideas dramatically. Diversification

131

continues in American higher education to this day, but most of the supreme diversification events took place during—or had their roots in—the 38-year period now under review.

Following the Civil War the educational innovations pioneered prior to the Land Grant College Act began at last to achieve favor. Moreover, in addition to the new land grant colleges and the eastern colleges that accepted the land grants, other new-type institutions broke ground. Research universities opened in Baltimore, Chicago, Palo Alto, and elsewhere. Vocationally oriented higher schools such as Tuskegee Institute for Practical Training of Negroes in Alabama and the Rochester Atheneum and Technical Institute in New York opened. New women's colleges embarked either—as happened at Vassar in 1865—as independent structures or—in settings such as Barnard, Radcliffe, and Pembroke—developed as coordinate colleges in institutions historically confined to the education of young males. Normal schools, which had started in New England as secondary schools, began to be converted in many states into two-year colleges. The precursors of present-day junior colleges made their debut. And numerous new black colleges emerged.

For the latter institutions the greatest boom came during the decade immediately following the Civil War—the so-called Reconstruction era. Promoted by a curious coalition of church missionaries and former Civil War military officers, this boom led to the founding of Howard University (named for General Oliver O. Howard), Fisk (named for General Clifton B. Fisk), Morehouse, Atlanta University, Talladega, and a host of others. Primarily, these colleges during the nineteenth century produced clergy and teachers for black churches and black schools. A few Native American institutions— Sheldon Jackson College, Indian University, and Bacone College among them—also appeared. Native American students also enrolled at the black institutions.

With the end of Reconstruction, the new black colleges in the South entered into difficult times. Beholden from the start to the white power structure, the colleges now became the pawns of white leaders who countenanced black higher education only to the degree that people associated with it did not threaten the whites' dominant position.

This phenomenon probably accounts for the success enjoyed by Booker T. Washington's Tuskegee Institute. Begun in 1881 Tuskegee reflected Washington's conviction that black people of his time could best benefit from vocational education. By the time of his death in 1915

Washington had built Tuskegee into an organization consisting of over one hundred buildings, a student body of fifteen hundred, an endowment of two million dollars, and an annual budget of $300,000. Washington thus belongs in the company of the great builders in higher education of this time—with the Harpers, the Gilmans, the Eliots, the Whites and the others so frequently mentioned. Washington's emphasis on the trades found a hearing throughout the South, and white leaders there seemed quite willing to allow the blacks their new industrial schools.

While black higher education was experiencing its ups and downs, the more general university movement in this country began to gain momentum. This momentum resulted not merely from the nation's technological needs but also from the demand for vastly improved facilities for educating professional men, business executives, civil servants, scientists, and scholars. As earlier reported, clergymen, lawyers, and physicians had largely been trained through the apprenticeship system; so also had businessmen and civil servants. Most intending scholars and scientists, however, travelled abroad—chiefly to Germany—for advanced instruction. So also did substantial numbers of the embryo professors from all over the world. Returning home, they promoted German educational ideas and ideals, and German influences upon American universities must therefore be traced.

The Rise of the Modern German University

Friedrich Paulsen, the University of Berlin philosopher who early in this century wrote the best available history of German universities translated into English, has called the University of Halle, which opened in 1694, the first modern university. (Another candidate for that title might be the University of Leyden, established in Holland more than a century earlier. See Chapter Four.) There followed in the eighteenth century the new University of Gottingen and its associated Gottingen Academy of Sciences. These and other Teutonic institutions that so influentially made the transition to modern education, however, lost some of their pre-eminence upon the founding of the Friedrich Wilhelm University at Berlin in 1809. Generally known as the University of Berlin, it arose from the ashes of the Napoleonic wars and immediately challenged the leadership of Halle, Gottingen, and the other great universities of the world.

Napoleon devastated the German states, and the humiliating treaty of peace that he imposed at Tilsit in 1807 drove the German peoples to a desperate effort to revive their spirits and their culture. In this crisis, the philosopher J.G. Fichte took to the platform of the great hall of Berlin's Academy of Sciences during the winter of 1807–1808 to deliver a series of fourteen "Addresses to the German People." Germany must realize its character and destiny, declared Fichte, through the conscious promotion of education. Education and only education, he insisted, could liberate all the potentialities—moral, intellectual, physical, economic—of Germans (1807, pp. 218ff). So cogent were Fichte's arguments and so pervasive his prestige that the German people heeded him and reached out to education as their means of regeneration. They reorganized the common schools, established compulsory education to the age of fourteen, rebuilt their plundered universities, and built new ones.

Fichte visualized the universities as the very crown of German civilization, and for their improvement he proposed two momentous ideas: first, that scholarly research be emphasized in every field of thought—even in literature and theology—and second, that every university teacher be also if not primarily a research scholar. Against this background the University of Berlin opened in 1809. A national catastrophe brought it into existence, but the way had been prepared for it by a hundred years of intellectual advances at Halle, Gottingen, and their sister universities. Emotionally of incalculable value as a national monument of renascence, Berlin sent its torrents of new energy into channels already deeply cut. Its founders, although chiefly philosophers and philologists, established chairs in physics, chemistry, geology, and other sciences to match those in the reanimated universities which the French had not succeeded in destroying. They also took over the existing Academy of Sciences and made it an organic part of the University, in this fashion concentrating the scientific leadership of Germany in the universities, rather than in independent societies as in England and France. Soon all twenty German universities, "the most intensely cultivated and most productive intellectual corporations the world has ever seen" (Huxley, 1896, p. 106), achieved world hegemony in all branches of learning.

Meanwhile the French universities and Oxford and Cambridge plodded along the classical road oblivious of the grass which had come to grow lustily down its middle. In a bitter tirade against the British backwardness, Huxley wrote:

> The foreigner who should wish to become acquainted with the scientific or the literary activity of modern England, would simply lose his time and his pains if he visited our universities with that object. And, as for works of profound research on any subject, and, above all, in that classical lore for which the universities profess to sacrifice almost everything else, why a third-rate, poverty-stricken German university turns out more produce of that kind in one year, than our vast and wealthy foundations elaborate in ten (1896, p. 104).

The classical curriculum alone did not account for the retarded condition of English education. No less important was the fact that the established church controlled its two ancient seats of learning. No one, for example, could be a candidate for a degree unless he were an Anglican, a requirement that remained until 1871. Nor did Oxford and Cambridge make adequate provision for advanced studies. They continued to devote their chief energies to the classical education of undergraduates. Quite naturally, therefore, American students preferred Germany, where they could prepare to become professors by earning the German degree of Doctor of Philosophy as a tangible evidence of scholarly preparation.

The French, as well as the British, had strong ties with the United States, but these, too, the German universities broke or seriously bent. During the second decade of the nineteenth century Ticknor, Bancroft, Everett, and Cogswell discovered Berlin, Halle, and Gottingen. Returning home after several years of enthusiastic discipleship at the shrine of German learning, they opened up a highway to Germany on which two hundred other Americans travelled by 1850. Some ten thousand young Americans followed them by 1914. Unattracted by somnolent Oxford and Cambridge, wary of French schools, and intensely stimulated by the buoyant German universities, they became with hardly an exception, as one of them expressed it, "the intellectual subjects of Germany" (Minot, 1912, p. 776).

Back home after their inspiriting German interlude, most of those who took the Ph.D. degree became professors and promptly initiated one of the most animated crusades ever embarked upon in American education: the effort to adapt American colleges and more particularly the rising universities to the purposes of scholarship and research. To this end they imported from Germany such devices as the lecture system, laboratory instruction, the seminar, the clinical method, the Ph.D. degree, the elective principle, the semester plan of arranging the academic year, and the methods employed in organizing instruction and research.

More significant by far must be accounted the knowledge, skills, and enthusiasm that Americans gained from the illustrious German professors under whom they studied. Cite any academic discipline, and the names of strategic German professors of the period come to mind: Leibig, Ostwald, and Wohler in chemistry; Blunstchli, Kniew, and Schmoller in economics; Mommsen, Niebuhr, and Ranke in history; Du Bois-Reymond, Schwann, and Virchow in the medical sciences; Helmholtz, Mayer, and Roentgen in physics; Heeren, Eichorn, and Holst in political science; Diez, Schleicher, and Zuess in philology; Hartmann, Liebmann, and Lotze in philosophy; Ebbinghaus, Fechner, and Wundt in psychology; Dilthey, Ihering, and Weber in social theory. England and France, of course, had their full share of definitive thinkers, too, but few of them had university posts. In any event, Americans predominantly studied with Germans and brought home German conceptions of scholarship and also of university organization.

The Rise of the American University

The name *university* first came into American thinking and planning during the Revolution, but its use expressed hope rather than accomplishments. The so-called universities of the time lacked present-day prerequisites of graduate training and research facilities, and long decades of urgent demands and persistent efforts by leading educators and laymen during the first two-thirds of the nineteenth century would be required before American universities emerged. Morison has noted, for instance, that Harvard's charter contained the Baconian notion of advancing learning, but not until the nineteenth century was the institution in a position to fulfill this part of its founders' plans (1936b, pp. 40ff). Thus at a "convention of literary and scientific gentlemen" held in New York City in 1830 George Bancroft, Harvard alumnus and a Ph.D. of the University of Gottingen, popularized the slogan "The University Idea", and at the same convention Henry

Dwight, son of the late eminent president of Yale, Timothy Dwight the Elder, exclaimed: "We need a University like those of Germany." About the same time Ticknor likened Harvard to a high school, a sentiment to be repeated as late as 1866, when another distinguished Harvard professor declared Harvard to be nothing more than a school for boys in a nation that urgently needed universities. Two years later Mark Pattison, Rector of Lincoln College, Oxford, could assert that "America has no universities." No one took issue with him, since he was saying no more than what Americans had been admitting for decades. A statement of Henry P. Tappan's written in 1851 continued to be true for at least another quarter of a century:

> In our country we have no universities. Whatever may be the names by which we choose to call our institutions of learning, still they are not universities. They have neither libraries and material of learning, generally nor the number of professors and courses of lectures, nor the large and free organization which go to make up Universities (1851, p. 50).

Finally in 1876, a century after the signing of the Declaration of Independence and 240 years after the founding of Harvard, the Johns Hopkins University opened in Baltimore. The flood gates behind which power for change had long been gathering had at last opened, and universities burst forth all over the nation.

Because of the unique American governmental structure, each of the fifty states of the United States defines its own educational standards and terminology, so the name *university* has no generally accepted meaning throughout the country. By and large, however, academic people think of universities as having three major characteristics: a commitment both to research and to teaching, professional schools, and graduate curriculums leading beyond the baccalaureate degree. Until the Civil War period graduate study and scholarly research had been virtually non-existent in American colleges. Students could undertake individual study after receiving the B.A., but they acquired the M.A. by paying a small fee and by staying out of jail for, usually, a period of three years.

The promoters of American universities comparable to those of Germany faced a major question: namely, should the new functions of advanced instruction and research be performed within existing colleges or should they be handled by new, post-collegial institutions? Should graduate education and research be separated from undergraduate education, or would it prove more effective if centered exclusively in graduate and research-oriented institutions? American educational leaders disagreed among themselves, and in attempting to find the answer they experimented with three courses of action.

Some, led by Daniel Coit Gilman of Johns Hopkins, the most fertile thinker of all the university presidents of the time, proposed the creation of graduate universities apart from undergraduate colleges. These, he suggested, should become three-year institutions. Others, led by Henry P. Tappan of the University of Michigan, William W. Folwell of the University of Minnesota, and William Rainey Harper of the University of Chicago, proposed to turn over the first two years of colleges to the secondary schools, thereby having the universities begin with the traditional junior year. Still others, led by Charles W. Eliot of Harvard, moved to expand the existing colleges into comprehensive universities which would undertake undergraduate and graduate instruction as well as research.

Of these three types of university the comprehensive university sponsored by Eliot has become standard. Had Gilman, Tappan, Harper, and their associates succeeded with either of their plans, general education would not be overwhelmed by specialized education, graduate education, and research as currently in most American universities. But although their proposals had the benefit of logic, they failed because of the stubborn will-to-life of the colleges and also because the combination of undergraduate and graduate instruction within a single institution offered clear economic advantages.

In a history-making reorganization in 1890, Eliot and his Harvard associates made the Faculty of Arts and Sciences responsible for all non-professional education from the beginning of the freshman year through the Ph.D. degree. The other eastern colleges, concurrently remodeling themselves into universities, adopted comparable plans, and the state universities followed their example. Today the comprehensive university flourishes from coast to coast. It has encompassed the undergraduate liberal arts college, has balanced it with variable undergraduate vocational colleges, and has erected graduate and professional schools above them. Most important of all, it engages in both teaching and research. Combining these functions has revolutionized American higher education. No long are universities simply institutions of higher *education*. Through research they even more faithfully venerate and minister to the higher *learning*.

The Acceleration and Elevation of Research

Today research has become so firmly established that everyone takes it for granted. Few know, it seems, that it had little status a century ago in the colleges of either the United States or England and that only during recent decades has it achieved its lofty eminence in both countries. Recall that the accepted approach for seeking knowledge during the medieval period consisted of the dialectical method and that universities continued their adherence to dialectic into the Renaissance, forcing factual investigators to establish their own scientific societies outside the universities.

Indeed, except for the beginnings made in Holland and Germany and to a lesser degree in a few other countries, the universities of the world played little, if any, direct part until late in the nineteenth century in the momentous progress of science. In England Clark Maxwell, who in 1871 became Professor of Experimental Physics at Cambridge, came to symbolize the changes in the status of university research in that country. Until his appointment, English empirical research had been conducted mainly by non-university investigators such as Darwin, Davy, Dalton, Faraday, and Huxley.

Controlled by the classicists and religionists, Oxford and Cambridge looked with unconcealed disdain upon what they considered to be the spiritually unprofitable and potentially heretical grubbings of the scientists. About 1890, for example, Benjamin Jowett, the famous master of Balliol College, Oxford University, sneered: "Research! A mere excuse for idleness; it has never achieved, and will never achieve, any results of the slightest value" (Smith, 1938, p. 737). In the same spirit until not too long ago students and not a few dons of Oxford and Cambridge referred to chemistry as "stinks," a designation coined over a century ago to express the dislike and hostility which they and university authorities felt for it and science in general.

Comparable attitudes held back factual investigation in the United States. While Thomas Jefferson sought to encourage the progress of science when he organized the University of Virginia, the academic world in this country never seriously sponsored scientific research until well after the Civil War. A member of the Yale Class of 1853 included the following anecdote, for instance, in his autobiography:

> (O)ne day in my senior year, looking . . . from my window in North College, I saw a student [of the Sheffield Scientific School] examining a colored liquid in a test-tube. A feeling of wonder came over me! What could it all be about? Probably not a man of us in the whole senior class had any idea of a chemical laboratory save as a sort of small kitchen back of a lecture-desk, like that in which an assistant and a colored servant prepared oxygen, hydrogen, and carbonic acid for the lectures of Professor Silliman. I was told that this new laboratory was intended for experiment, and my wonder was succeeded by disgust that any human being should give his time to pursuits so futile (White, 1906, Col. 1, p. 290).

Despite the occasional courses in sciences such as those given by Benjamin Silliman, the idea of research being a recognized function of American colleges jelled slowly. Even President Eliot of Harvard had his doubts about its value:

> Professor C. L. Jackson relates that when he was a young teacher of Chemistry in the seventies he asked Eliot if he might be relieved of the duty of teaching one class in order to prosecute certain investigations. The President, in his stately manner, propounded a question to which an answer can seldom be given— "What will be the results of these investigations?" They would be published, was the reply. The President wanted to know where. Mr. Jackson named a German chemical journal. "I can't see that that will serve any useful purpose here," said Eliot, and therewith dismissed the matter (James, 1930, Vol. 2, p. 19).

The research idea advanced slowly, and as late as 1909 a distinguished scientist who visited the University of Minnesota reported that,

> . . . the regents generally regarded research as a private fad of a professor, like collecting etchings or playing the piano, and they rarely interfered with it so long as (the professor) . . . did not ask for money (Slosson, 1910, p. 246).

With the opening of the Johns Hopkins University in 1876, a new day dawned, and Gilman's success there convinced Eliot and other administrators that the research function could no longer be neglected.

After Johns Hopkins, research achieved primacy at three other newly-launched universities: Clark University, which opened in 1889, Stanford, which began instruction in 1891, and the University of Chicago, which followed a year later. The three men who headed these widely-heralded institutions had no doubts at all about the importance of research. Indeed, they gave it the place of honor. Harper of Chicago wrote in 1895:

> It is not enough that instructors in a university should merely do the class and lecture work assigned them. This is important, but the university will in no sense deserve the name, if time and labor are not also expended in the work of producing that which will directly or indirectly influence thought and life outside the university. . . . The first obligation resting upon the individual members who comprise it is that of research and investigation (p. 11).

G. Stanley Hall made similar statements at Clark. In his *Life and Confessions of a Psychologist*, he wrote:

> (R)esearch is his [a person's] highest function. . . . As man is the highest and best and as mind is the best thing in him, so research is the supreme function of mind, the true heir of the kingdom and of all the promises (1923, pp. 538, 539).

David Starr Jordan at Stanford went further and asserted that teaching and research must be completely intermingled:

> Investigation is the basis of all good instruction. No second-hand man was ever a great teacher, and I very much doubt if any really great investigator was ever a poor teacher (1891, p. 14).

Clearly the research point of view had not only finally prevailed but also become paramount in these university settings. Simultaneously, however, impressive improvements catalyzed the education function. Four of them require describing.

Educational Advances

Recent scholarship has made it clear that, while the university made its advances during the late nineteenth century, the education function and the old American literary colleges did not fall by the wayside. To the contrary the colleges more than held their own during this period, and university leaders found it to their advantage to collaborate with their counterparts in the literary colleges (Axtell, 1971; Burke, 1982; Hawkins, 1971; McLachlan, 1978).

During the period under review, four preeminent advances not only contributed to diversification in the education function but also to its considerable strengthening. They were: the reconstruction of professional education, the inauguration of new teaching methods, the further evolution of the elective principle, and the initiation of undergraduate specialization. Each will be sketched in turn.

Until about a century ago few American physicians and lawyers had attended college or professional school. Moreover, since the states placed few restrictions on them, many people with little but apprenticeship training set themselves up as practitioners. Their number included numerous able and conscientious people but also many incompetents and charlatans.

The professional schools of the period, furthermore, gave nothing comparable to present-day training. The medical course, for example, consisted in many instances of a three-month set of lectures repeated three years in succession. During the remaining nine months of the three-year period students served as apprentices, and at the end of the third year they exhibited their knowledge in oral examinations. Henry James has reported the experience of his brother, William, when he took them at Harvard in November 1868:

> In a large room a number of professors sufficient to examine in the nine principal subjects disposed themselves at suitable intervals. The students circulated singly from one to the next and were quizzed on a new subject at each station of the journey. Every ten minutes a presiding functionary sounded a bell and the candidate moved along. When the bell had pealed nine times . . . the examiners were expected to be ready to vote. This they did without consultation. . . . Each had a piece of cardboard that was white on one side and marked with a black spot on the other. The Dean

called the name of a candidate and pronounced a formal question
and command—"Are you ready to vote?—Vote!" The nine
examiners simultaneously thrust forward their cards. If the Dean
counted not more than four black spots, the candidate received his
degree, he could hang out his sign and work his ignorance at will
on the patients who came to him, for under the laws as they then
were a School diploma conferred the right to practice (1930, Vol.
1, pp. 275ff).

Two years later Eliot, newly inaugurated as president of Harvard,
proposed that written examinations be substituted for the orals, but the
dean of medicine responded that his students did not write well enough.
In short, not even university-affiliated professional schools gave
adequate instruction. The superb group of New Educators who, along
with Eliot, came into university presidencies during this period set
diligently about the task of correcting this shocking situation. They
succeeded brilliantly, Eliot considering his achievements in this sector
his most significant.

The universities that already had professional schools often began
by appointing full-time deans, and their presidents backed them in their
devoted efforts to elevate professional education. The universities which
had not yet organized professional schools often did so or else they
reached out and brought those in their vicinities into affiliation. Next,
they required high school graduation for admission and later increasing
amounts of college work, some in time coming to require the
bachelor's degree. Concurrently they extended the length and vastly
augmented the content and quality of professional curriculums, and
medicine added the internship.

No developments in American higher education have been more
spectacular and far-reaching than those in professional education. They
have thoroughly reformed American professional men and women, and
to the traditional triad of professional schools have been added units for
the training of business executives, educators, dentists, engineers,
nurses, and a score of other specialists. The huge strides that
professional education has made since 1868 make William James's
experience at the Harvard Medical School seem antediluvian.

Before the influx of German influences, most American college
teachers used only the recitation method of instruction. Young
professors returning from Germany, however, brought back the lecture
system and employed it despite the objections of conservatives such as

President Noah Porter of Yale, who opposed it for lower classmen and warned that "for the more advanced students of a college, and even for students of professional schools, instruction by lecturing should be sparingly applied" (1870, p. 127). Chemistry professors also began to employ the laboratory method that Professor Justus Leibig had developed at the University of Giessen. So also did all of the other sciences. In turn the burgeoning social sciences and also the literary subjects adopted the seminar, one of the first apparently being those established in the early 1870s by the historians Henry Adams at Harvard and Charles Kendall Adams at the University of Michigan. The case method developed at the Harvard Law School beginning in 1870 and later spread to other fields, especially to business administration. Meanwhile geology adopted the field trip; engineering, the summer camp; biology, the experiment station; and all departments, the term paper.

By means of these and other new methods college and university teaching improved so markedly that James Freeman Clarke could observe at the Harvard commencement dinner of 1886:

> Formerly, the only business of a teacher was to hear recitations, and make marks for merit. Now he has the opportunity of teaching. This is one of the greatest discoveries of modern time— that the business of a teacher is to teach (Morison, 1937, p. 347).

Not only did the reformers among the professoriate improve their classroom teaching and testing, but they also sent their students to study in the college libraries, whose collections they insisted be constantly improved. In 1858 the trustees of Columbia voted to open the library for ten rather than nine hours a week, and about the same time librarians began to be concerned with the circulation of their books rather than with merely protecting them. Some librarians, however, such as John Langdon Sibley of Harvard (1856 to 1877) gave up their custodial responsibilities reluctantly. A friend of Sibley's meeting him on the street one day, asked him why he looked so happy. He replied, so the story goes, "All the books are in excepting two. Professor Agassiz has those, and I am going after them" (Brough, 1953, p. 2).

The greatest educational advance came not in methods but in content. The reformers of the period of exploration had succeeded in establishing new college curriculums parallel to the traditional literary curriculum, but the elective principle served as an open sesame for the sciences, the social sciences, the modern languages, and the arts. Moreover, as knowledge proliferated, professors widened and deepened their courses.

Recall that in 1825 both the University of Virginia and Harvard pioneered the elective principle—Virginia by establishing separate curricula from among which students could choose, Harvard by permitting students to substitute a modern language for Greek. Two further expressions of the elective principle now developed—the "free elective" and the "group elective" systems. The former has had infinitely more publicity, but few institutions other than Harvard practiced it. The Lawrence Scientific School, Harvard's other undergraduate unit during the Eliot regime, did not. Moreover, Harvard College abandoned it in 1910.

When Eliot became president of Harvard in 1869, he began to work for the extension of the limited elective system that had been in operation in one form or another since 1825. Not until the 1880s, however, did he get the faculty and governing boards to approve a wider election of courses. Though called "free," the Eliot scheme did not give students complete freedom of course selection. In entrance examinations they had to demonstrate acceptable knowledge and abilities in English and a foreign language. If they failed, they took courses in English and in French or German.

Free election ended just after Eliot's retirement. His successor, A. Lawrence Lowell, immediately moved to scuttle it, and the faculty without delay adopted the group elective system which had been developing at Pennsylvania, Princeton, Yale, and most small eastern colleges. Eliot assumed that students would select their courses wisely, but most faculty members over the country disagreed. They contended that free election permitted serious-minded students with special bents to gorge themselves in single departments and that it also encouraged lazy students to concoct curricula made up entirely of elementary courses. To hamper these indisputable tendencies, faculties slowly fabricated not only the group elective system but also the correlative system of majors. The former, they maintained, would ensure educational breadth, the latter depth.

The group system, involving what today are commonly referred to as distribution requirements, limits the choices available to students by requiring that they elect a prescribed number of courses within each of several groups of subjects—the most common groupings now being the sciences, the social sciences, and the so-called humanities. No better example exists of meritorious academic statesmanship in American history. Authors of the group system accomplished the extremely difficult task of circumventing the entrenched classicists by dividing up the curricular cake in such a way that every subject got a slice. By means of the group system educators avoided one of the dangers of free election—overspecialization. To impede the other—superficiality—they devised the major system.

To require undergraduates to study at least one subject in depth, the universities and somewhat later the colleges adopted the principle of concentration or majoring. Gilman, Harper, and Jordan introduced it at Johns Hopkins, Chicago, and Stanford, whence it travelled to other institutions. As part of his 1910 reforms A. Lawrence Lowell established it at Harvard, and promptly thereafter it spread to other New England institutions. Soon it covered the country to the degree that nothing is more typical of American college education than majoring.

Students could not begin to major, of course, until professors led the way. Those trained in Germany had been specializing for a long while, but single-subject professors did not come upon the American scene in influential numbers until toward the end of the nineteenth century. Professor Oliver March during his thirty-seven years on the faculty of Northwestern University beginning in 1862, for instance, taught botany, chemistry, geology, Greek, logic, mineralogy, physics, and zoology, and Professor Allen C. Thomas of Haverford College at one time or another from 1878 to 1912 taught American history, Biblical literature, constitutional law, English history, English literature, political economy, and religion and also served part of the time as librarian and business manager. Similarly, when in 1872 David Starr Jordan began his career as professor of natural history at Lombard College (later merged with Knox College), he found that, to use his own words:

> My "chair" demanded classes in Zoology, Botany, Geology, Mineralogy, Chemistry, Physics, Political Economy, Paley's "Evidences of Christianity," and, incidentally, German and Spanish! I also had charge of the weekly "literary exercises," consisting of orations and the reading of essays . . . with a class in Sunday School as a good measure (1922, Vol 1, p. 105).

Contrast the not untypical teaching range of these professors with the following 1933 description of the fragmentation in chemistry written by Dean Charles S. Slichter of the University of Wisconsin Graduate School:

> We not only have "scientists," we have "chemists." We not only have "chemists," we have "colloid chemists." We not only have "colloid chemists," we have "inorganic colloid chemists." We not only have "inorganic colloid chemists," we have "aerosol inorganic colloid chemists." We not only have "aerosol inorganic colloid chemists," we have "high temperature aerosol inorganic colloid chemists," and so on indefinitely until the scientist is fractionated to a single paragraph of his doctor's thesis (1933, pp. 97–99).

The results of this new ideal of specialization proved both desirable and undesirable. On the credit side stand the unmistakable improvement of the subject matter in advanced courses, the employment of infinitely better methods of teaching, the weeding out of the playboys, and—above all else—the contribution it made and increasingly continues to make to meeting the knowledge needs and the skilled manpower needs of society. The debit side, however, has at least one serious entry: namely, the narrowness to which specialization so frequently has led.

In contemplating the nation's need for scientists, engineers, and other specialists in 1886, Justice Oliver Wendell Holmes suggested that perhaps "we need specialists even more than we do civilized men," but he went on to urge that "if a man is a specialist it is more desirable that he should also be civilized" (1887, p. 77). Mr. Holmes's plea and that of others, however, did not halt the subjugation of general education to specialized education either in the United States or in Europe. Thus in 1930 the Spanish philosopher Ortega y Gasset declared in an address at the University of Madrid:

> Civilization has had to await the beginning of the twentieth century, to see the astounding spectacle of how brutal, how stupid, and yet how aggressive is the man learned in one thing and fundamentally ignorant of all else. Professionalism and specialism . . . have smashed the European man into pieces. . . . The guilt of the universities is not compensated for by the

prodigious and brilliant service which they have undeniably
rendered to science (1944, pp. 61,58).

The complex but also crucial problem of producing specialists who are
also well-educated, broad-gauged men and women remains to be solved
by the universities of all nations.

The Spread of Impersonalism

German conceptions largely dominated the period of
diversification, and in addition to the results already dealt with they
profoundly affected American higher education by reinforcing a trend
away from "the collegiate way of living." Brought from England to the
colonial colleges, the collegiate way had long been cherished but not by
the educational reformers of the late nineteenth century. German
university educators asserted, moreover, that their responsibility related
only to the training of the student's mind. They had no interest in
students as persons. What students did with their time outside of class
hours or indeed between matriculation and final examination, no official
of the German university knew or cared.

Many of the older American professors had been clerics, and as
such they were as much interested in the state of their students' souls as
in the contents of their minds. New-type faculty members, on the other
hand, rebelled against patrolling the unruly dormitories, praying with
the repentant, or punishing the miscreants. They sought the newly-
prized label of the professoriate, the doctorate of philosophy, and when
they had acquired it, they devoted their time and their energies to
research and to their professional societies rather than to students and
their souls. Trained in Germany or devoted to German ideals, they
formed a vanguard of a great army of college teachers who led the
onslaught upon paternalism by leaving students to their own devices.

Francis Wayland began the attack at Brown in 1842; Tappan
followed him at Michigan ten years later; F.A.P. Barnard joined them at
Mississippi, Alabama, and Columbia; Andrew Dickson White at
Cornell added the force of his tremendous prestige to the new point of
view; and Eliot, fresh from his study of European education, read in his
inaugural address at Harvard in 1869 the death sentence of the old order.
Students were to be considered adult men who needed no personal

interest from their instructors. The paternalism of the past thus gave way to almost complete indifference.

This mood spread through all avenues of student life. The old and deeply-ingrained interest in the housing of students vanished. At the newly opened Vanderbilt University in Nashville, Tennessee there appeared the following statement in its 1875 catalogue:

> There are no dormitories connected with the institution, and none are contemplated, except as may hereafter be supplied in connection with the Divinity School. For the generality of young men, the dormitory is unsatisfactory in its results. In the opinion of most persons best qualified to judge, it is injurious to both morals and manners. The Board believes it far safer to disperse young men among the private families of an intelligent and refined community, and have adopted this policy.

The disciplinary rule books grew thinner and thinner. Finally, in 1886, Harvard adopted the continental philosophy of student life *in toto* by announcing that attendance at classes would no longer be taken for juniors and seniors and that they would be required to pass only course examinations. Impersonalism had set in with a vengeance.

Consider, for instance, the decline in compulsory chapel. Although a few of the old-time colleges continued to require chapel attendance into the second half of the twentieth century, the ancient institution began to disintegrate when "godless" Cornell in 1868 and Johns Hopkins in 1876 opened without it. President Gilman posted this notice on Hopkins's bulletin boards: "A brief religious service will be held every morning at 8:45 in Hopkins Hall. No notice will be taken of the presence or absence of anybody" (Franklin, 1910, p. 220). Ten years later Harvard abandoned compulsory chapel, and most other colleges have followed suit.

Almost unanimously, the educational reformers disapproved dormitory life. To them it seemed to be the cause of the disorders which so frequently gave them sleepless nights; and, because student housing had long since been abandoned by German authorities, they abandoned it, too. Amherst tore down its largest and newest dormitory and permitted fraternities to monopolize student housing with the result that by 1904 not one Amherst senior and only two juniors and six sophomores lived in dormitories. President Tappan of Michigan, as one of the first acts of his administration, abandoned Michigan's only dormitory and converted it into a classroom building, and in Cambridge Eliot allowed the existing ones to run down and permitted Harvard students to live in rooming houses or in the "Gold Coast" apartments built by private entrepreneurs.

In short, the most prized of all the characteristics of the old American literary college, its collegiate way of living, came to be enjoyed by a diminishing proportion of students. The rest moved into rooming houses or rode the trolley cars to and from home. They filled the stadia on Saturday afternoons, where they yelled themselves hoarse in the belief that they were experiencing college life. They were, but it now revolved about the extracurricular activities, which were mushrooming and diversifying fantastically.

The extracurriculum, either faculty approved or surreptitious, has been a part of student life since the time of Plato's Academy, but during the half century between the end of the Civil War and the beginning of the Great Depression it swelled to elephantine proportions on every American campus. Sports had been banned in the old-time college along with all other amusements except decorous debates, but educational reformers removed the prohibitions because, among other things, they believed that athletics would produce a socially-acceptable release of student energies and thus reduce the number and intensity of riots and rebellions. Sports might also clear students' minds and thus improve their intellectual concentration.

A crew race between Harvard and Yale in 1852 may have initiated intercollegiate athletics, but in any event in 1858 four New England colleges organized the first athletic conference. After the Civil War baseball captured the imagination of the country and of college students, and soon thereafter football took the center of the collegiate stage. By the end of the nineteenth century colleges were fielding intercollegiate teams in a dozen sports. Meanwhile, however, the administrators and professors who had welcomed sports perceived that they had cast out the devils of riot and rebellion only to have the new devils of commercialism and hypocrisy replace them. Undergraduate interest in intellectual activities, they also observed, had improved not a whit.

Fraternities boomed along with athletics and became no less troublesome. They had begun as literary societies, some of which possessed libraries that shamed those owned by the colleges. Long before the advent of Dale Carnegie, however, the changing pattern of American life transmogrified them into clubs chiefly interested in training their members in the arts of winning friends and influencing people. Here the educational reformers—especially those associated with state universities—also miscalculated. Since German students lived around town in rented rooms, they concluded that their American counterparts should, too. American undergraduates responded, however, by inventing the fraternity house.

Fraternities had much to do with the increasing emphasis upon athletics, but they also promoted extracurricular enterprises in general: student newspapers, magazines, and yearbooks, glee clubs, mandolin clubs, and drama clubs, proms, house parties, and informal dances. By 1900 the extracurriculum, among undergraduates at least, had decisively triumphed over the curriculum. At Columbia, for example—so the story went—the "sharp boys" limited their attendance to the hours between ten and one, at Yale they never scheduled a course which met above the first floor of a college building, and at Harvard they made it clear the "C" constituted the "gentleman's grade."

The impersonalistic reaction against paternalism and the extracurricular diversification that resulted blended with the other changes reported in this chapter to produce the present-day conglomerate diversity that baffles not only foreigners but also many Americans. Technological, equalitarian, and other social pressures as well as German influences, however, inevitably led the old literary colleges to share the scene with institutions that offered vocational training through a myriad of courses made available to young men and women of all classes in land grant colleges, normal schools, technical institutes, and women's colleges. Such pressures not only precipitated the creation and rapid growth of comprehensive universities for the training of professionals, scholars, and scientists, they also led to the emergence of still another important structure in the American higher educational landscape, the junior (later called the community) college.

The Beginnings of the Junior College

In an address at the 1915 meeting of the North Central Association Dean James Rowland Angell of the University of Chicago put into circulation an expression that soon became a slogan, namely "the Junior College movement." Nineteen years earlier President William Rainey Harper of the same university had used the term "'junior college' . . . to cover the work of the freshman and sophomore years." Later he wrote that he had chosen it "for lack of a better term," but it took hold and spread so rapidly that by 1915 Dean Angell could refer to the resulting Junior College movement (Harper, 1905, p. 378).

Because William Rainey Harper made early use of the term "the junior college," writers of the history of the junior college movement frequently refer to him as the father of the junior college. Had Harper lived to see the appearance and growth of the two-year colleges of today, however, he would probably deny his alleged fatherhood.

Harper believed that the freshman and sophomore years of the historic American college should be pushed back into the secondary schools, but he had no notion that they would be set apart in two-year structures. Until 1903 he advocated a six-year high school, but during the last several years of his life he accepted the emerging idea that the period of secondary education should consist of two three-year units. It seems clear that he never desired or even imagined that two-year colleges would appear. When he died in 1906, none had.

Junior college historians also refer to Henry Philip Tappan, president of the University of Michigan from 1852 to 1863, and to William W. Folwell, president of the University of Minnesota from 1869 to 1884, as progenitors of today's two-year colleges, but, much like Harper, they did not propose or even contemplate today's junior or community college. Harper, Tappan, and Folwell conceived instead a reconstructed educational system that would include a six-year secondary school similar to the German gymnasium.

On December 21, 1852 President Tappan delivered his inaugural address as the first executive head of the University of Michigan. He had been on the faculty of the institution that grew into New York University, and he had been one of the leaders of the movement to further the university idea by establishing a new university in New York City. He had also gone abroad to study the educational systems of England, France, and Germany and written a widely-read book in 1851 entitled *University Education*, wherein he lauded the German program. Universities, he insisted, should divest themselves of collegial education. If the people of Michigan had accepted the Tappan proposal, the state would have generated a six-year secondary school system similar to Germany's. Before he could initiate these changes, however, Tappan lost his presidency; and with his departure the structure of secondary and higher education in Michigan remained unchanged.

The second campaign got underway six years later at the University of Minnesota. Its sponsor, President William W. Folwell, proposed it in his 1869 inaugural address and soon called it "The Minnesota Plan." Under Folwell's plan the first two years of the University curriculum belonged properly in the secondary schools. Minnesotans liked Folwell's plan no better than the people of Michigan liked Tappan's, however, and Folwell resigned in 1884.

The scene shifts to Chicago in the early nineties. In May 1889 John D. Rockefeller had pledged $800,000 for the building of a new Baptist university on the ashes of the bankrupt University of Chicago which Stephen Douglas had helped institute in 1859. Rockefeller and his Baptist associates in the reorganization agreed unanimously that the new University of Chicago should be headed by William Rainey Harper, at the time thirty-two years of age and Professor of Semitic Languages at Yale. Harper had graduated from Muskingum College before he had reached fourteen years of age and had taken his Ph.D. at Yale before turning nineteen, and he had been intimately involved in the Chicago venture from the beginning. For example, he had done yeoman service in helping raise the additional $400,000 needed to confirm Rockefeller's gift. After his election to the presidency in September, however, Harper took five months to decide whether or not he'd accept.

Rockefeller and the other members of the Board of Trustees wanted a college, but Harper wanted a university and only a university. As he conceived it, the new institution should not be concerned with undergraduate instruction but, instead, should be what he called "a great research university" devoted entirely to graduate and professional teaching and investigation. Negotiations proceeded for five months and ended in a compromise: the new institution would be a combined college and university. Harper made it clear, however, that he intended to move as rapidly as possible to slough off the freshman and sophomore years, and he proceeded immediately to make plans toward that end. Among other things he divided the four undergraduate years down the middle, calling the freshman and sophomore years "the academical college" and the junior and senior years "the university college." Then in 1896 he changed these designations to "junior college" and "senior college." In sum, he set the stage for Chicago to cease being a combined or consolidated university and to become instead a bifurcated university.

Harper did not stop with setting the stage. Indeed, he had put his Herculean energies to work toward the end of dropping the freshman and sophomore years even before the University of Chicago opened in October 1892. In one of the "Official Circulars" which announced to the public how the new university would operate he outlined one of the most ambitious, most dazzling plans of educational organization that any American has ever had the imagination to conceive. He called it "University Affiliations."

Harper envisioned an educational empire not unlike the industrial empire already created by the principal benefactor of the University of Chicago, John D. Rockefeller. The operations of the Standard Oil Company extended from coast to coast, but Harper largely limited his ambitions to the "inland empire" of the Middle West. He dreamed of the University of Chicago as the axis about which would rotate an imposing number of secondary schools which would, he planned, add two more years of work and of colleges which, he hoped, would drop their junior and senior years. Nor did he merely dream. He drafted a plan of action and set about bringing it to consummation.

The affiliated colleges, he wrote in "Official Bulletin Number Two" published in April 1891, would be "situated at different points" geographically but would "in every case" function with "standards, curriculum and regulations" exactly the same as "those of the University of Chicago." This meant that the University of Chicago would organize the programs of these affiliated colleges, write the examinations to be taken by their students, and generally treat them as branch institutions. They would, or course, drop their junior and senior years and hence become junior colleges. They would associate themselves, moreover, with secondary schools and thus become six-year structures. At the end of their six-year programs they would confer the "title" of Associate in Arts; and those of their students who desired more advanced instruction would continue at the University of Chicago.

The affiliated academies fell into two groups—those owned and operated by the University of Chicago and those owned and operated by their own boards of trustees but under the supervision of the University of Chicago. The former group never expanded beyond the single school originally included in the plan—the Morgan Park Academy in one of the Chicago suburbs. The second group at the height of the enterprise numbered ten schools—five in Chicago, two in other Illinois communities, two in Indiana, and one in Wisconsin. Soon, however,

Harper and his associates added a third group with a "looser relation . . . described and designated by the term of 'co-operation.'" Cooperation meant that the University of Chicago would accept the graduates of these schools without examination but would in turn expect to have some weight in determining their curricula, teaching methods, and overall procedures. In 1903 a total of 129 schools belonged to this third group. The great majority were located in twelve Middle Western states, but New York accounted for one, Pennsylvania and California for two each, and Colorado for three.

Harper also helped establish at least three new six-year affiliated secondary schools: Bradley Polytechnic Institute, which opened early in 1897 at Peoria, Illinois with Harper holding the position of President of the Faculty; Lewis Institute in Chicago, which opened the previous September with Harper on its board of trustees; and Joliet High School, which in 1901 at Harper's suggestion added two additional years to its four-year curriculum. Bradley continued to operate under the Harper plan until 1920, when it organized a four-year undergraduate college, and in 1946 changed its name to Bradley University. Lewis Institute began to change over to a four-year program in 1902 and complete the switch in 1918. Then in 1940 it merged with Armour Institute of Technology to become the Illinois Institute of Technology. Joliet High School, however, continued the Harper vision of a six-year high school, the last two of which were designated the Joliet Junior College. Some call it "the first public junior college." A more accurate name might be "the oldest surviving junior college."

Harper's circle of intimates shared his enthusiasm for the affiliation scheme, but many members of the Chicago faculties disliked it enough to attack it. The small colleges meanwhile recognized it as a threat to their existence, and the maturing state universities of the "inland empire" looked upon it with growing suspicion. Opponents of the plan believed, and not without reason, that Harper had embarked upon the business of making the University of Chicago the educational dictator of the Middle West with powers resembling those in the French university system and the University of London. For such centralization they had no taste at all, and so they continued to flout his efforts.

Harper continued his course, however, into the twentieth century; and in the next chapter that story will be continued. Suffice it to comment here that the efforts of Harper, Gilman, Eliot, White, and their colleagues to establish a new kind of university in America led to a number of structural changes, changes which had major impact upon the nation in the twentieth century and which account for the diverse nature of American higher education today.

Bibliographic Notes

The closer one approaches to the present the more voluminous becomes the list of new studies. Jarausch (1983) edits, for instance, a helpful book comparing changes occurring in higher education in England, Germany, Russia, and the United States in the nineteenth and twentieth centuries. The book is divided into four parts: the dynamics of expansion, the diversification of institutions, the opening of recruitment, and the process of professionalization. Authors provide a good amount of quantitative data in this publication. Another look at change during this time comes from the Handlins (1970), who discuss the impact of Darwin's theories on higher education's role as "custodian of culture." Stone (1971) edits a book-length collection of chapters on the rise of the American university, paying particular attention to the period 1890–1910.

Stevenson (1983) writes about Noah Porter's efforts, too often ignored, to change Yale after 1871. Thelin (1976) takes a social historian's look at student life in Ivy League institutions. Horowitz (1987) describes the various student sub-cultures that typified college life, including those of blacks, women, and Jews.

A number of recent books have dealt with President Charles William Eliot at Harvard. The Hawkins (1979) book portrays Eliot's educational career, for instance, from the time of his entrance to Harvard as a freshman in 1849 to his death in 1926. Special attention goes to the impact Eliot had on educational policy, not only at Harvard but also nationwide. Smith (1986) in his opening chapter also traces Eliot's contributions to Harvard. Fleming writes a chapter in Bailyn's (1986) book on the role Eliot played in the late nineteenth century changes at Harvard. Powell (1980) studies Eliot's role in national educational change in the late nineteenth century. Included is material on the development of the "Normal Course" at Harvard during the 1890s. Cremin (1988) opens his Chapter 8 with comments on Eliot's inaugural address and shows how Eliot's remarks pointed to new ways universities would take in their use of knowledge. Wagner's chapter in

Goodenow and White (1981) compares Eliot's and Booker T. Washington's views on black higher education.

Stetar (1985) covers an oft-neglected subject: the status of higher education in the South following the Civil War. The institutions themselves suffered economic deprivation and political interference but carried on their work in ways different from other regions. Cremin (1980) writes about the damage done to education in the South as a result of the Civil War but shows, too, the rise of new institutions throughout the period. Anderson (1988) writes about black education after the Civil War, showing how black leaders and their white allies struggled to provide education to the newly-freed slaves. Attention also goes to the model provided black education by Hampton Institute. Shannon (1982) writes about the unfortunate treatment blacks received from Tennessee legislators in distributing land grant funds for which they were eligible

Rudolph (1977) gives good detail to the changes that occurred in the curriculum and to ways that the curriculum was taught after the Civil War. These changes led by the turn of the twentieth century to what Rudolph calls disarray in the curriculum. Kimball (1986) also studies the curriculum during this period, paying particular attention to the liberal studies, which their advocates during this period began describing as the "liberating" studies.

Herbst (1989) continues his history of teachers and teacher education into the period after the Civil War, noting the effort to professionalize the field. In Illinois this meant seizing "upon the cultivation of educational research and science" (p. 145). A move toward the preparation of secondary school teachers and administrators and the subsequent deserting in some instances of elementary school teachers by these schools Herbst portrays as "betrayal." The book edited by Goodlad, Soder, and Sirotnik (1990) provides chapters on the history of normal schools and of other settings where teacher education took place. Harcleroad and Ostar (1987) also follows the rise of the normal schools after the Civil War as well as certain other special interest institutions.

The Harcleroad and Ostar book relates to Johnson's (1981) paper in which he set out to correct "misconceptions" he found in the historical literature on the early land grant colleges. Findlay (1982) also writes about the land grant institutions, especially the distribution of funds after 1862. Madsen has a chapter in Anderson (1976) describing the "myth and reality" of the land grant university. He provides a most helpful one-chapter review of the history of this institution. Hyman (1986) uses three actions by the federal government—the 1787 Northwest Ordinance, the 1862 Land Grant College Act, and the 1944 GI Bill—as examples of America's "singular" effort to improve access to opportunity to its people.

Others have written about the rise of the state universities during this period. Findlay shows how presidents of the old private colleges perceived these new institutions as a threat. Lang (1978) writes about the short-lived People's College that opened in 1858 and in some ways served as a precursor to the land grant colleges that followed.

Still another kind of institution—the bible college—began to emerge in this period. Carpenter and Shipps (1987), having shown the role of religion in higher education during earlier periods, turn to the rise of the bible colleges after 1880.

Diener's (1985) documentary history of the junior/community college includes Barnard's 1871 proposal for a sort of junior college system in Washington, D.C. and Burgess's (1884) proposals for extended secondary schools.

Finkelstein (1983 and 1984) notes the rise of a new class of junior faculty member after the Civil War. Rather than the temporary individuals waiting for work elsewhere, junior faculty by this time saw themselves as occupying the lower rung on an academic ladder to which they would devote their lives. Wolfle (1973) chronicles the emergence of "professional" scientists in American higher education and the sources of support that made possible that emergence. Church (1974) writes about one group of faculty, the economists, whose behavior in the early years of their existence he explains as an effort to influence public thinking.

The Winter 1971 edition of *The Journal of Higher Education* contains several papers on "The Liberal Arts College in the Age of the University." Axtell takes to task those historians who claim that the old colleges, faced by the new universities, simply died after the Civil War. To the contrary, he insists, these institutions played an important role alongside the new institutions. Hawkins studies the role of these colleges from the perspective of university presidents, some of whom saw themselves as collaborating with or supporting the colleges rather than abolishing them.

Potts (1971) finds some colleges, especially those of Baptist orientation, resisting the secular tendencies historians are more apt to describe for this period. McLachlan (1978) takes issue with the claim that the old colleges declined in number after the Civil War and that universities became the dominant American institution of higher education by the end of the nineteenth century.

Bishop (1987) seeks to refute the accusation that, with the founding of the Johns Hopkins University, institutions began a de-emphasis of teaching. At JHU at least, Bishop finds the first generation of faculty members committed both to teaching and to research.

Burke (1982) continues his search for data into the post-Civil War period, showing, among other things, that contrary to traditional histories of the period, graduate and agricultural enrollments remained small while enrollments in the smaller liberal arts colleges increased.

Oleson and Voss (1979) edits a series of essays on changes that occurred in the organization of knowledge in the United States between 1860 and 1920. These changes coincided with the rise of the American university and thus offer insight into the growth of that institution during those years. Hawkins (1979) stresses the interlocking importance of research and teaching in the newly emerged American university of the late nineteenth century. Utilitarian values of the American society also prevailed.

Women's higher education after the Civil War took new turns and raised new controversies. Gordon (1990) writes about the generation of women who attended college during the Progressive Era, with special attention to the University of California, the University of Chicago, Vassar, and Sophie Newcomb and Agnes Scott Colleges. Horowitz (1984) portrays the opening of new women's colleges during this period and shows how women's enrollments grew as a result. Solomon (1985) presents data on enrollments and the curriculum during this period, especially in the context of women. Brown (1988) writes about the ascension during 1882–1884 of Martha Carey Thomas to the presidency of Bryn Mawr. Butcher (1986) follows the rise of women's rights publications and its connection with women's higher education. Hague (1984) writes about the increasing status of women at the University of Wisconsin between 1875 and 1900. Palmieri (1983a) describes Henry and Pauline Durant's founding in 1875 of Wellesley. Palmieri also writes in 1983b about Wellesley's preference for women on its faculty and the impact these women had on and off the Wellesley campus. Conway (1974) shows how women's colleges during this period raised their graduates' aspirations beyond the household, putting pressures on existing professions and encouraging the establishing of new ones. Wein (1974) also writes about these changes, giving special attention to the activities of the Association of Collegiate Alumnae, (established in 1881), Bryn Mawr College under Carey Thomas, and Wellesley College under Alice Freeman Palmer. Gordon (1975) provides data and commentary on the characteristics of the "first ten classes" at Smith College.

Walsh (1977) continues into this period her history of women's struggle to enter the medical professions. As they gained this access they also suffered a backlash from their male critics. Gordon (1986) describes the role played by Annie Nathan Meyer in the founding and development of Barnard College. Zschoche (1989) deals with the controversial views of Dr. Edward Hammond Clarke as to the appropriate curriculum, given the status of their health, offered women students. Perkins (1983) contrasts white and black female teachers in the South after the Civil War. Whites taught as an antidote to "idleness and boredom" (p. 21) and tended to teach for only a few years. Blacks taught out of a sense of duty and expressed the desire to devote their lives to teaching.

Rossiter (1982) describes stages through which women passed between 1868 and 1907 in their struggle to gain access to doctoral education. Glazer and Slater (1986) shows the barriers facing women seeking entrance to the professions after 1890.

Johnson (1974) writes about legal and medical education in general during the nineteenth century, showing how by the end of the century formal schooling had replaced apprenticeship as the road to these professions. Stevens (1983) studies legal education in the United States higher education starting with the 1850s, showing how higher standards and more formal approaches to this education contributed to the quality of the graduates. Leedmerer (1985) shows how research became a greater part of medical professional practice after the Civil War as part of the effort to raise the status of medicine from the low rank to which it had fallen at mid-nineteenth century.

CHAPTER EIGHT

A New Status: 1900–1945

> Supported by other sectors of society, particularly after World War I, academicians entered the "real world" of modern America. Yet at the same time they entered an imaginary world in which only technical expertise gained through a college education could solve the world's problems. Ironically, as American higher education has moved into the mainstream of American life, its faculty, its research and training, its graduates, and its potential personal and social benefits have been put on a pedestal.
>
> (Levine, 1986, p. 38)

During the nineteenth century the United States spread from a narrow strip of territory on the Atlantic seaboard over the largest land mass ever developed in such a brief period. Across the continent America built railroads and highways, established communities, cultivated farms, dug mines, and constructed factories and other buildings beyond the most fanciful dreams of the founding fathers. They laid the foundation for a common culture upon the single national language that they taught to wave after wave of immigrants; they entered upon the most ambitious and humane program for improving the lot of common people ever attempted by any nation; they organized and erected free schools, churches, hospitals, libraries, art galleries, and universities. As their numbers grew from a total of five million people in 1800 to about seventy-six million in 1900, they settled much of the arable land of the country, and when the frontier disappeared, they sought other opportunities for their talents and their urge for a better life. They found them chiefly through education.

After 1900 social changes continued at an even faster pace. Before the availability of power machinery about 90 percent of the world's manpower went into raising and processing food, but the modern power saltation steadily reduced that proportion. About 1875 the number of Americans employed in agriculture fell for the first time below the number engaged in non-agricultural pursuits, and since then the percentage has plummeted below 10 percent. Correspondingly, population flowed from the hinterlands into the mobile and cosmopolitan cities, making the United States largely an urban culture. From this base it spread out from the cities into wider and wider suburbias.

These changes suggest the magnitude of the educational task that twentieth-century American society faced, but the accelerating trend to urbanization alone had additional effects. The American people began to send their children to school for longer periods than ever before in history, because they had nowhere else to send them. Urban children could seldom assist their families financially as could farm children. Child labor in the cities virtually disappeared, and employment for youth, especially in the inner city ghettoes, grew more and more scarce. Seventy-seven percent of the eighteen- and nineteen-year-old youth of 1920 had full-time jobs, but less than forty-three percent of the same age group found work in the period immediately preceding the Second World War. Surplus young people of earlier generations could move west, but in the twentieth century free land virtually disappeared. During the Great Depression of the 1930s the young jobless continued their schooling, went to CCC camps or to NYA project centers, or rotted in idleness. For all of these reasons—demographic, economic, and social—American higher education in the period 1900–1945 was marked most dramatically in terms of the changed status it experienced.

The Widening Impact of Colleges and Universities

American colleges and universities increased spectacularly in number during their era of exploration, and their variety and functions expanded greatly during the period of diversification. The rate of expansion during the twentieth century accelerated all the more.

This healthy status of postsecondary education in America did not always exist, but times have changed. Until the middle of the nineteenth century the traditional colleges appealed only to young men destined for the so-called learned or literary professions, a fact that explained their once-common designation as "literary seminaries." By 1945, however, their successors were preparing men and women who became corporation executives, politicians, labor leaders, ship captains, police officers, social workers, nurses, and members of hundreds of other respected occupations.

Some of these people were not "college graduates" in the ordinary sense. Instead they participated in the manifolding number of short courses organized for agriculturists, businessmen, civil servants, labor leaders, journalists, and dozens of other occupational groups. They typify the phenomenal expansion of postsecondary educational activities during this period. The more these activities expanded, the more intertwined higher education became in the national life. In the decades that followed they have achieved the status of epicentric institutions: practically every other institution in society looks to them for its leaders and its highly skilled personnel. They therefore influence the nation in ways and in extent undreamed of in other centuries and far beyond comparison with those of other nations.

American higher education has expanded prodigiously during the twentieth century, and its variety has proceeded apace. Philanthropy has increased, and during 1900 to 1945 it created a number of new institutions (Reed, Bennington, Sarah Lawrence, and the California Institute of Technology among them) as well as added to its support for the already existing ones. Land grant colleges expanded into state universities, technical institutes into comprehensive colleges, and two-year normal schools into four-year teachers colleges. In these many ways did the status of American higher education change during the first four and a half decades of the twentieth century.

The Period Prior to World War I

With the start of the new century leaders in American higher education could look forward to continuing growth not only in terms of enrollment but also in programs and institutions. This growth began early and was well underway by the start of World War I.

The Changing Role of Civil Government: The beginning of the twentieth century coincided with two trends which affected the relationship between civil government and American higher education. In one case rivalries had become more fierce between institutions, especially between state universities and land grant colleges in states that had both and between both of these institutions and the normal schools over their respective roles in teacher education. These rivalries coincided with a move, begun in Andrew Carnegie's steel mills but later extended to education, toward "scientific management" and efficiency. To the scientific managers of that period, institutional rivalries stood in the way of efficiency and required reducing. State governments undertook this task and were assisted by federal government specialists.

Applied to education the calls for scientific management and efficiency had an ominous ring. Take, for instance, this quotation of Stanford's Elwood P. Cubberley from his highly influential 1916 book, *Public School Administration*:

> Our schools are, in a sense, factories in which the raw products (children) are to be shaped and fashioned into products to meet the various demands of life. The specifications for manufacturing come from the demands of twentieth century civilization, and it is the business of the school to build pupils according to the specifications laid down. This demands good tools, specialized machines, continuous measurement of production to see if it is according to specifications, the elimination of waste in manufacture, and a large variety in the output (p. 338).

Cubberley's frame of reference was the school as factory, but others wanted to apply some of this same thinking to higher education. Samuel Paul Capen, higher education specialist for the United States Bureau of Education, expressed it this way:

> The field of higher education has until very recently seldom been invaded by the educational investigator. Efficiency tests and statistical measurements have been applied with increasing frequency to the work of the lower schools, and a voluminous literature in which the results are recorded has already grown up. The literature of higher education, however, is still preponderatingly of the naively philosophical order. The majority of those who write about the college and university are apparently committed to the method in vogue before the "Novum Organum" burst through the thickets of scholasticism (1916, p. 7).

Leaders in state government struggling with rivalries between institutions found Capen's procedures most helpful, and they called on him and his colleagues in the U.S. Bureau of Education for advice on how they should proceed. In deciding how to advise these state leaders the Capen group engaged in comparative cost accounting, a procedure aimed at determining the costs of various functions within an institution, even down to the clock hour costs of individual faculty members, and comparing these costs with those at other institutions, both on a national and within-state basis. All of this activity occurred without access to modern-day computers and the conceptual sophistication left much to be desired, but nevertheless state leaders acted on the basis of results generated (U.S. Bureau of Education, 1916).

Among the outcomes of these efforts was the rise of a new generation of state coordinating boards for higher education. By these measures state leaders hoped to reduce wastage and duplication and to avoid some of the penalties of institutional rivalry. As Capen wrote in the context of one of his state reports, "The value of some central coordinating machinery is that it can study State educational problems in a nonpartisan spirit for the purpose of determining what is and what is not needed and that it can bring state institutions to comply with its conclusions" (1916, p. 61). New York exemplifies states that had some form of state coordination much earlier, but in the first two decades of the twentieth century several states (including Florida, Iowa, West Virginia, Mississippi, Oklahoma, Idaho, Kansas, North Dakota, Montana, and Washington) developed new forms of state coordination. Perhaps most extreme was Kansas, which in 1913 established a State Board of Administration having control over the university, the land grant college, the three normal schools, the school of mines, the school for the deaf, the school for the blind, and the penal institutions.

The Rise of Prominent National Organizations: While state leaders sought greater control over the feuding institutions within their borders, another form of coordination was occurring among various institutions and groups within American higher education. One such group, the Association of American Universities, began operation in 1900 in response to a request from officials at the University of Berlin for help in comparing the quality of baccalaureate degrees from the various American colleges and universities of that time. AAU thus began its life in an accrediting capacity but later gave that activity over to the regional accrediting agencies.

Other national organizations had their beginnings during this time, including the National Association of State Universities, which had its first meeting in 1895, and the Association of Land Grant Colleges, which was organized the same year that AAU got underway. Meanwhile the nation's colleges in 1915 developed their own organization, the Association of American Colleges, giving them a national voice in the American higher education system.

One new national organization established during this period began speaking out for faculty members within the American system. In 1913 Professor Arthur O. Lovejoy and his associates at the Johns Hopkins University wrote to colleagues at nine other institutions proposing formation of a national professorial organization which would have as its purpose "to promote a more general and methodical discussion of educational problems of the university; to create means for the authoritative expression of public opinion of the profession; and to make possible collective action, on occasions when such action seems called for." ("A National Association of University Professors," 1914, p. 458) From this letter came formation of the American Association of University Professors. Having elected John Dewey as its first president, AAUP by 1917 had established twenty committees with responsibilities ranging from honorary degrees to study in South America. A large number of cases during World War I relating to academic freedom led it, however, to turn its attention increasingly in that direction.

In 1915 the AAUP Committee on Academic Freedom and Tenure issued its "General Declaration of Principles," in which it made clear the status which the professoriate, in the eyes of its new association, had achieved. "(O)nce appointed," the Committee declared, "the scholar has professional functions to perform in which the appointing authorities have neither competency nor moral right to intervene." (AAUP, 1961, pp. 865–66). Trustees in a civilized society had no more right to control the conclusions reached in their work by professors than did the President of the United States in respect to the decisions reached by judges in Federal courts. Determining the worthiness of faculty work must come, the Committee insisted, from a faculty member's peers. No other party was qualified to make such a decision. AAUP did not immediately win approval of these ideas from its administrative counterparts, but its 1915 statement made clear the direction it would take.

Institutional Developments—The Universities: "For both public and private research universities," wrote Geiger (1986, p. 40), "the two decades before the First World War brought far-reaching changes." These changes occurred largely because research universities benefited from the economic growth occurring nationally during that time. Public universities benefited from a fourfold increase in funding from state sources, while private institutions improved their success at fund raising from private sources.

Among the public universities, the bellwether institutions during this period were Michigan and Wisconsin. Michigan had prospered during the Angell years, and it continued under his successors. In Wisconsin the Governor, Robert La Follette, and the President of the University, Charles Van Hise, had remained friends since their student days at the University. Now in positions of authority, the two friends took advantage of their proximity in Madison to bring the University into greater involvement in affairs of the state. Faculty members served on state government committees to help draft the reform legislation which marked the La Follette administration. Meanwhile Van Hise reached out to families throughout the state, making especially effective use of agricultural extension agents to improve the quality of farming within the state. The borders of Wisconsin became the borders of the University, and in the process "the Wisconsin Idea" reached its peak.

In order for research at Michigan, Wisconsin, or elsewhere to occur, faculty members needed some release from their teaching responsibilities. This opportunity began to occur in some institutions during the period before World War I. Increasing availability of private money often made these changes possible.

The move to more research within the universities was matched by changes in medical education. As discussed earlier, nineteenth-century medical education in the United States left much to be desired; and leaders in the field took steps early in the twentieth century to correct the problem. The 1911 Carnegie Foundation report by Abraham Flexner gave focus to these efforts, and numerous low-quality medical schools, especially those not associated with universities, disappeared.

Institutional Developments—The Colleges: The changes within the colleges took place both in the form of new institutions and of alterations in the old.

Reed College came on the scene during these years and offered an antidote to some of the problems confronting older institutions. The first Reed president, William Trufant Foster, had worked as a dean at Harvard and knew the struggles that belabored Adam Lawrence Lowell, Woodrow Wilson, and other presidents of that time in fighting the influence of the so-called "gentlemen's C" and the extracurriculum. Foster vowed that Reed would avoid those difficulties. The College under his influence engaged in no intercollegiate athletics. It had no fraternities or sororities. Its students came to its Portland campus to learn, and Foster set out to provide an atmosphere where that learning would suffer from a minimum of distractions.

Alexander Meiklejohn when he became the President of Amherst recognized the same problem as had Foster. "In a hundred different ways," Meiklejohn commented,

> . . . the friends of the college, students, graduates, trustees and even colleagues, seem . . . so to misunderstand its mission as to minimize or falsify its intellectual ideals. The college is a good place for making friends; it gives excellent experience in getting on with men; it has exceptional advantages as an athletic club; it is a relatively safe place for a boy when he first leaves home; on the whole it may improve a student's manners; it gives acquaintance with lofty ideas of character, preaches the doctrine of social service, exalts the virtues and duties of citizenship. All these conceptions seem to the teacher to hide or to obscure the fact that the college is fundamentally a place of the mind, a time for thinking, an opportunity for knowing (1920, pp. 32–33).

These were challenging times for the liberal arts colleges. They had held their own during the nineteenth century against the rise of the universities, but as these latter institutions continued to grow in stature college leaders became concerned. Universities pressed them from above, but at the same time normal schools and junior colleges had begun to press them from below. Normal schools had begun in Massachusetts in the 1830s and during the nineteenth century had remained basically secondary schools preparing teachers for primary education. By this time, however, the normal "schools" began conceiving of themselves as "colleges," at least to the extent that they might start offering some postsecondary education. The former state normal school at Greeley, Colorado, became, for example, Colorado State Teachers' College. Iowa State Teachers College achieved postsecondary status. Other examples appeared in Michigan, Montana, Illinois, and New York, all before 1910. Meanwhile at least eight states began certifying their normal schools to offer college-level work (McDowell, 1919, p. 20). In some cases these former normal schools became four-year institutions, but in other cases the institutions joined the junior college movement, which definitely gained momentum during this pre-World War I period.

Institutional Developments—The Junior Colleges: If one conceives of the junior college as evolving in some good measure from an extension of secondary education into the thirteenth and fourteenth grades, then the junior college movement began earlier than the twentieth century. Numerous private academies made this extension on their way either to two-year or four-year college status. Public school districts in Indiana, Michigan, and Colorado during the nineteenth century extended their offerings beyond the twelfth grade. Even a public university in Indiana (Vincennes), established in 1804, found it difficult to extend itself beyond the fourteenth grade and remained as late as 1990 a two-year institution.

Elsewhere major universities in selected regions gave support to the junior college movement by reaching agreements with struggling four-year private institutions to admit to third-year status students who had completed two years at the private institution. These arrangements occurred in Missouri through the University of Missouri, in Texas through Baylor University, and probably in other settings. Meanwhile William Rainey Harper continued until his death in 1906 to expand his various plans for affiliation, both with private colleges in the region and with public school districts.

The oldest continuously-operating public junior college in the United States began with Harper's encouragement in Joliet, Illinois, in 1901. The Joliet principal, J. Stanley Brown, admired Harper and saw at Joliet the opportunity to put Harper's ideas into action. The school district enjoyed strong financial support from its community and had built a new secondary school building with space available for a junior college. Brown thus moved ahead with Harper's plan and soon had college-level courses and students in place at Joliet.

California led all states during this period in the development of junior colleges. The state at that time had two universities, both some fifty miles apart in the San Francisco Bay region, and could offer little else but a few private institutions and normal schools to meet the demand elsewhere in the state. The California Assembly thus approved legislation in 1907 permitting school districts to establish junior colleges, and in 1910 Fresno opened the first such institution in California. Fresno Superintendent C.L. McLane foresaw a wide range of courses for the new institution, including not only the usual academic subjects associated with the first two years of the university curriculum but also courses in agriculture, manual training, domestic science, teacher training, and other fields (McClane, 1930). Alexis F. Lange had much to do with popularizing the junior college in California. Lange came to the University of California from the University of Michigan in 1890 as a professor of English, but his developing interest in the junior college prompted California President Benjamin Ide Wheeler to move Lange into Education. From that vantage point Lange traveled up and down the state spreading the gospel of the new institution.

As his conception of the junior college matured, Lange came to see it as serving roles far beyond the preparation of students for transfer to the university. It could, for one thing, serve what Lange called that "great mass of high school graduates, who can not, will not, should not, become university students." Such an institution had as its controlling purpose provision of "a reasonably complete education, whether general or vocational" (cited in McDowell, 1919, p. 25).

Lange's statement appeared in an important study undertaken just before the start of the war and published in 1919. In that study F.M. McDowell identified four kinds of junior college: (1) the lower divisions of universities, (2) normal schools that now offered two years of postsecondary work, (3) public secondary schools that extended their offerings beyond the twelfth grade, and (4) private colleges offering instruction only through the fourteenth grade. Universities in twelve states—Arkansas, California, Idaho, Indiana, Illinois, Iowa, Kansas, Michigan, Minnesota, Missouri, Texas, and Washington—officially recognized junior colleges in their region. Numbers of new institutions—especially in the public realm—were increasing dramatically, McDowell finding a 168 percent growth in numbers during 1914–17 alone (1919, p. 67).

Moves Toward Curricular Coherence: The changes noted in the early decades of the twentieth century in junior college curricula had their counterparts elsewhere in American higher education. College and university leaders inherited from the nineteenth-century curricula a state of disarray, growing largely from abuse of the elective principle. This principle permitted Harvard's Eliot and others during the nineteenth century to open curricula to new subject matter, but other problems did arise. Some students sought the easiest approach possible, usually taking a wide range of courses having no relationship to each other but reputed to require a minimum effort on the students' part. Students in this instance may have obtained breadth in their studies but no depth. Other students took the opposite extreme of restricting their study to a narrow range of courses, perhaps even within a single discipline. Students in this instance obtained depth but no breadth. New leaders appeared who set out to correct some of these abuses.

While Yale, Cornell, Wesleyan in Connecticut, City College of New York, and other institutions had taken the lead earlier, Harvard after 1909 under President Adam Lawrence Lowell signalled this effort to achieve greater coherence in undergraduate education. Under the Harvard plan students met established distribution requirements as well as developing a concentration (major) in a specific field. In order to meet the distribution requirement, the seventeen courses that a student needed to qualify for the Harvard baccalaureate degree had to include six courses outside his field of concentration. The field of concentration, in turn, consisted of six courses taken within a single division of the University. The distribution requirement met the need for breadth; concentration served the need for depth.

Both Lowell at Harvard and Wilson at Princeton experimented with new residence plans for the undergraduates. Their thinking brought their institutions back into an English collegiate mode, the more impersonal German model apparently not serving the universities well at the undergraduate level. Wilson introduced not only a house plan to Princeton but also a corps of "preceptors," instructors chosen for their teaching ability and their personality as these characteristics would enhance undergraduate learning. The preceptors worked with students in small groups of four or five and tried to encourage student interest in affairs of the mind.

Princeton students faced more required courses than Harvard's. At Princeton freshman-year courses were completely prescribed; the sophomore year contained a mixture of required and elective courses; and the junior and senior years called for students to take three of their courses in a specialized field, leaving only one course for work outside their specialty.

Student Life During the Prewar Period: As can be seen from the struggles with the curriculum and from proposals arising at Reed and Amherst, students during this period did not always take their studies seriously. One group of students, however, did take their politics seriously. These were times when student socialists began organizing on a national scale. Their numbers were never large, but the names of some them remain familiar today. They include Paul Blanshard, Clarence Darrow, Heywood Broun, Paul Douglas, Walter Lippmann, Jack London, Edna St. Vincent Millay, Inez Milholland, Lewis Mumford, John Reed, Upton Sinclair, Norman Thomas, and others. All of these people belonged to the Intercollegiate Socialist Society, Sinclair having conceived it and London serving for awhile as its national president. ISS would produce in later generations student organizations important to the student movements of their times—the Student League for Industrial Democracy in the 1930s and the Students for a Democratic Society in the 1960s.

Perhaps making a bigger impact than the student socialists were the numbers of women who found their way into college during the years leading to 1920. During these years women gained the right to vote, and with this greater societal attention to the rights of women came an increase in the percentage of women enrolled in American higher education. This percentage declined in ensuing decades, however, and did not reach the 1920 level again until the 1980s (Newcomer, 1959).

These were the times of the great debate between Booker T. Washington and W.E.B. Du Bois. Born into a slave family, Washington looked upon manual work as the vehicle whereby blacks could best rise in status within American society. His approach opened the doors of higher education to many who might not otherwise have considered such an option. Du Bois came from a family in the North, had attended Fisk and Harvard, and believed that efforts should focus on that "talented tenth" among black youth who could learn and benefit from the same liberal arts education received by whites. Du Bois was concerned that black higher education should be of the same quality as that received by whites.

World War I

As Europe went to war in the second decade of the twentieth century, Americans at first could not decide on which side they belonged. This dilemma loomed large among academics, many of whom had great respect for the German university which had so influenced universities in the United States. Only with the increasingly belligerent behavior of the German submarine fleet did Americans become sufficiently incensed as to know on which side they should fight. Once having made that decision, however, they took a strong stand. Everyone, they concluded, should do his or her part for the war effort. Anyone who did not fell under suspicion. For the generation that later lived through the war in Vietnam, the superpatriotism of Americans and the loyalty expected of her academics during World War I stand in stark contrast.

Perhaps typical of the fervor with which Americans greeted the start of the war was the speech delivered by the University of Washington's President Henry Suzzallo on the night after war was declared. Suzzallo's speech had been preceded by a parade of 15,000 people through the streets of downtown Seattle, another 100,000 lining the streets and cheering them as they passed. Following the march 8,000 of the paraders filed into a downtown arena for a program chaired by the President of the University. "We are gathered here to affirm a cause," Suzzallo declared.

> That cause is the sacredness of our national liberties and our national rights. For years, as becomes a just people, it has leashed its indignation, patiently gathered testimony and heard the guilty. The evidence is now in and the judgment is war.

Because Americans were now at war, Suzzallo continued, they had a responsibility to fall unquestioningly into line behind the people who now led the nation's war effort. "There is no place," he proposed, "for further . . . debate. There is no time for further discussion. It is for us, for you and me, my countrymen, to execute the supreme verdict delivered into our hands" (*Seattle Times*, April 8, 1917).

Faculty members and administrators alike considered it appropriate to join the government in promoting the war effort. Some of the younger men joined their students in the military services. Their older colleagues placed their expertise and their laboratories at the disposal of appropriate federal and state government agencies. President Hadley summarized Yale's mobilization in the following memo:

> Have placed laboratories at disposal of Government, organized research committee for National Defense Council, and promised leave of absence to instructors needed by Government. Have organized four year course for training reserve artillery officers, aviation unit already in service, naval training unit, and motor boat patrol for Long Island Sound. Will graduate at once any senior called to service of the Government. Have formed Emergency War Council, consisting of President, Secretary, Treasurer, Deans of College and Scientific School, and Military Science professor, with authority to deal with any situation which may arise without waiting for approval of faculty (Gruber, 1975, p. 100).

While these activities began, President Hadley and his counterparts elsewhere had to deal with faculty members whose loyalty to the war effort anyone had reason to doubt. President Nicholas Murray Butler at Columbia took a strong stand on the issue. Any professor, he warned, who could not commit his "whole heart and strength" to the war effort could expect a speedy separation from the University, if his or her actions were judged unlawful or treasonable. Psychologist J. McKeen Cattell—who had feuded with Butler and the Trustees for years—became one of the casualties of Butler's threat. Using University stationery, Cattell wrote to several Congressmen, arguing against the sending of draftees (of whom Cattell's son was one) to the battlefields of Europe against their will. His action cost him his position at Columbia. Others who left during the war years included several other respected members of the Columbia faculty—including Charles Beard and Henry W.L. Dana (Gruber, 1975; Summerscales, 1970).

The Columbia experience contrasts with an event at Harvard. Concern arose that an alumnus would refuse to give $100,000 to the Cambridge institution because of the presence there of the pro-German Professor Hugo Munsterberg, but President Lowell kept Munsterberg at Harvard, explaining:

> It is sometimes suggested that the principles are different in time of war; that the governing boards are then justified in restraining unpatriotic expression injurious to the country. But the same

problem is present in war time as in time of peace. If the university is right in restraining its professors, it has a duty to do so, and it is responsible for whatever it permits. There is no middle ground. Either the university assumes full responsibility for permitting its professors to express certain opinions in public, or it assumes no responsibility whatever, and leaves them to be dealt with like other citizens by the public authorities according to the laws of the land (Hofstadter and Metsker, 1955, p. 503).

Organizing higher education to help fight the war took time, and in many respects the organizing was still proceeding when the war ended. Perhaps typical of some of the futility of those times was the Student Army Training Corps, which involved bringing millions of young men to college and university campuses where they would receive training and take courses that would prepare them for war service at the point where the nation needed them. This program got underway in May of 1918. By mid-autumn a world-wide outbreak of the deadly swine flu struck the campuses where the men were training. Living and working in close, temporary quarters, the recruits fell easy prey to the virus and many lost their lives. By the time this threat had passed the war had ended and few if any SATC recruits had found their way into active duty.

The Period Between the Wars

With the war behind them college and university leaders could return to their primary tasks. In this undertaking they enjoyed a number of successes, despite a depression that brought the American economy to its knees.

The Increasing Role of Research in the American University: "By 1920," wrote DeVane, "the universities had reached a stage of maturity." According to Devane:

The organization as a whole had become compact and was certainly more orderly. The major departmental lines had been marked out, and within the department the hierarchy had been established, from the full professor at the top to the lowest instructor. The complex organization that was now the university was usually managed by a large bureaucracy presided over by a secular president who naturally could not maintain his scholarship in his busy office. He in turn was responsible to a board of trustees, largely made up of alumni lawyers and businessmen (1965, p. 74).

For Thorstein Veblen (1918) the "maturation" to which DeVane referred represented a step in the wrong direction. Veblen took issue with the "Captains of Industry" who now dominated boards of trustees and with the "Captains of Erudition" whom the boards hired as their presidents. From Veblen's perspective universities would fare better without their boards, their presidents, and the business-oriented principles they brought to the higher learning.

The maturation to which DeVane referred included a growing strength within the professional and graduate schools as well as an increasingly important role for the research function. Aided by a new commitment on the part of wealthy foundations—especially those supported by Carnegie and Rockefeller—to the increasing of knowledge, the private American universities of the twenties and thirties gave new attention to their research function.

Some of this momentum began with the establishing in 1916 of the National Research Council. The Council at its founding and during World War I had a primary commitment to organizing the nation's research effort in behalf of the war but with the signing of the armistice the Council continued in existence and aided in furthering university research. Much of the support for the Council after the war came from the foundations (Geiger, 1986).

Symbolic of the new status of graduate education and research was the establishing of the California Institute of Technology. The combination of private money from several sources, postwar support from the National Research Council, and success in luring some of the nation's outstanding scientists to Pasadena led Caltech quickly to the forefront of American universities during the twenties (Geiger, 1986).

While much of the research activity occurred within private institutions during this period, the pattern changed toward the end of the Depression. By this time private institutions were feeling the effects of the economic downturn, while public institutions with their broader financial base fared better. California, Minnesota, and Michigan showed special resiliency, with the result that university research within these states assumed a role of relative importance (Geiger, 1986).

The Changing Status of the Normal School: While universities continued their maturation, the normal schools that had begun their work as secondary institutions in the nineteenth century continued their climb to postsecondary status following World War I. As Harcleroad and Ostar wrote:

> The pressure for additional opportunities for higher education during the early 1900s and particularly after World War I led many students to attend nearby normal schools and teachers colleges and to press for broadening the curriculum in additional fields. This also caused continual pressure for collegiate status for all previously specialized institutions, especially institutes of technology, normal schools, and teachers colleges (1987, p. 42).

In 1918, according to Harcleroad and Ostar, "27 degree-granting colleges existed in 14 states" (p. 43). These institutions set a pattern during the next two decades, wherein normal schools increasingly assumed the title of teachers' colleges and, following in the thirties and forties, colleges of education. As the demand for secondary school teachers grew, the teachers colleges expanded their curricula in the arts and sciences, thereby giving them more and more the character of something other than a normal school.

Growth of the Junior College Movement: The demand for access to higher education influenced not only the normal schools but also the junior colleges. In 1920 the U.S. Commissioner of Education, Philander Priestly Claxton, invited a group of junior college leaders to a national meeting in St. Louis. At this meeting Claxton called attention to the increased enrollments to be expected during the twenties in American higher education. Claxton proceeded to endorse the junior colleges as a primary vehicle for serving that enrollment growth.

From this meeting came not only a recognition that junior colleges could help meet the enrollment growth of those times but also that in order to coordinate their efforts they would need some sort of national organization. That organization appeared a year later with the establishment of the American Association of Junior Colleges in 1921.

While many of the junior colleges of this time—especially those in the public domain—still retained their ties to the secondary school, they left no doubt of their intention to identify with the higher education system. "The junior college," AAJC declared in 1925, "is an institution offering two years of strictly collegiate grade" (quoted in Thornton, 1972, p. 53).

Nor did the junior colleges necessarily limit themselves to the lower division curriculum of the university. Student interest in the transfer function of junior colleges remained primary, but meanwhile vocational courses were offered as the new institutions sought out their niche within the American system (Brint and Karabel, 1989). Meanwhile courses for students who would not go beyond the junior college assumed the unfortunate title of "terminal."

Publications during this period gave further credence to the junior college movement. Koos in 1925 produced *The Junior College Movement* and Eells in 1930 *The Junior College*, both major contributions to their field. Also in 1930 AAJC began publication of *The Junior College Journal* with Eells as its first editor.

Changes on the College Scene: The further rise of the junior college movement paralleled developments among the four-year colleges. Rudolph (1962) attributed much of the change during this period to the progressive education followers of John Dewey. Bennington College appeared in 1932, for instance, and set out to provide a setting "where such values of progressive education as initiative, self-expression, creative work, independence, and self-dependence could be accommodated" (Rudolph, 1962, p. 476). At Bennington, Rudolph continued, "professors were charged with the responsibility of closing the gap (between the curriculum and the extracurriculum), of making work and play, classroom and theater, classroom and poetry journal, one undifferentiated experience" (pp. 476–77). Other new institutions of a decidedly experimental nature appearing during this time included Black Mountain (Duberman, 1973) and Sarah Lawrence Colleges.

Older institutions meanwhile tried a number of new ideas. Swarthmore under Frank Aydelotte developed an honors program patterned after that at Oxford (Aydelotte, 1973). Arthur Morgan took over the reins at Antioch and introduced a highly successful cooperative education plan there. Alexander Meiklejohn moved to the University of Wisconsin and for a few years headed an experimental unit that provided his students a more coherent undergraduate learning experience (Brennan, 1988). The University of Minnesota, joining junior college leaders in recognizing that some students appearing at the doorstep would probably never graduate from a baccalaureate institution, established its two-year General College in 1932 (Rudolph, 1962, pp. 478–79).

Curricular Developments: Some of the curricular changes occurring within the college ranks had their counterparts in the universities. Especially notable were the Contemporary Civilizations and Great Books courses that emerged during World War I at Columbia. The Contemporary Civilizations course evolved from a War Department request for instruction on "war issues" for its Student Army Training Corps and was the only surviving element in a three-part effort to develop general courses—each extending over two years—in the sciences, humanities, and the social sciences. Its goals continued to challenge curriculum builders for decades thereafter.

At the same time that the Contemporary Civilizations course appeared, Carl Erskine developed a Great Books course at Columbia that influenced not only faculty and students at Columbia but also became a part of the curriculum that Robert Maynard Hutchins advocated at the University of Chicago during the 1930s. Mortimer Adler, a friend of Hutchins who had been exposed to the Erskine course at Columbia, convinced the new Chicago president that they should teach such a course together at Chicago. Hutchins found great merit in this course and used his eloquence and position in academic circles to encourage its spread elsewhere (Hutchins, 1936; Ashmore, 1989).

The Great Books course was just one of the changes undertaken by Hutchins at Chicago. Convinced that general education belonged appropriately in the eleventh through the fourteenth years of a student's education, Hutchins began admitting a carefully selected cadre of secondary school juniors to the undergraduate college at Chicago and awarding them baccalaureates four years later. He hoped that other universities would follow, but none did, leading his successor to end the experiment.

Presidents and professors might thus experiment with curricular change, but students also contributed their part during this period. Barnard students in 1921–22 generated a proposed new curriculum for their institution, and those at Dartmouth followed suit a short while later. Similar reports appeared at Harvard, Yale, Bowdoin, Oregon, Northwestern, Vassar, and elsewhere. Harvard's student council between 1926 and 1946 actually completed five separate reports on the curriculum at their institution, that of 1939 later claiming an influence on the Harvard faculty's 1945 *General Education in a Free Society* (Harcleroad, 1948).

Impact of the Great Depression: Some of these student reports on the curriculum appeared during the 1930s, a time of great strain not only for higher education but for every other sector of society. The market crash of 1929 had no immediate strong effect on American colleges and universities, but by 1932 they had begun definitely to feel its impact. Enrollments fell during 1932–34 but then began a rise that continued into the start of World War II. With jobs in short supply, people looked to higher education as an alternative. The federal government through its National Youth Administration subsequently made a number of work-study options available to students (Levine, 1986).

Unfortunately, the state governments and the private sources that funded higher education could not provide the support needed by the colleges of those times. Among the faculty the practice grew that everyone would take a salary reduction rather than see some colleagues lose their positions altogether. Educational leaders called for a winnowing of the curriculum, suggesting that general courses enrolling large classes should take the place of specific subject matter courses in which only a handful would enroll.

The AAUP recognized the need for faculty members to address these issues, and in 1937 its Committee Y on the Effect of Depression and Recovery on Higher Education issued its 543-page report. The authors by 1937 thought they could detect signs of recovery. Faculty employment, except at the lower ranks, held steady. Institutions had lowered salaries in recent years but now had begun rebuilding them toward previous levels. Although faculty morale had indeed suffered, the quality of instruction did not appear to have declined.

Bothersome to Committee Y, on the other hand, was the failure of administrators adequately to involve their faculty members in the difficult decisions that had been made during those times. Also bothersome was the tendency of American higher education, even in these troubled times, to continue its expansionist tendencies when it might better have consolidated some of its efforts. Committee members also expressed concern that state government had increased its central role in the coordination of public higher education, a trend that the Committee found distressing. "If the analysis presented . . . elevates one conclusion above all others," the Committee warned, "it is that effective work on the part of public institutions can be achieved only if a tradition develops among their supporters that will serve as a buffer to protect these colleges and universities from the control pressures that are exerted upon them" (AAUP, 1937, p. 477).

Perhaps indicative of the growing strength of AAUP was acceptance in 1940 by the Association of American Colleges of AAUP's Statement of Principles of Academic Freedom and Tenure. Later adopted by a host of other agencies, this basic statement set a standard for all of American higher education for years to come.

Student Life: Student life during the Great Depression proved often difficult, but prior to the Depression students had a lively time. Labeled by Lee (1970) "Mad, Bad, and Glad," the 1920s generation of students enjoyed their cars, their clothes, their new dance steps, and the Saturday afternoon football game as no previous generation had done. Although a student poll taken at the University of Texas between 1919 and 1921 indicated that students considered "sex irregularities," drinking, gambling, smoking, and dancing to be sinful, students did not allow their definition of sin to interfere with their fun (Lee, 1970, pp. 34–35).

While all of this activity took place, some students found the doors to universities they might have attended closed to them. Jews and students of color alike came face to face with surprisingly open declarations of bias against their enrollment in some of the most prestigious institutions in the land. Applicants who didn't fit the white, upper-class, Anglo-Saxon preferences of the times faced quotas and biases that prevented many from seeking the education for which they were qualified (Wechsler, 1981; Strum, 1984; Synnott, 1979a & b).

The Great Depression also had its influence on students, forcing some to forego the college experience and thousands of others to struggle in poverty. Government funding for work-study kept many of them off the ranks of the unemployed and permitted them to continue their studies, but only a certain number could benefit from these programs. Once they had finished their education, moreover, the graduates encountered a labor market that could not absorb them. Bitterness resulted.

With the American economic system in difficulty, youth cast about for alternatives. Some came to see Communism as the appropriate choice, and their activities during the thirties provided the fodder for much on which Joseph McCarthy and others feasted two decades later. Student leftist organizations, some of them derivatives of student movements that preceded World War I, grew across the country.

Looking abroad, students could see another war approaching, and thousands of them sent out the warning to national leaders that should another war occur they would not fight it. This movement began possibly at Oxford in England, where a group of students signed a petition declaring they would "not fight for King and country in any war" (quoted by Lee, 1970, p. 62). American students picked up this theme. Organized by the National Student League and the League for Industrial Democracy, strikes occurred nationwide against the approach of war.

Despite their protests the Oxford students a few short years later found themselves fighting a war they had vowed they would not fight. Their American counterparts followed in 1941.

World War II

The shock of Pearl Harbor awakened students and faculty alike to the need to become involved in the war effort. In time the majority of male students received their call, and civilian student populations on campus assumed a decidedly feminine character. Lee reported, for example, that by 1944 the University of Wisconsin had nine women students to every male and Ohio State University four (1970, p. 76).

Despite the departure of their male students (and those women, too, who entered war service during that period), the campuses remained busy places. Much as in World War I the institutions developed special courses relating national defense topics to the conventional peacetime curriculum. War-industry workers took short-term, engineering-related courses on campus, and intensive language courses also appeared. Army and Navy personnel appeared on many campuses, where they participated in ASTP and V-12 programs. Four hundred twenty institutions by 1943 could report the presence of military training personnel on campus. These "students" at that time numbered 288,000 (Lee, 1970, p. 76).

As the war neared a close it became obvious to government and educational leaders that colleges and universities would play major roles in the postwar era. The economy could not absorb the numbers of veterans who would shortly return home looking for work. Might they go to college instead? University researchers, given access to government funding, had proven capable of making major strides in the generation of new knowledge and new techniques. Might the partnership between academe and the national government that had worked so well in wartime also prove productive in peacetime? Might the status of American higher education further change? Whatever happened, expansion lay in the future, not only in terms of enrollments but also in terms of functions performed.

Bibliographic Notes

Recent literature on the 1900 to 1945 history of American higher education is especially helpful in that it has provided a number of publications dealing with a selected period or with a selected topic important to the period. Levine (1986), for example, focuses on American higher education during 1915–1940. "American culture," according to Levine, "is a culture of aspiration" (p.14), and he sets out to show the role higher education played in responding to that aspiration. Included are chapters on World War I, the junior colleges, and the Great Depression. Jarausch (1983) edits a book on this century containing chapters by Burke on expansion, Herbst on diversification, Angelo on social transformations, and Light on professional schools. Abraham Flexner and Arthur Morgan made important contributions to American higher education in this century, and Wheatley (1988) and Sealander (1988) provide further insight into their work. Another valuable contribution of this sort is Geiger's (1984, 1986) study of the emergence of the American research university. Geiger's study, which ends with 1940, shows the primary role played by private capital during this period in developing and supporting the research function.

Lazerson's (1987) documentary history provides excellent background for the period. It includes excerpts from Booker T. Washington and W.E.B. Du Bois on the "talented tenth" controversy, Charles Van Hise on "the Wisconsin Idea," Alexander Meiklejohn on the liberal arts college, and Abraham Flexner on medical education. Meiklejohn receives more extended attention in Brennan (1988), which deals with Meiklejohn's presidency at Amherst between 1912 and 1923.

Turning to the curriculum, Kimball (1986) shows how twentieth-century American higher education continued to reflect both oratorical and philosophical concepts of the liberal arts, concepts which had prevailed since Greek times.

More materials have appeared specific to Harvard. Powell's (1980) history of the Harvard School of Education, for example, illustrates some of the challenges facing these units when operating within major research universities, including the need to attract capable students, the struggle for funding, the expectation that faculty members and their students will produce quality and research, and other such issues. Smith (1986) shows the role Harvard played both in academic and sociopolitical matters in the United States during the twentieth century.

A much-awaited biography of Robert Maynard Hutchins (Ashmore, 1989) provides good background on university life and issues at Yale and Chicago during the first half of this century as well as insight into Hutchins the man and the positions he took in academic discourse.

Finkelstein (1984) writes about the professoriate, which underwent "consolidation" during the twentieth century, leading to a more secure and prominent position within American higher education.

Lagemann (1983) contributes a history of the Carnegie Foundation for the Advancement of Teaching, showing Andrew Carnegie's role, the part Henry S. Pritchett and other leaders played in operating the Foundation, and criticisms that it received.

Turning to students, Horowitz (1987) continues her study of undergraduate student life into the twentieth century, showing the organizations and activities students established as antidotes to the pressures of the classroom and responses attempted by institutional officials. Included is a chapter on women's role in the student culture. Wechsler (1981) studies the impact four new groups—the poor, female, Jewish, and black students—had on the more traditional American college student culture. Strum (1984) investigates the extent of discrimination occurring at Syracuse University starting in the 1920s. Synnott (1979a&b) identified instances of discrimination in admissions policies at Harvard, Yale, and Princeton during the first half of this century and the changes that occurred later.

Interest in the higher education of people of color remains high. Pearson (1983) draws on the 1938–56 writings of Charles S. Johnson to describe the status of black colleges during that period. Shannon (1982) continues into the twentieth century his account of the frustrations experienced by blacks in sustaining higher education in Tennessee. Wagoner (1981) also continues his analysis of Harvard President Charles William Eliot's influence on black education into the twentieth century, especially his emphasis on academics and the need to provide equal education to blacks and to whites. Anderson's (1988) book contains several sections on black higher education through 1935, including chapters on support from northern philanthropists, on the role of the black normal schools, and on "liberal culture" as a core of the curriculum. For documents on the "talented tenth" controversy between Booker T. Washington and W.E.B. DuBois, see Lazerson (1987). See also Olivas (1982), who studies the precarious status of colleges developed in recent decades for Native Americans, Chicanos, and Puerto Ricans.

Another expanding literature deals with higher education for women. Gordon (1990) continues her account of women's higher education during the Progressive era into this period. Butcher (1986) recounts the criticisms directed toward women attending college early in the twentieth century. Palmieri's chapter in Lasser (1987) similarly shows the concern raised during this time that college-educated women were less apt to marry. In another publication Palmieri (1983b) focuses on "academic women" at Wellesley between 1895 and 1920, a period when the College succeeded in attracting an outstanding female faculty. Horowitz (1984) and Solomon (1985) continue their histories into the twentieth century, Horowitz building her material around prominent women's colleges through the 1930s and Solomon showing the role women played in each of the decades into the eighties. McCandless (1987) writes about student life for women attending Southern colleges during this same period and finds authorities of that time patterning a curriculum and an extracurriculum that would preserve traditional expectations for Southern womanhood. Glazer and Slater (1986) continue their study of women's entrance into the professions to 1940, showing where the greatest opportunities, however limited, might lie. Science offered this opportunity, as did psychiatric social work. Stevens (1983) shows how legal education, now that its place within American higher education was established, evolved during the twentieth century. Among the issues were the use of the case method and the role of the state bar in the education and certification of lawyers.

Leedmerer's (1985) history of American medical education gives excellent detail to the twentieth century, including conditions leading to and following the Flexner report, the increase of private funding, the rise of the teaching hospital, and the continuing dependence of medical education on outside funding for its survival.

CHAPTER NINE

Expansion: 1945–1990

> We have created the world's first system of universal access to higher education. It provides entrance somewhere to virtually all who wish to enroll and offers an almost unlimited choice of subjects to be studied. This system of higher education, with its openness, diversity, and scholarly achievement, is the envy of the world. Unencumbered by suffocating ideology, the vitality and integrity of the American college and university are unmatched.
>
> (Ernest Boyer, 1987, p. 2)

Many of the conditions to which Ernest Boyer could point so proudly in 1987 derived from improvements after 1945. Before the war Americans did not talk of providing "universal access to higher education," but after the war they did. Enrollments had expanded during the past century, but after 1945 the pace of that expansion accelerated rapidly. Growth occurred after 1945 in practically all phases of American higher education. This expansion brought higher education more and more to the attention of the American public, an attention from which academe more often than not benefited but in some instances suffered.

Postwar Boom and Fears of Communism— 1945–1960

Impact of the G.I. Bill: Government leaders had learned from their experiences in World War I the kinds of civil unrest that could arise if returning veterans did not find work. Moreover, as a way of making the military draft more acceptable to the general public, in 1940 Congress had guaranteed reemployment to veterans who at the time of conscription held jobs. Government leaders came to realize, however, that the nation could not hope to employ the numbers of job seekers that peacetime would bring. Writers of the Final Report of the Conference on Post-War Adjustment of Civilian and Military Personnel anticipated in 1943, for example, that "(w)ithin the first year of the demobilization process there will exist the likelihood, if not the certainty, of a large volume of unemployed, involving as many as 8 or 9 million" (Olson, 1974, p. xi).

Drawing on examples from Wisconsin and Canada, government planners came to see educational and training programs as offering a proper response to the needs of postwar veterans. Encouraged by the American Legion and the American Council on Education, Congress and President Roosevelt on June 22, 1944 completed action on Public Law 346, the Servicemen's Readjustment Act, better known as the G.I. Bill. This action had a dramatic impact on American colleges and universities.

Dormitory rooms by the autumn of 1946 had filled to overflowing. Space intended for one person now accommodated two or three, and larger facilities usually intended for two absorbed four to six. Closets of any size served a new purpose, and gymnasiums suddenly filled with bunk beds in which slept those who couldn't fit into one of the closets. Enrollment in American higher education had reached 1,365,000 in 1939. By 1946 it had expanded to two million. Under the Korean G.I. bill of the 1950s another 1,166,000 veterans enrolled in college (Babbidge and Rosenzweig, 1962, p. 24).

These two G.I. bills produced an enormous change in American higher education. Before World War II American colleges and universities attracted primarily the sons and daughters of the middle and upper classes. The G.I. bills made it possible for an entirely new sector of American society to pursue higher education, and once the members of that generation had gone to college they most certainly wanted their daughters and sons to follow. The massive enrollment build-ups of the 1960s and 1970s are a direct outcome of the increases in enrollment generated by the post-World War II GI bills.

The Truman Report: With opportunities generated by the G.I. Bill increasing, the American people needed a new look at their system of higher education. That "new look" appeared in 1947 in the form of a

six-volume report from the President's Commission on Higher
Education, better known as the Truman Commission. Entitled *Higher
Education for American Democracy*, the report called for dramatically
expanding access to a college education. "We shall have to educate more
of our people at each level of the educational program," the authors of
the report declared, "and we shall have to devise patterns of education
that will prepare them more effectively than in the past for responsible
roles in modern society" (1:23). In order to achieve such an outcome
some attention would have to be paid to the cost for students. "The
American people should set as their ultimate goal," the report
continued, "an educational system in which at no level—high school,
college, graduate school, or professional school—will a qualified
individual in any part of the country encounter an insuperable economic
barrier to the attainment of the kind of education suited to his aptitudes
and interests" (1:36).

The Truman Commission proposed a broad mandate for
American education. The curriculum, heretofore seriously biased toward
Western culture, should reflect worldwide perspectives. Separate
facilities for the education of blacks and whites were intolerable.
National priorities should not lean so far toward the sciences that other
branches of academe suffered neglect. If education were to serve a wider
population, it followed that more and more American citizens would
need access to education beyond the twelfth grade to the fourteenth
grade. At least 50 percent of the population, according to the report,
could benefit from education through the fourteenth grade.

*Growth Within the Community Colleges and the Teachers'
Colleges*: In calling for greater access to education through the
fourteenth grade, the Truman Commission gave new support to the
junior colleges. It also gave credibility to a new name for these
institutions.

The authors of the Truman report proposed that henceforth the
junior college should call itself the "community college." Such an
institution would serve the full educational needs of its entire
community, whatever they might be. The report further proposed that
every state that had not already done so make it possible for school
districts to extend their secondary schools through the fourteenth grade,
thus creating a much-expanded national system of community colleges.
While not every state responded immediately to this advice, the open
support of the Truman Commission helped community colleges

continue their move to national prominence. Their growth until 1955 was gradual, but between then and 1970 their numbers grew spectacularly.

Meanwhile the teachers' colleges continued to change in stature. The demand for secondary school teachers became so great, in fact, that the teachers' colleges could justify vastly increasing their faculty in the arts and sciences. In the process a good number of these institutions made the transition from teachers' colleges to state colleges. A few moved to university status, a pattern that increased during the 1960s and 1970s. As enrollments increased nationwide these institutions—along with the community colleges—absorbed much of the mass of new students now seeking higher education. Also helping to absorb these numbers were a number of new public comprehensive colleges and universities.

Emergence of the National Science Foundation: World War II not only produced new students, it also gave a boost to research. Faculty members and administrators during World War II contributed in many ways to the war effort through their research efforts. Much as the National Research Council in World War I gave direction to university research in behalf of that war, so did the National Defense Research Committee assume this duty during World War II. From the efforts of the National Defense Research Committee came the realization that the research expertise of American academics, combined with the financial resources of the federal government, could produce outcomes valuable to the well-being of society.

Efforts began to establish an organization for peacetime that would continue the partnership found so productive during the war. Those efforts bore fruit in 1950 with the establishment of the National Science Foundation. Since that time NSF has served as a major source of funding for higher education research.

Curricular Change—the Harvard Report: Another initiative emerging during the postwar years came from the Harvard faculty. "We are faced," the Cambridge professors argued, "with a diversity of education which, if it has many virtues, nevertheless works against the good of society by helping to destroy the common ground of training on which any society depends." (Harvard, 1945, p. 43) That "common ground" to which the Harvard faculty referred existed in part of a society's heritage, "an inherited view of man and society which it is the

function, though not the only function, of education to pass on."
(p. 45) The report paid tribute to the methodology of science and to the
mutual importance of breadth and depth in the curriculum. Labeled by
Daniel Bell "the bible of general education," the Harvard report attracted
attention around the nation as college and university leaders looked
anew for ways to bring coherence to their curricula (Bell, 1962, p. 39).

Academic Freedom During the McCarthy Era: While some
academics struggled with curricular change, others faced threats to their
academic freedom. These threats grew from fears in the American
society that a conspiracy existed for the overthrow of their government
and its replacement with people committed to the doctrines of Marx and
Lenin. Some citizens were further convinced that faculty members had a
role in this conspiracy. To be sure, some portion of the intelligentsia of
the forties and fifties had toyed earlier with Communism. Some portion
of them now taught on college and university campuses. It behooved
political leaders, regardless of whether or not the academics still held
firm to Marxist beliefs, to label as them conspirators and to put them
to trial.

Schrecker (1986) attributed President Truman's March 27, 1947,
signing of Executive Order 9835 calling for a new loyalty-security
program for federal government employees as having a significant effect
on the later attacks on academics. This order gave Presidential credence
to suspicions of a conspiracy and permitted government agencies to
enter more fully into the search for its perpetrators. Meanwhile
Congressional leaders conducted their own searches within the general
public as did their counterparts at the state government level.

While the chase after Communists spread nationwide, two
instances—both occurring on the West Coast—deserve special
attention. In the case of the University of Washington the State
Legislature had established its own investigating committee just
nineteen days before President Truman signed Executive Order 9835,
and committee members were confident that they could find
Communists on the University campus. They found only a few, but in
the process that followed faculty careers were permanently destroyed
(Sanders, 1979).

The same legislature that established the investigating committee
in Washington also dictated that all state employees sign an oath
disclaiming membership in organizations advocating strikes or
overthrow of the government. This idea of oaths found favor with

numerous conspiracy-hunters, including the Regents of the University of California. When the Regents required University faculty members to sign loyalty oaths they encountered resistance which, similar to the Washington situation, brought national attention to the institution and endangered faculty positions. Only when the California Supreme Court on October 17, 1952, struck down the loyalty oaths did that controversy end (Gardner, 1967).

At the national level efforts by the House Un-American Activities Committee and by Senator Joseph McCarthy brought national attention to the hunt for Communists within government and academe. Within higher education these practices brought havoc to the careers of faculty members who had shown interest at an earlier time in Marxist thinking. Neither the mechanisms on campus nor those at the national AAUP level proved capable of preventing the damage.

Sputnik and the 1958 National Defense Education Act: Toward the close of the 1950s, the national government took action of a different sort, this action aimed at strengthening the nation's defense effort but in the process setting precedents for federal assistance to education that would affect the next several decades dramatically. When the Soviet Union in 1957 succeeded in launching its tiny Sputnik space satellite, the nation and Congress became alarmed. Until Sputnik entered the skies Americans had assumed their technical superiority worldwide. That the Soviet Union had "won" the race to space and that such a victory constituted a threat to the national security of the United States provided Congress with the rationale for passing the National Defense Education Act (NDEA) of 1958. If America must defend itself from this new threat in the heavens, it would start that defense with its educational system.

NDEA contained numerous provisions important to higher education. One of those provisions made it a matter of national policy that "no student of ability will be denied an opportunity for higher education because of financial need" (Babbidge and Rosenzweig, 1962, p. 50). Loan and graduate fellowship programs provided financial assistance to students; and for those students receiving the loans who later taught in the fields of science, mathematics, engineering, and foreign languages the Act made possible forgiveness for up to half of the amount of money borrowed. Other features of NDEA provided support for language and area centers, advanced study institutes, and for improving counseling and guidance in primary and secondary schools (Henry, 1975).

The Tumultuous Sixties

Proponents of NDEA justified its passage primarily on the basis of the threat to national defense, but educational leaders also found it timely as enrollments rose in the 1960s. Not only were the numbers increasing; higher percentages of those graduating from secondary school were choosing to go to college. The G.I. bills and the Truman Report encouraged college for a much wider spectrum of the American public, and colleges and universities could now expect their enrollments to grow dramatically.

Massive growth did occur during the 1960s, especially within the community colleges and the comprehensive colleges and universities, which absorbed the largest portion of the enrollment increase. New community colleges appeared at times during this decade at the rate of one a week, creating openings for a mass of new students. Medsker and Tillery (1971, p. 18) reported almost a doubling of community colleges during the 1960s, the number increasing from 656 in 1960 to an estimated 1,100 by 1970.

Having set the precedent with the National Defense Education Act, members of Congress felt more comfortable using federal money to support education in a wider variety of ways than they had in the past. Presidents Kennedy and Johnson encouraged legislators in these efforts, Johnson making a special effort to make his mark as an "Education President" by pushing Congress for programs. In 1963 alone Congress passed the Vocational Education Act, the Higher Education Facilities Act, and the Health Professions Act. In 1965 it found in civil rights and access to higher education for those who had previously been denied it a new rationale for massive increases in support for higher education. Also in 1965 the National Endowments for the Humanities and for the Arts appeared. A year later Congress approved the National Sea Grant College Program and the Adult Education Act. In 1967 it passed the Educational Professions Development Act. Once Congress had decided it could legitimately fund education, it did so in a big way.

1967 also marked the establishing of the first of two commissions funded by the Carnegie Foundation for the Advancement of Teaching and chaired by former University of California President Clark Kerr. A total of 175 reports emerged from these two groups—the Carnegie Commission on Higher Education and after 1973 the Carnegie Council on Policy Studies in Higher Education—covering a wide array of topics important to American higher education at this point in its history. Never before or since has such a comprehensive study of American higher education occurred; and many of the national, state, and local decisions affecting American higher education made during the 1970s and the early 1980s reflected the thinking of the Carnegie groups.

The decade of the 1960s also saw the development of new institutions especially for students of color, some of them with federal government support. In 1968, for instance, the Navajo Nation opened its own community college, setting an example for other tribes which in subsequent years established their own institutions. Efforts to start colleges specifically for Hispanics also occurred, Hostos College in the South Bronx providing one example of what such institutions might accomplish (Olivas, 1982).

The Years of Protest: The rush of students to campus produced many pressures, a good number of them generated by the students themselves. These pressures began early in the 1960s and in most of these early cases originated with student concerns for civil rights. Perhaps indicative of some of this early student pressure was a story from Greensboro, North Carolina that appeared in the February 2, 1960, edition of the *New York Times*. "A group of well dressed Negro college students," the *Times* reported, "staged a sitdown strike in a downtown Woolworth store today and vowed to continue it in relays until Negroes were served at the lunch counters." "We believe,"the students continued, "since we buy books and papers in the other part of the store we should get served in this part." The sit-ins in North Carolina gained support nationwide and generated other such efforts. On February 17 the Congress for Racial Equality announced its widened support for the sit-ins, and on March 28 students from Southern University sat in at an S.H. Kress lunch counter in Louisiana. By July 25 the eating places in Greensboro had been desegregated.

As the struggle for civil rights intensified college and university students of all colors entered into the activity with enthusiasm. Forays into the South involved them in freedom rides and voter registration drives, sometimes at cost of their lives. Participation in these programs gave students experiences of lasting impact and the inspiration to fight for human rights wherever they found the need.

As it developed, some of those needs existed on college and university campuses well outside the South. Students in Berkeley in September of 1964, for instance, found their right to distribute political literature at the gates to campus denied and in the weeks that followed gained national attention in their struggle to regain those rights. Sit-ins on the Berkeley campus and the ensuing struggle for authority between students, faculty, administrators, and city and state officials captured the attention of the American public nationwide. Only when some of the students took their pressure for "free speech" too far did the student movement at Berkeley lose its momentum. In the process, however, students developed ideas and strategies for protest that served them well in other settings. In the United States and abroad the protest movement gained strength, and over the next seven or eight years protests occurred on hundreds of campuses.

A number of national student organizations became active during these years. The Students for a Democratic Society emerged in 1960 from the ashes of the old Student League for Industrial Democracy and took a leading role in the protest movement. So, too, did the Student Nonviolent Coordinating Committee, which also appeared in 1960. The Council for Racial Equality also attracted students nationally.

Encouraged by the local chapter of SDS, a major explosion occurred at Columbia University in 1968. In this instance students demonstrated not only over civil rights issues but also in opposition to the war in Vietnam. The major civil rights issue had to do with access for community members to a new gymnasium under construction at the edge of campus, while the war issue revolved about University involvement in defense-related research. Buildings were occupied, police entered the fray, and campus life lost all semblance of normalcy.

The Downturn of the 1970s

As the 1970s opened, an air of apprehension pervaded all of higher education. Would the protests continue? Would they worsen? What effect was the unrest having on public attitudes toward higher education? Relations between the Nixon administration and higher education were becoming increasingly strained, and funding for the nation's colleges and universities had lost its momentum.

Hope that the worst of the student protests had passed did not survive for long. Matters became even worse, in fact. Violence in Santa Barbara in April of 1970 led to the death of a student. President Nixon's decision a month later to send American troops into Cambodia produced reactions on campuses throughout the nation, the most serious occurring at Kent State University, where several days and nights of unrest led the Ohio governor to bring National Guard troops to campus. In a moment of tension the troops fired on the students, resulting in the deaths of four students and injuries to nine others. A short while later a confrontation between police and students at Jackson State College led to two more student deaths and injuries to at least eleven others (President's Commission, 1971, pp. 273–74, 430–32). These tragic events brought home to everyone the seriousness of the situation. Yet the war dragged on, and the protests continued.

Meanwhile, other issues arose. Students during those times, for example, had little patience with courses that did not meet their tests for relevance, and their criticisms led faculties on many campuses to reduce their general education and other curricular requirements. In the place of these requirements students in some instances created their own degree programs, selecting courses which best fit their needs as they perceived them. Programs in the humanities and foreign languages suffered particularly.

The protest years undoubtedly damaged the image of American higher education. Viewed by some leaders as a major contributor to the well-being of an increasingly knowledge-based society and therefore a critical element in the future of American society (Machlup, 1962; Kerr, 1963; Bell, 1973), higher education by this time also attracted attention as a setting where conflict and controversy could rise to levels requiring police intervention and resulting in death and injury. For a good portion of the general public and for the political figures who capitalized on the fears of that public, this more negative image of higher education proved very real. "There has been," reported the Carnegie Commission on Higher Education in 1973, "a basic erosion of affection for and interest in education, including higher education" (p. 6).

It didn't help that during the 1970s the nation suffered several economic downturns that had serious effects on higher education. Earl

Cheit in 1971 published *The New Depression in Higher Education*, in which he found two-thirds of all the colleges and universities in the nation either in financial difficulty or heading in that direction. President Nixon in February of 1971 came forth with a hold-the-line budget that offered little hope for increased help from federal sources. State funding for higher education declined sharply. Business support for education in 1971 dropped 9 percent. Fearing what might lie ahead, the Association of American Colleges developed guidelines for the termination of tenured faculty members. Tenure itself came under further study. Given the shortage of funding, tensions grew between public and private institutions as they competed for students and for dollars.

Faced with these uncertainties faculty members looked more favorably at collective bargaining. The number of institutions with collective bargaining contracts increased from nine in 1968 to 156 in 1973. Taking note of the trend, AAUP in May of 1972 voted overwhelmingly to enter into collective bargaining, and with the American Federation of Teachers and the National Education Association they moved forward to organize faculties across the land. Wherever state governments passed legislation making possible faculty collective bargaining and wherever faculty members in public or private institutions considered themselves vulnerable or inadequately involved in institutional affairs, a faculty union became a reasonable option.

With the winding down of the war in early 1973 came a winding down of the student protests themselves. National organizations in a number of cases lost their momentum, SDS, for example, splitting into several increasingly radical factions and in the process losing the general student support it had received earlier. Most students, with the war behind them, succumbed to what some called "the fatigue of the seventies."

All was not gloom in the 1970s. Perhaps most encouraging was renewal by Congress in 1972 of the Higher Education Act. As time came to review the 1965 Act, a major decision involved the form that new federal funding for higher education might take. One option involved grants of funds directly to the institutions, the other the directing of that money to the needy students who attended these institutions. Congress eventually chose the second of these options, and in the autumn of 1973 some 500,000 freshmen enrolled with the help of the first basic opportunity grants, which were a part of the new legislation. Before long American colleges and universities, especially those in the private domain, came to realize a sizable portion of their income from this federal source.

The 1972 amendments also strengthened efforts on the part of government to improve college and university responses to the need for affirmative action. As recipients of federal funding, institutions had a responsibility to follow federal laws relating to affirmative action. Title IX of the 1972 amendments gave substance to women's demands for an equal place in academe, and tensions over this issue increased as the decade continued.

The later seventies also saw further changes in the curriculum. Faculty members and deans, recognizing that they had gone too far in responding to student criticisms of the curriculum, began to restore some of the coherence they had lost. Declines in the study of foreign languages slowed. At Harvard Dean Henry Rosovsky and his colleagues began work on a new "core curriculum" that would reassert an institution's responsibility to provide structure to the undergraduate learning experience (Keller, 1982). Numerous other institutions undertook these efforts, a trend that continued and strengthened in the 1980s.

Financial conditions rose and fell. Private institutions found ways to cope with the changed financial situation, and state legislatures when they could increased their appropriations to public higher education. Both sectors benefited from the financial aid measures of the 1972 Higher Education amendments. Institutions also raised tuition and fees; costs for students within one four-year period during the seventies increased 40 percent. Such steps helped institutions at least to keep pace with a rising inflation rate.

Other problems plagued the later 1970s. Student scores on admissions tests continued to decline. Recruiting scandals within intercollegiate athletics led to calls for a crackdown, for stronger leadership from college and university presidents, and for some greater control over the spiraling costs of these programs. Student defaults on their government loans also generated alarm. States that did not satisfactorily adjust their educational systems to reduce discrimination faced pressures either to change their systems or to lose federal government funding. Faculty members found their positions threatened, and during one two-year period AAUP received 1,100 complaints from academics seeking Association help. It didn't help that faculty members who had benefited so richly from salary increases in the 1960s now lost ground to increases in the cost of living. The academic job market had stabilized and could no longer absorb the numbers of people produced by the graduate schools. Demand declined, supply increased, and academics paid the price.

Some signs of encouragement appeared. The enrollment of women and students of color increased, women accounting in 1978, for example, for 90 percent of the enrollment growth of that year and black student enrollments actually doubling during the 1970s. Job opportunities for graduates, at least at the undergraduate level, improved. Meanwhile the decline in college admission test scores slowed.

The rise of collective bargaining among college and university faculty members which greeted the start of the 1970s also slowed as the 1980s approached. State governments proved reluctant to pass the necessary enabling legislation, and the question of whether faculty members in certain institutions should legally be considered a part of institutional management began working its way through the courts. Finally in February of 1980 the Supreme Court ruled that faculty members at Yeshiva University did indeed perform managerial functions and therefore could not avail themselves of collective bargaining. This decision seriously slowed collective bargaining among Yeshiva's sister private institutions.

Probably the most important court decision of the seventies came in June of 1978, when the Supreme Court decided that the University of California at Davis had erred in allowing racial quotas to lead to the denial of admission of a white student, Allan Bakke, to its medical school. Colleges and universities were justified, the Court declared, in considering the race, geographical origins, and other such characteristics of student applicants as a means of creating a more diverse student body, but they could not use quotas as the device for achieving that diversity.

Racial issues also played a role in the resurgence of student protest that marked the later years of the 1970s. Students focused their concern on the policies of apartheid in South Africa. Colleges and universities with large investments should divest, the students insisted, from companies doing business in South Africa.

Another form of student unrest arose toward the end of the decade in the form of protest among Iranian students over the policies of their

Shah, some students supporting and others condemning their national leader. Iranians at this time had become the largest foreign student group in the United States, and when relations between Iran and the United States deteriorated, so did the status of the Iranian students. When the Shah was eventually overthrown, many of these students sought asylum in the United States, while others returned home to participate in the religious revolution there.

As President during the late 1970s Jimmy Carter faced the problems of apartheid and religious upheaval in Iran, but he also gave attention during those years to the place of education in national affairs. His campaign for the presidency included a promise to give cabinet-level status to education within his administration, and in 1979—following Congressional approval to establish a separate United States Department of Education—he welcomed Shirley Hufstedler as the first Secretary of Education in his cabinet.

Another issue of national policy toward education during the Carter presidency related to the rising costs of attending college and the role the federal government should play in helping families meet those costs. Special alarm arose among middle-class families who on the one hand faced costs they hadn't heretofore encountered and on the other had the political clout needed to generate political action toward meeting those charges. As one strategy these parents and their political allies sought tax relief for college expenses, but in the end they settled instead for various forms of federally supported student financial aid for which their sons and daughters were now eligible.

The nation was moving in a more conservative direction. A taxpayer revolt in California led to passage in June of 1978 of Proposition 13, which on the one hand reduced local property taxes dramatically but on the other placed California institutions of higher education, especially the community colleges, in serious jeopardy. Meanwhile measures of student attitudes showed them also moving in a more conservative direction.

When Jimmy Carter ran for reelection in 1980 he encountered a conservative American public that preferred and elected the conservative Californian, Ronald Reagan. American higher education, which had turned increasingly to Washington, D.C., now faced political challenges of a different sort.

The Eighties—Responding to a Conservative Trend

For those individuals concerned that the federal government had become too deeply involved in the affairs of American higher education, the election of Ronald Reagan bode well. President Reagan believed strongly that the federal influence over all of American society had become excessive. In the context of education, for example, he vehemently disagreed with President Carter's establishment of a separate Department of Education and early announced his intention of doing away with it. As it developed, no such action occurred.

President Reagan inherited not only a department of education, he also confronted a period of serious, double-digit inflation. The early years of his administration were marked by efforts within the federal government, therefore, to reduce that inflation, efforts that proved successful but in the process also generated a recession probably deeper than anything experienced by American higher education since the 1930s.

For academic leaders the recession spelled special problems. A 1979 monograph predicted a coming decade of "reduction, reallocation, and retrenchment," a prediction that proved frighteningly accurate for the early years of the decade. Mortimer and Tierney, who wrote this report, based their prediction in part on the anticipated declines in enrollment that would result from declines in the 18–24 age group anticipated for the 1980s. As it developed, enrollment declines did not occur, largely because of larger enrollments of women, adults, part-timers, and foreign students, but reduction, reallocation, and retrenchment did occur because of the recession. The availability of new money for new programs slowed, forcing college and university leaders to reduce funding in one program if they hoped to increase it in another. Numerous institutions, both public and private, found it necessary to place themselves in a status of financial exigency, leading to the termination both of programs and of faculty and staff. Some institutions had to close their doors.

In the midst of the recession there appeared a report prepared for the U.S. Department of Education that reawakened the interest of the American public in its educational system. Prepared by a committee chaired by the President-elect of the University of California, David P.

Gardner, *A Nation at Risk* focused on primary and secondary education. Inevitably, however, the calls for reform also reached higher education. These calls appeared in several forms and came from several directions, both inside and outside academe.

From the inside there appeared calls from the students, from various academic organizations, and from individuals. Students demanded anew that their institutions divest in companies doing business in South Africa, a proposal that produced far better response in the 1980s than it had in the 1970s. The Association of American Colleges called for "integrity" in the undergraduate curriculum, having noted "mounting evidence that undergraduate programs in American colleges and universities were afflicted by serious weaknesses" (1985, p. i). A National Institute of Education study called for greater student involvement in their learning, a theme also stressed by Alexander Astin in his 1985 book, *Achieving Educational Excellence.* Ernest Boyer (1987) charted the dimensions of undergraduate education as he viewed them from the perspective of the Carnegie Foundation for the Advancement of Teaching. Allan Bloom (1987) took issue with a curriculum that emphasized relativism and gave too much attention to non-essentials, leading to "the closing of the American mind." Allan Hirsch (1987) found reason to question the "cultural literacy" of Americans and proposed a list of terms that in his judgment all literate Americans should find familiar.

From the outside came other criticisms. Congress and the media found that scandals in intercollegiate athletics had increased in their severity and demanded attention, if not by academe then by the government. Congress also expressed continuing alarm at the increasing level of defaults on student loans and initiated efforts to change the trend. William Bennett, who became the United States Secretary of Education in 1985, used his position as a "bully pulpit" from which to mount numerous calls for change in all sectors of education. State governors also entered the discussion, one of their conclusions leading to the expectation that colleges and universities would increase their efforts to measure what their students learned. The resulting pressure for assessment became an important part of the dialogue as American higher education moved into the decade of the 1990s (Hutchings and Marchese, 1990).

A Concluding Word

By September of 1990 enrollment in American colleges and universities had reached 13,043,118. The 3,535 institutions that constituted American higher education were spending annually a sum in excess of ninety-seven billion dollars ("The Nation," 1990, p. 3). American higher education had become a massive undertaking.

In becoming larger had American higher education maintained its quality? Chester E. Finn, Jr., was not sure. "Rising tuition, declining productivity, dubious practices, and slipshod quality," he commented, "have grown so pervasive in academe that public pressure is mounting for government officials to take some sort of action" (Schuster, Miller et al., 1989, p. 180).

And so the debate continues. Readers of this volume will recognize the constant quest aimed at improving higher learning. The Greeks struggled with it, as did educators in Europe during the Middle Ages and the Reformation and their successors in America. The history of higher education tells a story about people seeking a better way of educating the best and the brightest of each succeeding generation. Such a story has no ending. Nor should it.

Bibliographic Notes

As one moves closer to the present time it becomes more difficult to find recent secondary materials of a purely historical nature. Writing or studying the history of American higher education since 1945 more properly involves one in reviewing primary source documents. Nevertheless several sources have appeared since 1980 that will prove helpful.

Lazerson's (1987) documentary history includes materials, for instance, from the Truman Commission's report on community college education, from Clark Kerr on the multiversity, and from the College Board on declining test scores of America's entering college freshmen.

Thompson (1984) compares material on American higher education written during 1962–1972 with that produced by "selected Victorian essayists in nineteenth century England" (p. 3). Some of the principles enunciated in the nineteenth century, she proposes, retain their merit today. Best (1988) takes a somewhat different approach in his study of changing markets and management styles as they reflected a "revolution" in American higher education during the period after World War II. Kimball (1986) uses his 1986 book as the basis for comments on reports appearing in the 1980s recommending changes in undergraduate education (1988).

Keller (1982) and Rosovsky (1990) provide insight into the inner workings of Harvard, Keller giving nice detail on the development of Harvard's core curriculum during the seventies and Rosovsky providing his readers with "an owner's manual" on the American research university of the 1980s.

Several authors focus on specific kinds of institution. Harcleroad and Ostar (1987) address the development of the public comprehensive college and university. The authors put this institution alongside the community college and the land grant institutions as representing unique American contributions to the structure of higher education. During 1945–90 they played a major role in absorbing the massive enrollment increases of those times. Goodchild (1986) tells of the struggle within Jesuit institutions to accept accreditation standards of the North Central Association. Diener's (1986) documentary history of the community college provides insight into the leadership provided by individuals and by civil government in the rise of community colleges to their present position within American higher education. Brint and Karabel (1989) explore the extent to which leaders of the community college movement in the twentieth century have, in seeking their place within the structure of American higher education, increasingly emphasized their vocational education function.

Cremin (1988) continues his discussion of the rise of the American university into the twentieth century, showing the role that graduates of these institutions played as academic leaders, the rise of the research function after World War II, the decisions institutions made as to whether they would remain basically undergraduate institutions or join the parade toward university status, changes in student role and student diversity, and the transformation of American colleges and universities from elite to popular institutions during this period.

Schrecker (1986) contributes an important study of academe's response to the threats of the McCarthy era, showing how ineffective it was in protecting academic freedom during those difficult years. In a more specific case McCormick (1989) details the removal of art professor Luella Raab Mundel at Fairmont State College in West Virginia during the McCarthy era.

Analyses of the protest years of the 1960s and early 1970s are also prominent in the more recent literature. Horowitz (1986) assesses the period of those protests and the impact they had on student cultures. Miller (1987) gives good detail to the protest years, showing the motives of movement leaders, their strategies, and their experiences. Bright (1989) provides his interpretation of what happened, giving frequent references to events at Duke. Rorabaugh (1989) focuses on the city of Berkeley, the University, and the social changes that occurred in that setting during the sixties.

In the context of federal government relations with higher education, Kerr (1984) studies presidential archival records as the source for comparing processes followed by various federal government groups in developing reports on higher education between 1946 and 1972. The role of academe in the espionage activities of the U.S. government between 1939 and 1961 appears in Winks (1987).

BIBLIOGRAPHY

Adams, Henry. *The Education of Henry Adams.* Boston: Houghton Mifflin, 1930.

Allmendinger, David F., Jr. "Mount Holyoke Students Encounter the Need for Life Planning, 1837–1850." *History of Education Quarterly* (Spring 1973), 19:27–46.

———. "New England Students and the Revolution in Higher Education, 1800–1900." *History of Education Quarterly* (Winter 1971), 11:381–89.

American Association of University Professors. "Report of the Committee on Academic Freedom and Tenure." In Hofstadter, Richard and Smith, Wilson (Eds.) *American Higher Education: A Documentary History.* Chicago: University of Chicago Press, 1961. Two volumes. 2:860–78.

———. Report of Committee Y. *Depression, Recovery, and Higher Education.* New York: McGraw-Hill, 1937.

Anderson, G. Lester. *Land Grant Universities and Their Continuing Challenge.* East Lansing: Michigan State University Press, 1976.

Anderson, James D. *The Education of Blacks in the South, 1860–1935.* Chapel Hill: University of North Carolina Press, 1988.

Aristotle. *Rhetoric* (Jowett translation). Oxford: Clarendon, [1885].

Ashmore, Harry S. *Unseasonable Truths: The Life of Robert Maynard Hutchins.* Boston: Little, Brown, 1989.

Astin, Alexander W. *Achieving Educational Excellence.* San Francisco: Jossey-Bass, 1985.

———, et al. *The Power of Protest.* San Francisco: Jossey-Bass, 1975.

Association of American Colleges. *Integrity in the College Curriculum: A Report to the Academic Community.* Washington: AAC, 1985.

Axtell, James. "The Death of the Liberal Arts College." *History of Education Quarterly* (Winter 1971), 11:339–352.

Aydelotte, Frank. *Breaking the Academic Lock Step.* New York: Harper and Brothers, 1944.

Babbidge, Homer D., and Rosenzweig, Robert M. *The Federal Interest in Higher Education.* New York: McGraw-Hill, 1962.

Bacon, Francis. "Novum Organum." In John M. Robinson (Ed.), *The Philosophical Works of Francis Bacon.* London: George Routledge & Sons, [1905].

Bailyn, Bernard, et al. *Glimpses of the Harvard Past.* Cambridge: Harvard University Press, 1986.

Baldwin, John W., and Goldthwaite, Richard A. (Eds.). *Universities in Politics: Case Studies from the Late Middle Ages and Early Modern Period.* Baltimore: The Johns Hopkins Press, 1972.

Beard, Charles A. and Mary. *The Rise of American Civilization.* New York: Macmillan, 1927. Two volumes.

Bell, Daniel. *The Coming of Post-Industrial Society.* New York: Basic Books, 1973.

———. *The Reforming of General Education.* New York: Columbia University Press, 1962.

Bennett, Charles A. "Is Teaching a Narcotic?" *The Bookman* (March 1929), 69:25–28.

Best, John H. "The Revolution of Markets and Management: Toward a History of American Higher Education Since 1945." *History of Education Quarterly* (Summer 1988), 28:177–89.

Bevan, Edwyn R. *History of Egypt Under the Ptolemaic Dynasty.* London: Methuen, 1919

Bishop, Charles C. "Teaching at Johns Hopkins: The First Generation." *History of Education Quarterly* (Winter 1987) 27:499–515.

Blackburn, Robert T., and Conrad, Clifton F. "The New Revisionists and the History of United States Higher Education." *Higher Education* (1986), 15:211–30.

Bloom, Allan. *The Closing of the American Mind.* New York: Simon & Schuster, 1987.

Boas, Louise Schutz. *Women's Education Begins.* Norton, Mass.: Wheaton College Press, 1935.

Boyer, Ernest L. *College: The Undergraduate Experience in America.* New York: Harper & Row, 1987.

Brennan, Robert T. "The Making of the Liberal College: Alexander Meiklejohn at Amherst." *History of Education Quarterly* (Winter 1988), 28:569–97.

Brint, Steven, and Karabel, Jerome. *The Diverted Dream: Community Colleges and the Promise of Educational Opportunity in America, 1900–85.* New York: Oxford University Press, 1989.

Brough, Kenneth J. *Scholar's Workshop: Evolving Conceptions of Library Service.* Urbana: University of Illinois Press, 1953.

Brown, Cynthia F. "'Putting a Woman in Sole Power': The Presidential Succession at Bryn Mawr College, 1892–94." *History of Higher Education Annual* (1988), 8:79–97.

Brubacher, John S., and Rudy, Willis. *Higher Education in Transition.* New York: Harper & Brothers, 1976. Third edition.

Bullough, Vern L. "Education and Professionalization: An Historic Example." *History of Education Quarterly* (Summer 1970), 10:160–69.

Burke, Colin B. *American Collegiate Populations: A Test of the Traditional Views.* New York: New York University Press, 1982.

Burnaby, Andrew. *Travels Through the Middle Settlements in North America in the Years 1759 and 1760.* London: T. Payne, 1760. Second Edition.

Burritt, Bailey B. *Professional Distribution of College and University Graduates.* Washington, D.C.: Government Printing Office, 1912.

Bury, J.B. *A History of the Eastern Roman Empire, From the Fall of Irene to the Accession of Basil I.* London: Macmillan, 1912.

Butcher, Patricia S. "Education for Equality: Women's Rights Periodicals and Women's Higher Education, 1849–1920." *History of Higher Education Annual* (1986), 6:63–79.

Butler, Georgina. "Byzantine Education." In Norman H. Baynes and H.L.B. Moss (Eds.), *Byzantium: An Introduction to East Roman Civilization.* Oxford: Clarendon Press, 1948.

Byrd William. *The Secret Diary of William Byrd of Westover.* Edited by L.B. Wright and Marion Tinling. Richmond: The Dietz Press, 1941.

Calkins, Earnest Elmo. *They Broke the Prairie.* New York: C. Scribner's Sons, 1937.

Canby, Henry Seidel. *Alma Mater*. New York: Farrar & Rinehart, 1936.

Capen, Samuel P. "Relation of the State College to the New Movements in Higher Education." *The Educational Record* (January 1930), 11:12–23.

———. "Recent Movements in College and University Administration," United States Bureau of Education, *Bulletin*, No. 46. Washington: Government Printing Office, 1916.

Carnegie Commission on Higher Education. *Priorities for Action: Final Report of the Carnegie Commission on Higher Education*. New York: McGraw-Hill, 1973.

Carnegie Council on Policy Studies in Higher Education. *Three Thousand Futures: The Next Twenty Years in Higher Education*. San Francisco: Jossey-Bass, 1980.

Carpenter, Joel A., and Shipps, Kenneth W. (Eds.). *Making Higher Education Christian: The History and Mission of Evangelical Colleges in America*. Grand Rapids: Wm. B. Eerdmans, 1987.

Catto, J.I. (Ed.). *The History of the University of Oxford: Volume I, The Early Oxford Schools*. Oxford: Clarendon Press, 1984.

Chaudri, Abdul G. *Some Aspects of Islamic Education*. Lahore (Pakistan): Universal Books, 1982.

Cheit, Earl. *The New Depression in Higher Education*. New York: McGraw-Hill, 1971.

Church, Robert L. "Economists as Experts: The Rise of an Academic Profession in America." In Lawrence Stone (Ed.), *The University in Society*. Princeton: Princeton University Press, 1974. Two volumes, 2:571–609.

Church, Robert L., and Sedlak, Michael W. "The Antebellum College and Academy." In *Education in the United States: An Interpretive History*. New York: Free Press, 1976. Pp. 23–51.

Clark, Burton. *The Distinctive College: Antioch, Reed, and Swarthmore*. Chicago: Aldine, 1970.

Clarke, M.L. *Higher Education in the Ancient World*. Albuquerque: University of New Mexico Press, 1971.

Cobban, Alan B. *The Medieval English Universities: Oxford and Cambridge to ca. 1500*. Aldershott: Scolar Press, 1988.

———. *The Medieval Universities: Their Development and Organization*. London: Methuen, 1975.

Committee on College and University Teaching. "Report." *AAUP Bulletin* (May 1933, Part II), 19:1–122.

Commons, J.R. *History of Labour in the United States.* New York: Macmillan, 1918–35. Four volumes.

Conant, James B. "Academical Patronage and Superintendence." *Harvard Education Review* (May 1938), 8:312–34.

Conway, Jill. "Perspectives on the History of Women's Education in the United States." *History of Education Quarterly* (Spring 1974), 14:1–12.

Couat, Auguste H. *Alexandrian Poetry Under the First Three Ptolemies.* Translated by James Loeb. London: W. Heinemann, 1931.

Cramer, Frederick H. "Why Did Roman Universities Fail?" *Harvard Education Review* (March 1939), 9:204–88.

Cremin, Lawrence A. *American Education: The Metropolitan Experience, 1876–1980.* New York: Harper and Row, 1988.

———. *American Education: The National Experience, 1783–1876.* New York: Harper and Row, 1980.

———. *American Education: The Colonial Experience.* New York: Harper and Row, 1970.

Cubberley, Elwood P. *Public School Administration.* Boston: Houghton Mifflin, 1916.

Dabney, Virginius. *Mr. Jefferson's University: A History.* Charlottesville: University Press of Virginia, 1981.

Daniel, Norman. *The Arabs and Mediaeval Europe.* London: Longman Group Ltd., 1975.

DeVane, William C. *Higher Education in the Twentieth Century.* Cambridge: Harvard University Press, 1965.

Dewald, Carolyn. "Greek Education and Rhetoric." In Michael Grant and Rachel Kitzinger (Eds.), *Civilization of the Ancient Mediterranean: Greece and Rome.* New York: Charles Scribner's Sons, 1988. Three volumes, 2:1077–107.

Dewey, John. "Education and Social Change." *The Social Frontier* (May 1937), 3:235–38.

Diehl, Carl. "Innocents Abroad: American Students in German Universities, 1810–1870." *History of Education Quarterly* (Fall 1976), 16:321–41.

Diehl, Charles. *Byzantium: Greatness and Decline*. Translated by Naomi Walford. New Brunswick: Rutgers University Press, 1957.

Diener, Thomas (Ed.). *Growth of An American Invention: A Documentary History of the Junior and Community College Movement*. Westport: Greenwood Press, 1986.

Diogenes Laertius (R.D. Hicks translation). The Loeb Classical Library. New York: G.P. Putnam, [1881]. Volume One.

Duberman, Martin. *Black Mountain: An Exploration in Community*. New York: Anchor Press, 1973.

Dunn, Edward T. "Henry Flynt and the Great Awakening at Harvard College (1741–1744)." *History of Higher Education Annual* (1983), 3:3–37.

Durant, Will. *The Reformation*. New York: Simon & Schuster, 1957.

———. *Our Oriental Heritage*. New York: Simon and Schuster, 1935,

Eby, Frederick, and Arrowood, Charles F. *The Development of Modern Education*. New York: Prentice-Hall, 1934.

Eells, Walter C. *The Junior College*. Boston: Houghton Mifflin, 1930.

Eliot, John. "A College Proposed for Massachusetts Bay, 1633." In Richard Hofstadter and Wilson Smith (Eds.), *American Higher Education: A Documentary History*. Chicago: University of Chicago Press, 1961, 1:5–6.

England, J. Merton. *A Patron for Pure Science: The National Science Foundation's Formative Years, 1945–57*. Washington: National Science Foundation, 1983.

Fahie, J.J. *Galileo: His Life and Work*. New York: James Pott & Company, 1903.

Feingold, Mordechai. *The Mathematicians' Apprenticeship*. Cambridge: Cambridge University Press, 1984.

Ferruolo, Stephen C. "'Quid dant artes nisi luctum?' Learning, Ambition, and Careers in the Medieval University." *History of Education Quarterly* (Spring 1988), 28:1–22.

Fichte, Johann G. "Addresses." In Edward H. Riesner, *Evolution of the Common School*. New York: Macmillan, 1930.

Findlay, James. "'Western' Colleges, 1830–1890: Educational Institutions in Transition." *History of Higher Education Annual* (1982), 2:35–64.

————. "The SPCTEW and Western Colleges: Religion and Higher Education in Mid-Nineteenth Century America." *History of Education Quarterly* (Spring 1977), 17:31–62.

Finkelstein, Martin J. *The American Academic Profession*. Columbus: Ohio State University Press, 1984.

————. "From Tutor to Specialized Scholar: Academic Professionalization in Eighteenth and Nineteenth Century America." *History of Higher Education Annual* (1983), 3:99–121.

Finn, Chester E., Jr. "Context for Governance: Public Dissatisfaction and Campus Accountability." In Jack H. Schuster, Lynn H. Miller and Associates, *Tomorrow's Campus: Perspectives and Agendas*. New York: Collier Macmillan Publishers, 1989. Pp. 180–89.

Flexner, Abraham. *Medical Education in the United States and Canada*. New York: Carnegie Foundation for the Advancement of Teaching, 1910.

Franklin, Fabian. *The Life of Daniel Coit Gilman*. New York: Dodd, Mead, 1910.

Fulton, John F., and Thomson, Elizabeth. *Benjamin Silliman*. New York: H. Schman, 1947.

Gabriel, Astrik (Ed.). *The Economic and Material Frame of the Medieval University*. Notre Dame, Ind.: The National Commission for the History of Universities, 1977.

Garbedian, Haig G. *The March of Science*. New York: Covici Friede Publishers, 1936.

Gardner, David P. *The California Oath Controversy*. Berkeley: University of California Press, 1967.

Geanakoplos, Deno J. *Byzantium: Church, Society, and Civilization Seen Through Contemporary Eyes*. Chicago: University of Chicago Press, 1984.

Geiger, Roger L. *To Advance Knowledge: The Growth of American Research Universities, 1900–1940*. New York: Oxford University Press, 1986.

————. "After the Emergence: Voluntary Support and the Building of American Research Universities, 1900–1940." *History of Education Quarterly* (Fall 1985), 25:369–81.

————. "The Conditions of University Research, 1900–1920." *History of Higher Education Annual* (1984), 4:3–29.

Glazer, Penina, and Slater, Miriam. *Unequal Colleagues: The Entrance of Women into the Professions, 1890–1940.* New Brunswick: Rutgers University Press, 1986.

Goodchild, Lester. "The Turning Point in American Jesuit Higher Education: The Standardization Controversy Between the Jesuits and the North Central Association, 1915–1949." *History of Higher Education Annual* (1986), 6:81–116.

Goodchild, Lester, and Wechsler, Harold S. (Eds.). *The ASHE Reader on the History of Higher Education.* Needham Heights: Ginn Press, 1990.

Goodlad, John I., Soder, Roger, and Sirotnik, Kenneth A. (Eds.). *Places Where Teachers Are Taught.* San Francisco: Jossey-Bass, 1990.

Gordon, Lynn D. *Gender and Higher Education in the Progressive Era.* New Haven: Yale University Press, 1990.

————. "Annie Nathan Meyer and Barnard College: Mission and Identity in Women's Higher Education." *History of Education Quarterly* (Winter 1986), 26:503–22.

Gordon, Sarah H. "Smith College Students: The First Ten Classes." *History of Education Quarterly* (Summer 1975), 15:147–67.

Grant, Michael, and Kitzinger, Rachel (Eds.). *Civilization of the Ancient Mediterranean.* New York: Charles Scribner's Sons, 1988. Three volumes.

Green, Vivian H.H. *History of Oxford University.* London: Batsford, 1974.

Gruber, Carol S. *Mars and Minerva: Wars and the Uses of the Higher Learning in America.* Baton Rouge: Louisiana State University Press, 1975.

Guralnick, Stanley. *Science and the Antebellum American College.* Philadelphia: American Philosophical Society, 1975.

Hadas, Moses. *Imperial Rome.* New York: Time Incorporated, 1965.

Hague, Amy. "'What If the Power Does Lie Within Me?' Women Students at the University of Wisconsin, 1875–1900." *History of Higher Education Annual* (1984), 4:78–100.

Hall, G. Stanley. *Life and Confessions of a Psychologist.* New York: D. Appleton, 1923.

Handlin, Oscar and Mary F. *The American College and American Culture.* New York: McGraw-Hill, 1970.

Harcleroad, Fred F. "Influence of Organized Student Opinion on American College Curricula: An Historical Survey,"

Unpublished doctoral dissertation, Stanford University School of Education, 1948.

Harcleroad, Fred F., and Ostar, Allan W. *Colleges and Universities for Change: America's Comprehensive Public State Colleges and Universities*. Lanham: University Publishing Associates, 1987.

Harper, William Rainey. "The Situation of the Small College." In *The Trend in Higher Education*. Chicago: University of Chicago Press, 1905. Pp. 349–90.

———. *Quarterly Calendar*. University of Chicago: March 31, 1895.

Hartwell, Henry, Blair, James, and Chilton, Edward. *The Present State of Virginia, and the College*. Edited by H.D. Farish. Williamsburg: Colonial Williamsburg, Inc., [1940].

"The Harvard Charter of 1650." In Richard Hofstadter and Wilson Smith (Eds.), *American Higher Education: A Documentary History*. Chicago: University of Chicago Press, 1961. Two volumes, 1: 10–12.

Harvard University Committee on the Objectives of a General Education in a Free Society. *General Education in a Free Society*. Cambridge: Harvard University Press, 1945.

Hawkins, Hugh. "University Identity: The Teaching and Research Functions." In Alexandra Oleson, and John Voss (Eds.), *The Organization of Knowledge in Modern America, 1860, 1920*. Baltimore: Johns Hopkins University, 1979. Pp. 285–312.

———. *Between Harvard and America: The Educational Leadership of Charles W. Eliot*. New York: Oxford University Press, 1972.

———. "The University-Builders Observe the Colleges." *History of Education Quarterly* (Winter 1971), 11:339–52.

Henry, David D. *Challenges Past, Challenges Present: An Analysis of American Higher Education Since 1930*. San Francisco: Jossey-Bass, 1975.

Herbst, Jurgen. *And Sadly Teach: Teacher Education and Professionalization in American Culture*. Madison: University of Wisconsin Press, 1989.

———. *From Crisis to Crisis: American College Government, 1636–1819*. Cambridge: Harvard University Press, 1982.

———. "Church, State, and Higher Education: College Government in the American Colonies and States Before 1820." *History of Higher Education Annual* (1981), 1:42–54.

————. "From Religion to Politics: Debates and Confrontations over American College Governance in the Mid-Eighteenth Century." *Harvard Educational Review* (August 1976), 46:397–424.

————. "The Eighteenth Century Origins of the Split Between Private and Public Higher Education in the United States." *History of Education Quarterly* (Fall 1975), 15:273–80.

————. "The First Three American Colleges: Schools of the Reformation." In Donald Fleming and Bernard Bailyn (Eds.), *Perspectives in American History*. Cambridge: Charles Warren Center for Studies in American History, 1974. 8:7–52.

Hirsch, E.D., Jr. *Cultural Literacy: What Every American Needs to Know*. Boston: Houghton Mifflin, 1987.

Hofstadter, Richard, and Metzger, Walter P. *The Development of Academic Freedom in the United States*. New York: Columbia University Press, 1955.

————, and Smith, Wilson (Eds.). *American Higher Education: A Documentary History*. Chicago: University of Chicago Press, 1961. Two volumes.

Holmes, Oliver Wendell. *Record of the Commemoration of the 250th Anniversary of the Founding of Harvard College*, 1887.

Holt, Henry. *Garrulities of an Octogenarian Editor*. Boston: Houghton Mifflin, 1923.

Horowitz, Helen L. *Campus Life: Undergraduate Culture from the End of the Eighteenth Century to the Present*. New York: Knopf, 1987.

————. "The 1960s and the Transformation of Campus Cultures." *History of Education Quarterly* (Spring 1986), 26:1–38.

————. *Alma Mater: Design and Experience in the Women's Colleges from Their Nineteenth Century Beginnings to the 1930s*. New York: Knopf, 1984.

Humelsine, Carlisle H. *The President's Report: Cross and Gown*. Williamsburg: Colonial Williamsburg, Inc., [1965].

Humphrey, David C. "Colonial Colleges and English Dissenting Academies: A Study in Transatlantic Culture." *History of Education Quarterly* (Summer 1972), 12:184–97.

Hussey, J.M. *Church and Learning in the Byzantine Empire, 867–1185*. New York: Russell and Russell, 1937.

Hutchings, Pat, and Marchese, Ted. "Watching Assessment: Questions, Stories, Prospects." *Change* (September/October 1990), 22:12–38.

Hutchins, Robert M. *The Higher Learning in America.* New Haven: Yale University Press, 1936.

Huxley, Thomas H. *Science and Education.* New York: D. Appleton, 1896.

Hyman, Harold. *American Singularity: the 1787 Northwest Ordnance, the 1865 Homestead Acts.* Athens: University of Georgia Press, 1986.

Ijsewijn, Josef, and Paquet, Jacques. *The Universities of the Late Middle Ages.* Leuven: Leuven University Press, 1978.

Isocrates. "Panathenaikos." In *Isocrates* (George Norlin tr.). New York: G.P. Putnam's Sons, [1929]. Four volumes.

Jaeger, Werner. *Paideia: The Ideals of Greek Culture.* New York: Oxford University Press, 1944. Three volumes.

Jarausch, K.H. (Ed.). *The Transformation of Higher Learning, 1860–1930.* Chicago: University of Chicago Press, 1983.

James, Henry. *Charles W. Eliot.* Boston: Houghton-Mifflin, 1930. Two volumes

Jencks, Christopher, and Riesman, David. *The Academic Revolution.* Garden City: Doubleday, 1968.

Jesse, Richard H. "University Education." In the National Education Association, *Journal of Proceedings and Addresses: Session of the Year 1892.* New York: National Education Association, 1893. Pp. 120–27.

Joad, C.E.M. *Thrasymachus.* New York: Dutton, 1925.

Johnson, Allen, and Malone, Dumas (Eds.). "Jonathan Edwards." In *Dictionary of American Biography.* New York: C. Scribner & Sons, 1930. Twenty-two volumes, 6:33.

Johnson, Eldon L. "Misconceptions About the Early Land-Grant Colleges." *Journal of Higher Education* (1981), 52:333–51.

Johnson, William R. "Education and Professional Life Styles: Law and Medicine in the Nineteenth Century." *History of Education Quarterly* (Summer 1974), 14:185–207.

Jordan, David Starr. *The Trend of the University.* Stanford: Stanford University Press, 1929.

———. *The Days of a Man.* Yonkers-on-Hudson: World Book Company, 1922. Two volumes.

————. *The Voice of the Scholar*. San Francisco: Paul Elder & Company, 1903.

————. "Ideals of the New American University." *The Forum* (September 1891), 12:12–17.

Karp, Alan. "John Calvin and the Geneva Academy: Roots of the Board of Trustees." *History of Higher Education Annual* (1985), 5:3–41.

Keller, Phyllis. *Getting at the Core: Curricular Reform at Harvard*. Cambridge: Harvard University Press, 1982.

Kelley, Brooks M. *Yale: A History*. New Haven: Yale University Press, 1974.

Kerns, Kathryn M. "'Farmers' Daughters: The Education of Women at Alfred Academy and University Before the Civil War." *History of Higher Education Annual* (1986), 6:11–28.

Kerr, Clark. *The Uses of the University*. Cambridge: Harvard University Press, 1963.

Kerr, Janet C. "From Truman to Johnson: *Ad Hoc* Policy Formulation in Higher Education." *Review of Higher Education* (Fall 1984), 8:15–54.

Kimball, Bruce. "The Historical and Cultural Dimensions of the Recent Reports on Undergraduate Education." *American Journal of Education* (May 1988), 96:293–322.

————. *Orators and Philosophers: A History of the Idea of Liberal Education*. New York: Teachers College, 1986.

Kittelson, James, and Transue, Pamela (Eds.). *Rebirth, Reform, and Resilience: Universities in Transition, 1300–1700*. Columbus: Ohio State University Press, 1984.

Knight, Douglas M. *Street of Dreams: Nature and Legacy of the Sixties*. Durham: Duke University Press, 1989.

Koos, Leonard V. *The Junior College Movement*. Boston: Ginn & Company, 1925.

Lagemann, Ellen C. *Private Power for the Public Good: A History of the Carnegie Foundation for the Advancement of Teaching*. Middletown: Wesleyan University Press, 1983.

Lane, Jack C. "The Yale Report of 1828 and Liberal Education." *History of Education Quarterly* (Fall 1987), 27:325–38.

Lang, Daniel W. "The People's College, the Mechanics' Mutual Protection and the Agricultural College Act." *History of Education Quarterly* (Fall 1978), 18:295–321.

Lange, Alexis F. "The Junior College." In the National Education Association, *Journal of Proceedings and Addresses*. Ann Arbor: National Education Association, 1915. Pp. 119–24.

Lawson, Ellen H. *Three Sarahs: The Documents of Antebellum Black College Women*. New York: E. Mellon, 1984.

Lazerson, Marvin. *American Education in the Twentieth Century: A Documentary History*. New York: Teachers College, 1987.

Leader, Damian R. *A History of the University of Cambridge. Volume I: The University to 1546*. Cambridge: Cambridge University Press, 1988.

Lee, Calvin B.T. *The Campus Scene, 1900–79*. New York: David McKay, 1970.

Leedmerer, Kenneth M. *Learning to Heal: The Development of American Medical Education*. New York: Basic Books, 1985.

Lentz, Tony M. *Orality and Literacy in Hellenic Greece*. Carbondale: Southern Illinois University Press, 1989.

LeStrange, Guy. *Baghdad During the Abbasid Caliphate*. Oxford: Oxford University Press, 1900.

Levine, David O. *The American College and the Culture of Aspiration*. Ithaca: Cornell University Press, 1986.

Linton, Ralph. *The Tree of Culture*. New York: Alfred A. Knopf, 1955.

Lloyd, G.E.R. "Greek Philosophy." In Michael Grant and Rachel Kitzinger (Eds.), *Civilization of the Ancient Mediterranean: Greece and Rome*. New York: Charles Scribner's Sons, 1988. Three volumes, 3:1585–636.

Lunsford, Terry F. *The "Free Speech" Crises at Berkeley, 1964–1965*. Berkeley: Center for Research and Development in Higher Education, 1965.

Lynch, John P. *Aristotle's School: A Study of a Greek Educational Institution*. Berkeley: University of California Press, 1972.

Lyte, H.C.M. *A History of the University of Oxford*. London: Macmillan, 1886.

Lytle, Guy F. "Patronage Patterns and Oxford Colleges." In Lawrence Stone (Ed.), *The University in Society*. Princeton: Princeton University Press, 1974. Two volumes, 1:111–49.

Machlup, Fritz. *The Production and Distribution of Knowledge in the United States*. Princeton: Princeton University Press, 1962.

Mango, Cyril. "Byzantium from Justinian to Theophilus." In David T. Rice (Ed.), *The Dawn of European Civilization*. New York: McGraw-Hill, 1965. Pp. 103–14.

Maqdisi, George. *The Rise of Colleges*. Edinburgh: Edinburgh University Press, 1981.

Marrou, H.I. *History of Education in Antiquity*. George Lamb translation. New York: Sheed and Ward, 1956.

Mather, Cotton. *Magnalia Christi American: or the Ecclesiastical History of New England*. London: T. Parkhurst, 1702.

McCandless, Amy T. "Preserving the Pedestal: Restrictions on Social Life at Southern Colleges for Women, 1920–1940." *History of Higher Education Annual* (1987), 7:45–67.

McClane, C.L. "Announcement of the First Junior College in California." *Junior College Journal* (November 1930), 1:94.

McCormick, Charles H. *This Nest of Vipers: McCarthyism and Higher Education in the Mundel Affair, 1951–52*. Urbana: University of Illinois Press, 1989.

McDowell, F.M. *The Junior College*. Washington: U.S. Bureau of Education Bulletin No. 35, 1919.

McLachlan, James. "The American College of the Nineteenth Century: Toward a Reappraisal." *Teachers College Record* (December 1978), 80:287–306.

———. "The Choice of Hercules: American Student Societies in the Early Nineteenth Century." In Lawrence Stone (Ed.), *The University in Society*. Princeton: Princeton University Press, 1974. Two volumes, 2:449–94.

Medsker, Leland, and Tillery, Dale. *Breaking the Access Barriers*. New York: McGraw-Hill, 1971.

Meiklejohn, Alexander. *The Liberal College*. Boston: Marshall Jones, 1920.

Mill, John Stuart. *Dissertations and Discussions: Political, Philosophical and Historical*. New York: Henry Holt, [1882].

Miller, Howard G. *The Revolutionary College: American Presbyterian Higher Education, 1707–1837*. New York: New York University Press, 1976.

Miller, James E. *Democracy in the Streets: From Port Huron to the Siege of Chicago*. New York: Simon and Schuster, 1987.

Milton, John. "Paradise Regained." In Merritt Y. Hughes (Ed.), *Paradise Regained, The Minor Poems, and Samson Agonistes.* New York: The Odyssey Press, [1937].

Minot, Charles S. "Antrittsvorlesung." *Science.* (December 6, 1912), 36:771–76.

Montgomery, Thomas H. *A History of the University of Pennsylvania from Its Foundation to A.D. 1770.* Philadelphia: George W. Jacobs & Company, 1900.

Moore, Frank G. *The Roman's World.* New York: Columbia University Press, 1936.

Moore, Kathryn M. "The Dilemma of Corporal Punishment at Harvard College," *History of Education Quarterly* (Fall 1974), 14:335–46.

———. "The War of the Tutors: Student-Faculty Conflict at Harvard and Yale, 1745–1771." *History of Education Quarterly* (Summer 1978), 18:115–27.

Morgan, Edmund S. *The Puritan Dilemma: The Story of John Winthrop.* Edited by Oscar Handlin. Boston: Little, Brown [1958].

Morison, Samuel Eliot. *Three Centuries of Harvard.* Cambridge: Harvard University Press, 1937.

———. *Harvard College in the Seventeenth Century.* Cambridge: Harvard University Press, 1936a. Two volumes.

———. *The Puritan Pronoas.* New York: New York University Press, 1936b.

———. *The Founding of Harvard College.* Cambridge: Harvard University Press, 1935.

Mortimer, Kenneth, and Tierney, Michael L. *The Three "R's" of the Eighties: Reduction, Reallocation, and Retrenchment.* Washington: American Association for Higher Education, 1979.

Mummford, Lewis. *Technics and Civilization.* New York: Harcourt, Brace, 1934.

Nakosteen, Medhi. *History of Islamic Origins of Western Education.* Boulder: University of Colorado Press, 1964.

"The Nation." *The Chronicle of Higher Education Almanac.* September 5, 1990.

"A National Association of University Professors," *Science* (March 1914), 39:458–59.

Naylor, Natalie A. "The Theological Seminary in the Configuration of American Higher Education: The Ante-Bellum Years." *History of Education Quarterly* (Spring 1977), 17:17–30.

———. "The Ante-Bellum College Movement: A Reappraisal of Tewksbury's *The Founding of American Colleges and Universities.*" *History of Education Quarterly* (Fall 1973), 13:261–74.

Neuman, Abraham. *The Jews in Spain.* Philadelphia: Jewish Publication Society of America, 1942. Two volumes.

"New England's First Fruits." In Richard Hofstadter and Wilson Smith (Eds.), *American Higher Education: A Documentary History.* Chicago: University of Chicago Press, 1961. Two volumes, 1:6–7.

Newcomer, Mabel. *A Century of Higher Education for American Women.* New York: Harper, 1959.

Norlin, George. *Isocrates, with an English Translation by George Norlin.* New York: G.P. Putnam's Sons, 1928. Three volumes, 2:391.

Northrup, Cyrus. *The Jubilee of the University of Wisconsin.* Madison: University of Wisconsin Press, 1904.

Novak, Steven J. *The Rights of Youth: American Colleges and Student Revolt, 1798–1815.* Cambridge: Harvard University Press, 1977.

———. "The College in the Dartmouth College Case: A Reinterpretation." *The New England Quarterly* (December 1974), 47:550–63.

Oleson, Alexandra, and Voss, John (Eds.). *The Organization of Knowledge in Modern America.* Baltimore: Johns Hopkins University Press, 1979.

Olivas, Michael. "Indian, Chicano, and Puerto Rican Colleges: Status and Issues." *Bilingual Review* (January–April 1982), 9:36–58.

Olson, Keith W. *The G.I. Bill: The Veterans and the Colleges.* Lexington: University of Kentucky Press, 1974.

O'Malley, John W. "The Jesuit Enterprise in Historical Perspective." In Rolando E. Bonachea (Ed.), *Jesuit Higher Education.* Pittsburgh: Duquesne University Press, 1989.

Ortega y Gasset, José. *Mission of the University.* Edited and translated by Howard Lee Nostrand. New York: W.W. Norton, 1944.

Palmieri, Patricia A. "From Republican Motherhood to Race Suicide: Arguments on the Higher Education of Women in the United

States, 1820–1920." In Carol Lasser (Ed.), *Educating Men and Women Together: Coeducation in a Changing World*. Urbana: University of Illinois Press, 1987. Pp. 49–64.

————. "Incipit Vita Nuova: Founding Ideals of the Wellesley College Community." *History of Higher Education Annual* (1983a), 3:59–78.

————. "Here Was Fellowship: A Social Portrait of Academic Women at Wellesley College, 1895–1920." *History of Education Quarterly* (Summer 1983b), 23:195–214.

Papalas, A.J. "Herodes Atticus: An Essay on Education in the Antonine Age." *History of Education Quarterly* (Summer 1981), 21:171–88.

Parsons, Edward A. *The Alexandrian Library*. London: Cleaver-Hume Press, 1952

Paschal, George W. *History of Wake Forest College*. Wake Forest: Wake Forest College, 1935.

Peabody, Andrew P. *Harvard Reminiscences*. Boston: Ticknor & Company, 1888.

Pearson, Ralph L. "Reflections on Black Colleges: The Historical Perspective of Charles S. Johnson." *History of Education Quarterly* (Spring 1983), 23:55–68.

Peeps, J.M. Stephen. "A B.A. for the G.I. . . . Why?" *History of Education Quarterly* (Winter 1984), 24:513–25.

Peirce, Benjamin. *A History of Harvard University*. Cambridge: Brown, Shattuck and Company, 1833.

Perkins, Linda M. "The Impact of the 'Cult of True Womanhood' on the Education of Black Women." *Journal of Social Issues* (1983, No. 3), 39:17–28.

Pierson, George W. *The Founding of Yale: The Legend of the Forty Folios*. New Haven: Yale University Press, 1989.

Piltz, Henry. *The World of Medieval Learning*. Translated by David Jones. Oxford: Basil Blackwell, [1981].

Porter, Noah. *The American Colleges and the American Public*. New Haven: C.C. Chatfield and Company, 1870.

Potts, David B. "Curriculum and Enrollments: Some Thoughts on Assessing the Popularity of the Antebellum Colleges." *History of Higher Education Annual* (1981), 1:88–109.

————. "'College Enthusiasm!' as Public Response, 1800–1860." *Harvard Educational Review* (February 1977), 47:28–82.

————. "American Colleges in the Nineteenth Century: From Localism to Denominationalism." *History of Education Quarterly* (Winter 1971), 363–80.

Powell, Arthur G. *The Uncertain Profession: Harvard and Its Search for Educational Authority*. Cambridge: Harvard University Press, 1980.

President's Commission on Campus Unrest. *Report*. New York: Avon Books, 1971.

Rashdall, Hastings. *The Universities of Europe in the Middle Ages*. Oxford: Clarendon Press, 1936. Three volumes.

Rensselaer Polytechnic Institute. *Bulletin* (March 1940).

Rice, T. Talbot. *Everyday Life in Byzantium*. London: Putnam's, 1967.

Richardson, Leon Burr. *A History of Dartmouth College*. Hanover: Dartmouth College, 1932. Two volumes.

Riley, Isaac Woodbridge. *American Thought from Puritanism to Pragmatism*. New York: H. Holt, 1914.

Robinson, E.I. *Alexander the Great*. New York: E.P. Dutton, 1947.

Robson, David W. *Educating Republicans: The College in the Era of the American Revolution, 1750–1800*. Westport: Greenwood Press, 1985.

————. "College Founding in the New Republic." *History of Education Quarterly* (Fall 1983), 23:323–41.

————. "The Early American College and the Wider Culture: Scholarship in the 1970s." *American Quarterly* (1980), 32:559–76.

Rorabaugh, William J. *Berkeley at War: The Sixties*. New York: Oxford University Press, 1989.

Rosovsky, Henry. *The University: An Owner's Manual*. New York: W.W. Norton, 1990.

Rossiter, Margaret W. "Doctorates for American Women, 1868–1907." *History of Education Quarterly* (Summer 1982), 22:159–83.

Rowse, A.L. *Oxford in the History of England*. New York: G.P. Putnam, 1975.

Rubin, Michael R., et al. *The Knowledge Industry in the United States, 1960–1980*. New Haven: Yale University Press, 1986.

Rudolph, Frederick. *Curriculum: A History of the American Undergraduate Course of Study Since 1636*. San Francisco: Jossey-Bass, 1977.

————. *The American College and University: A History.* New York: Alfred A. Knopf, 1962.

Rudy, Willis. *The Universities of Europe, 1100–1914.* Rutherford: Fairleigh Dickinson University Press, 1984.

Rury, John, and Harper, Glenn. "The Trouble with Coeducation: Mann and Women at Antioch, 1853–1860." *History of Education Quarterly* (Winter 1986), 26:481–502.

Sale, Kirkpatrick. *SDS.* New York: Random House, 1973.

Sanders, Jane. *Cold War on Campus.* Seattle: University of Washington Press, 1979.

Sarton, George. *A History of Science.* Cambridge: Harvard University Press, 1952, 1959. Two volumes.

Schachner, Nathan. *The Medieaval University.* A.S. Barnes & Company, Inc., 1938.

Schneider, Franz. *Teaching and Scholarship and Res Publica.* Berkeley: The Pestalozzi Press, 1938.

Schrecker, Ellen W. *No Ivory Tower: McCarthyism and the Universities.* New York: Oxford University Press, 1986.

Schuster, Jack H., Miller, Lynn H., and Associates. *Governing Tomorrow's Campus: Perspectives and Agendas.* New York: Collier Macmillan Publishers, 1989.

Scott, Anne F. "The Ever Widening Circle: The Diffusion of Feminist Values from the Troy Female Seminary, 1822–72." *History of Education Quarterly* (Spring 1979), 19:3–23.

Sealander, Judith. "'Forcing Them to Be Free': Antioch College and Progressive Education in the 1920s." *History of Higher Education Annual* (1988), 8:59–78.

Shannon, Samuel H. "Land-Grant College Legislation and Black Tennesseeans: A Case Study in the Politics of Education." *History of Education Quarterly* (Summer 1982), 22:139–57.

Simon, John Y. "The Politics of the Morrill Act." *Agricultural History* (1963), 37:103–11.

Singer, Isadore (Ed.). *Jewish Encyclopedia.* New York: Funk and Wagnalls, 1906. Twelve volumes.

Slichter, Charles S. "Polymaths: Technicians, Specialists, and Genius." *Sigma Xi Quarterly* (September 1933), pp. 97–99.

Sloan, Douglas. *The Scottish Enlightenment and the American College Ideal.* New York: Teachers College Press, 1971.

Slosson, Edwin E. *The American Spirit in Education.* New Haven: Yale University Press, 1921.

———. *Great American Universities.* New York: Macmillan, 1910.

Smith, Logan P. "Oxford." *The Atlantic Monthly* (June 1938), 161:731–40.

Smith, Richard N. *The Harvard Century: The Making of a University to a Nation.* New York: Simon and Schuster, 1986.

Smith, William A. *Ancient Education.* New York: Philosophical Library, 1955.

Smith, Wilson. "Apologia pro Alma Matre: The College as a Community in Antebellum America." In Stanley Elkins (Ed.), *The Hofstadter Aegis.* New York: Alfred Knopf, 1974. Pp. 125–53.

Solomon, Barbara M. *In the Company of Educated Women: A History of Women in Higher Education in America.* New Haven: Yale University Press, 1985.

Stetar, Joseph M. "In Search of a Direction: Southern Higher Education after the Civil War." *History of Education Quarterly* (Fall 1985), 25:341–67.

Stevens, Robert B. *Law School: Legal Education in America in the 1850s to the 1980s.* Chapel Hill: University of North Carolina Press, 1983.

Stevenson, Louise L. "Between the Old-Time College and the Modern University: Noah Porter and the New Haven Scholars." *History of Higher Education Annual* (1983), 3:39–57.

Stiles, Ezra. *The Literary Diary.* New York: Charles Scribner's Sons, [1901]. Three volumes.

Stites, Francis N. *Private Interest and Public Gain: Dartmouth College Case.* Amherst: University of Massachusetts Press, 1972.

Stone, James C. *Portraits of the American University, 1890–1910.* San Francisco: Jossey-Bass, 1971.

Stone, Lawrence (Ed.). *The University in Society.* Princeton: Princeton University Press, 1974. Two volumes.

Story, Ronald. "Harvard Students, the Boston Elite, and the New England Preparatory System, 1800–1870." *History of Education Quarterly* (Fall, 1975), 15:281–98.

Strum, Harvey. "Discrimination at Syracuse University." *History of Higher Education Annual* (1984), 4:101–22.

Summerscales, William. *Affirmation and Dissent*. New York: Teachers College Press, 1970.

Swanson, Robert N. *Universities, Academics, and the Great Schism*. Cambridge: Cambridge University Press, 1979.

Synott, Marcia G. *The Half-Opened Door: Discrimination and Admissions at Harvard, Yale, and Princeton, 1900–1970*. Westport: Greenwood Press, 1979a.

———. "The Admission and Assimilation of Minority Students at Harvard, Yale, and Princeton, 1900–1950." *History of Education Quarterly* (Fall 1979b), 19:285–304.

Tappan, Henry P. *University Education*. New York: G.P. Putnam, 1851.

Tarn, W.W. *Alexander the Great*. Cambridge: University Press, 1948.

Tewksbury, D.G. *The Founding of American Colleges and Universities Before the Civil War*. New York: Teachers College Press, Columbia University, 1932.

Thelin, John R. *Cultivation of Ivy: A Saga of the College in America*. Cambridge: Schenkman, 1976.

Thomas, Carla. "I. Philosophical Anthropology and Educational Change: Wilhelm Von Humboldt and the Prussian Reforms." *History of Education Quarterly* (Fall 1973), 13:219–47.

Thompson, Jo Ann. *The Modern Idea of the University*. New York: Peter Lang, 1984.

Thomson, Robert P. "Colleges in the Revolutionary South: The Shaping of a Tradition." *History of Education Quarterly* (Winter 1970), 10:399–412.

Thornton, James W., Jr. *The Community Junior College*. New York: John Wiley and Sons, 1972. Third edition.

Totah, Khalil A. *The Contribution of the Arabs to Education*. New York: Teachers College Press, Columbia University, 1926.

Tritton, Arthur S. *Materials on Muslim Education in the Middle Ages*. London: Luzac and Company, 1957.

Tucker, Lewis L. *Connecticut's Seminar of Sedition: Yale College*. Chester: Pequot Press, 1974.

Tyler, William S. *A History of Amherst College, 1821–1891*. New York: F.H. Hitchcock, 1895.

United States Bureau of Education. *A Survey of Educational Institutions of the State of Washington*. Bulletin No. 26. Washington: Government Printing Office, 1916.

United States National Commission on Excellence in Education. *A Nation at Risk: The Imperative for Educational Reform.* Washington: The Commission, 1983.

United States President's Commission on Higher Education. *Higher Education for American Democracy.* Washington: Government Printing Office, 1947.

Van Amringe, John H., et al. *A History of Columbia University: 1754–1904.* New York: Columbia University Press, 1904.

Veblen, Thorstein. *The Higher Learning in America.* New York: Hill and Wang, 1918.

Vine, Phyllis. "Preparation for Republicanism: Honor and Shame in the Eighteenth Century College." In Barbara Finkelstein (Ed.), *Regulated Children/Liberated Children: Education in Psychohistorical Perspective.* New York: Psychohistory Press, 1979.

———. "The Social Foundations of Eighteenth Century Higher Education." *History of Education Quarterly* (Winter 1976), 16: 409–24.

Wagner, David S. (Ed.). *The Seven Liberal Arts in the Middle Ages.* Bloomington: Indiana University Press, 1983.

Wagoner, Jennings L., Jr. "Honor and Dishonor at Mr. Jefferson's University: The Antebellum Years." *History of Education Quarterly* (Summer 1986), 26: 155–79.

———. "The American Compromise: Charles W. Eliot, Black Education, and the New South." In R. Goodenow and A. White (Eds.), *Education and the Rise of the New South.* Boston: Hall, 1981. Pp. 26–46.

Walden, John W.H. *The Universities of Ancient Greece.* New York: Charles Scribner's Sons, 1909.

Walsh, Mary R. *Doctors Wanted: No Women Need Apply: Sexual Barriers to the Medical Profession, 1835–1975.* New Haven: Yale University Press, 1977.

Warch, Richard. *School of the Prophets: Yale College, 1701–1740.* New Haven: Yale University Press, 1973.

Watts, W. Montgomery. *The Influence of Islam on Medieval Europe.* Edinburgh: Edinburgh University Press, 1972.

Wayland, Francis. *Thoughts on the Present Collegiate System in the United States.* Boston: Gould, Kendall, and Lincoln, 1842.

Wechsler, Harold S. "An Academic Gresham's Law: Group Repulsion as a Theme in American Higher Education." *Teachers College Record* (Summer 1981), 82:567–88.

Wein, Roberta. "Women's Colleges and Domesticity." *History of Education Quarterly* (Spring 1974), 14:31–47.

Wells, H.G. *The Outline of History: Being a Plain History of the Life of Mankind.* New York: Macmillan, 1921.

Wertenbaker, Thomas J. *Princeton, 1746–1896.* Princeton: Princeton University Press, 1946.

Wheatley, Steven C. "Abraham Flexner and the Politics of Reform." *History of Higher Education Annual* (1988), 8: 45–58.

White, Andrew Dickson. *Autobiography.* London: Macmillan, 1906.

Whitehead, Alfred North. *Science and the Modern World.* Cambridge: University Press, 1928.

Whitehead, John S., and Herbst, Jurgen. "How to Think About the Dartmouth College Case." *History of Education Quarterly* (Fall 1986), 26: 333–49.

Whitehead, John S. *The Separation of College and State: Columbia, Dartmouth, Harvard, and Yale.* New Haven: Yale University Press, 1973.

Winks, Robin W. *Cloak and Gown: Scholars in the Secret War, 1939–61.* New York: Robin Morrow and Company, 1987.

Wolfle, Dael. *The Home of Science: The Role of the University.* New York: McGraw-Hill, 1973.

Wooten, Cecil W. "Roman Education and Rhetoric." In Michael Grant and Rachel Kitzinger (Eds.), *Civilization of the Ancient Mediterranean: Greece and Rome.* New York: Charles Scribner's Sons, 1988. Three volumes, 2:1109–20.

Wright, Louis B. *The First Gentlemen of Virginia.* San Marino: The Huntington Library, 1940.

"The Yale Report of 1828." In Richard Hofstadter and Wilson Smith (Eds.), *American Higher Education: A Documentary History.* Chicago: University of Chicago Press, 1961. Two volumes, 1: 275–91.

Zschoche, Sue. "Dr. Clarke Revisited: Science, True Womanhood, and Female Collegiate Education." *History of Education Quarterly* (Winter 1989), 29:545–69.

INDEX

231